THE SECRETS OF LAW

The Amherst Series in Law, Jurisprudence, and Social Thought

EDITED BY

Austin Sarat, Lawrence Douglas, and Martha Merrill Umphrey

The Secrets of Law

Edited by

AUSTIN SARAT

LAWRENCE DOUGLAS

MARTHA MERRILL UMPHREY

STANFORD LAW BOOKS

An imprint of Stanford University Press • Stanford, California

Stanford University Press
Stanford, California

Library of Congress Cataloging-in-Publication Data

The secrets of law / edited by Austin Sarat, Lawrence Douglas, and Martha Merrill Umphrey.
pages cm. — (The Amherst series in law, jurisprudence, and social thought)
Includes bibliographical references and index.
ISBN 978-0-8047-8259-3 (cloth : alk. paper)
1. Law and secrecy. 2. Law in literature. 3. Secrecy in literature. I. Sarat, Austin, editor of compilation. II. Douglas, Lawrence, editor of compilation. III. Umphrey, Martha Merrill, editor of compilation. IV. Series: Amherst series in law, jurisprudence, and social thought.
K487.S43S43 2012
340'.115—dc23

2011052154

Typeset at Stanford University Press in 10/14.5 Minion

For my son Ben
with love and the hope that he will understand (AS)

Acknowledgments

The essays contained in this book were originally prepared for and presented as a seminar series at Amherst College. We are grateful to our Amherst College colleagues David Delaney, Nasser Hussain, and Adam Sitze for their intellectual companionship. We thank our students in Amherst College's Department of Law, Jurisprudence & Social Thought for their interest in the issues addressed in this book. Finally, we would like to express our appreciation for generous financial support provided by Amherst College.

Contents

Contributors

RICHARD BURT is Professor of English at the University of Florida

LAWRENCE DOUGLAS is the James J. Grosfeld Professor of Law, Jurisprudence and Social Thought at Amherst College

LINDSAY FARMER is Professor of Law at the University of Glasgow

BERNADETTE MEYLER is Professor of Law at Cornell Law School

ALASDAIR ROBERTS is the Jerome L. Rappaport Professor of Law and Public Policy at Suffolk University Law School

AUSTIN SARAT the William Nelson Cromwell Professor of Jurisprudence and Political Science and Professor of Law, Jurisprudence and Social Thought at Amherst College

EDWARD STEIN is Professor of Law at Cardozo Law School

MARTHA MERRILL UMPHREY is Professor of Law, Jurisprudence and Social Thought at Amherst College

MELANIE L. WILLIAMS is Professor of Law at the University of Exeter

THE SECRETS OF LAW

Transparency and Opacity in the Law: An Introduction

MARTHA MERRILL UMPHREY

AUSTIN SARAT

LAWRENCE DOUGLAS

The website of WikiLeaks.org, the international organization that publishes data and diplomatic cables closely guarded by various governments and corporations, has described its project as follows:

> WikiLeaks is a multi-jurisdictional public service designed to protect whistleblowers, journalists and activists who have sensitive materials to communicate to the public.
> . . .
> We believe that transparency in government activities leads to reduced corruption, better government and stronger democracies. All governments can benefit from increased scrutiny by the world community, as well as their own people. . . .
> The power of principled leaking to embarrass governments, corporations and institutions is amply demonstrated through recent history. The public scrutiny of otherwise unaccountable and secretive institutions forces them to consider the ethical implications of their actions. Which official will chance a secret, corrupt transaction when the public is likely to find out? What repressive plan will be carried out when it is revealed to the citizenry, not just of its own country, but the world? When the risks of embarrassment and discovery increase, the tables are turned against conspiracy, corruption, exploitation and oppression. Open government answers injustice rather than causing it. Open government exposes and undoes corruption. Open governance is the most effective method of promoting good governance . . .
> What conscience cannot contain, and institutional secrecy unjustly conceals, WikiLeaks can broadcast to the world.[1]

This manifesto contains several themes and lines of argument apposite to a consideration of law and secrets. Most prominent among them is a valorization of transparency in governance. In "datadumping" tens of thousands of secret military documents concerning the Afghanistan war and hundreds of thousands of U.S. embassy cables,[2] WikiLeaks' founder Julian Assange asserted his place in the annals of journalism alongside Daniel Ellsberg (of *Pentagon Papers* fame) as an heroic defender of democratic values.[3] Those values, WikiLeaks asserts, depend upon clear and honest communication between governing social and political institutions and the wider public, both to protect against corruption and to ensure that the consent of the governed is meaningful and effective.[4] By contrast, WikiLeaks equates "secrecy" with oppression, unaccountable authoritarianism, and (more generally) injustice. The revelation of secret information is, from this point of view, an unarguable good, as it punishes corruption and deters those who might otherwise act for their own good at the public's expense.

Such a position presupposes that one can clearly distinguish justice from injustice on the basis of a moral distinction between the "principled" leaking of secrets and their "unjust" concealment. The "principle" in principled leaking may be difficult to articulate fully,[5] but it seems to resonate on at least two levels of meaning. It may, on the one hand, emerge out of the idea that there will be agreement, in at least some instances, that certain substantive acts or practices are corrupt or unjust (fraud, coercion, illegitimate violence). On the other hand, the justification and justice of leaking may follow more generally from a theory of governance that equates official secrecy with antidemocratic practices, regardless of the content of the secret (whether immoral or not). Either way, one can read in the assertion of principle an implicit acknowledgment that the revelation of secrets requires justification—that "leaking" secrets—particularly if they are damaging to the institutions holding them—might be immoral.

The third theme in WikiLeaks self-description is, perhaps paradoxically, that those individuals airing secrets through WikiLeaks who wish to remain—or who must remain—cloaked in anonymity ought to be accorded the most stringent protections available, even from WikiLeaks itself (through its "cutting-edge cryptographic technologies"):

> Our servers are distributed over multiple international jurisdictions and do not keep logs. Hence these logs cannot be seized. Anonymization occurs early in the WikiLeaks network, long before information passes to our web servers. Without specialized global internet traffic analysis, multiple parts of our organization and volunteers must conspire with each other to strip submitters of their anonymity.

Critics might suggest that what is good for the goose ought to be good for the gander: that if WikiLeaks values transparency as a general matter, it cannot embrace secrecy at its very core.[6] Even under the more limited claim that WikiLeaks values the revelation of secrets whose substance is immoral, relying on anonymous sources whose integrity is impossible to gauge can fatally compromise the organization's legitimacy.[7] Yet for our purposes the more interesting implication arising from this conundrum is that it suggests that transparency relies on a prior opacity: that sources will not expose corruption without protection, and that secrecy necessarily lies at the heart of WikiLeaks' production of truth.[8] In other words, secrecy and transparency are not opposites, but rather stand in a fraught but inescapable relationship with one another.

These three themes—the importance of transparency to democratic governance, the moral ambiguity of both guarding and revealing secrets, and the opacity that may be a precondition for transparency—highlight the allures as well as the dangers of keeping and exposing secrets. As humans we seem haunted by a desire—not always insatiable, but often compelling—to know and uncover knowledge kept from us,[9] and law is one of the signal terrains upon which clashes over secrets play out.[10] Moreover, if law is, as Marianne Valverde has suggested, "a privileged site in which people either seek the truth themselves or comment on the truth-seeking efforts of others,"[11] it also depends upon and incorporates certain kinds of secrecy into its workings even as it acts as a lever to uncover the secrets of others.

The essays in this interdisciplinary volume explore the ways law both traffics in and regulates secrecy and describe its place in both the workings of law and in our imaginings of it. Our contributors pose questions about the ways law overtly and covertly produces zones of secrecy, about the relation between secrecy and justice, and about how we represent and read the opacity of law's interpretive and representational processes. If the denizens of WikiLeaks struck a nerve in releasing such vast amounts of information,[12] it is because they laid bare our deep ambivalence—our longing and our fear—over the revelation of secrets at a highly charged legal and political moment.

What Is a Secret?

Both alluring and forbidding, secrets are set apart from the world of the everyday;[13] and, like other things we hold sacred, are ambiguous in the sense that they consist of an unknown onto which we project both our desires and our fears.[14] As Sissela Bok puts it, "[A]midst the vastness of all that we are conscious of not knowing, or of trying to ascertain, we experience as secret the spaces from which we feel shut out."[15] Secrecy is at once necessary for human flourishing and yet may also threaten it. "Secrecy," Bok writes, "is as indispensable to human beings as fire, and as greatly feared. Both enhance and protect life, yet both can stifle, lay waste, spread out of all control. Both may be used to guard intimacy or to invade it, to nurture or to consume. And each can be turned against itself; barriers of secrecy are set up to guard against secret plots and surreptitious prying, just as fire is used to fight fire."[16]

As several of the chapters below suggest, our ambivalence about intentional secrecy in particular is profound. While secrets are not necessarily "ethically negative,"[17] their set-apartness provokes suspicion and a tendency to magnify their significance.[18] As we imagine them, "secrets provide the unobservable weapons of the devious."[19] Sometimes we think of secrecy as a kind of poison or infection whose risks multiply because of its tendency to spread.[20] At the same time, we defend our own capacity for secrecy passionately in arguing that a world without secrets is a world deeply destructive of the human. Imaginative culture provides parable after parable detailing the soul-destroying effects of complete transparency.[21]

Intentional secrecy is often distinguished from the more diffuse concept of privacy, notoriously defined by Samuel Warren and Louis Brandeis in its most general sense as "right to be let alone."[22] Bok argues that the defining trait of secrecy is precisely this effort to conceal. "To keep a secret from someone . . . ," she writes, "is to block information about it or evidence of it from reaching that person, and to do so intentionally: to prevent him from learning it, and thus from possessing it, making use of it, or revealing it."[23] Secrecy is, in her view, different from privacy, which she defines as "the condition of being protected from unwanted access by others—either physical access, personal information, or attention."[24] Liberal societies are deeply invested in the idea that individuals need secrecy for "protection of what we are, what we plan, what we do, and what we own"—particularly vis-à-vis the intrusions of the state.[25] Edward Shils even more emphatically distinguishes the two concepts. "Privacy," he argues, "is the voluntary withholding of information reinforced by a willing indifference. Secrecy is the compulsory withholding of knowledge, reinforced by the prospect of sanctions for disclosure."[26]

And yet if one defines secrecy not with reference to the intentional acts of individuals but from the point of view of the audience from whom knowledge is concealed, one can coherently link secrecy with opacity—with the obscure, impenetrable, or ineffable rather than the concealed. This broader conceptualization of secrecy raises a set of epistemological issues that complicate an easy embrace of transparency in governance and law—issues arising from, for example, the complexity of the human psyche,[27] or the slippery nature of language and representation itself.[28] As a number of our contributors suggest, words on a page or images in a text alone cannot guarantee access to meaning; often to decipher law's secrets one must read between the lines of a report or search further in the historical record; and even then, one can find no guarantee of clarity or transparency.

Secrecy, Transparency, and Governance

However elusive the ideal of transparency may be, it remains central to the project of accountable governance in liberal democracies. Indeed there is a long tradition in political and legal theory extolling the value of transparency. Christopher Kutz has argued that, as far back as ancient Rome,

> as a principle, an ideal, the public nature of law went hand in hand with the nature of the republic itself. Indeed the very idea of a Republic, of *res publicae*, things pertaining to the public—supports the idea of matters of public concern being regulated by public rules, as opposed to the *arbitrario*—the raw will of the ruler . . . . The need to know law is a function of the structure of the state, and its basic purpose in creating coherent social order, in which ruler and subject can locate themselves.[29]

Jeremy Bentham echoes these ideas in utilitarian terms: "Publicity," he argues,

> [is] the very soul of justice. . . . It keeps the judge himself, while trying, under trial. Under the auspices of publicity, the cause in the court of law, and the appeal to the court of public opinion, are going on at the same time. . . . It is through publicity alone that justice becomes the mother of security. By publicity, the temple of justice is converted into a school of the first order, where the most important branches of morality are enforced, by the most impressive means: — into a theatre, where the sports of the imagination give place to the more interesting exhibitions of real life.[30]

For Bentham, publicity is the antidote both to unchecked power and to fantasies of the exercise of power untempered by a connection to the realities of its exercise in the world.

However venerable the pedigree of transparency, Alisdair Roberts argues that in fact democracies achieved a basic level of transparency only in the late nineteenth century.[31] Prior to that, governments operated under a strong presumption of secrecy. Slowly, though, the most advanced democracies began to mandate disclosure, a move toward managing rather than simply asserting the privilege of state secrecy.[32] In the United States, scandals of the 1960s and 1970s associated with the conduct of the Vietnam War[33] spawned legal tools to help citizens break the veil of government secrecy. The best known of these is the Freedom of Information Act, initially enacted in 1966 and subsequently amended, which establishes presumptive access for any person to existing, unpublished federal agency records on any topic.[34] FOIA contains, however, certain exemptions, the most significant of which preserves a zone of secrecy around national security information.[35] Particularly after the 9/11 attack, Roberts argues, "security organizations continued to exist in enclaves where the logic of transparency did not apply."[36]

Nonetheless, Amy Gutmann and Dennis Thompson argue that "the reasons officials and citizens give to justify political actions, and the information necessary to assess those reasons, should be public. This principle of publicity is a fundamental requirement of deliberative democracy."[37] They agree with Bentham that publicity both "motivates public officials to do their duty . . . [and] encourages citizens to deliberate about public policy and enables officials to learn about and from public opinion."[38] Moreover, they also endorse Kant's view that a policy is unjust if making it public would defeat its purpose. It loses moral legitimacy if it cannot be disclosed to those who are affected and bound by it, and on whose behalf it is enacted.[39] Building on that foundation, Gutmann and Thompson argue that in a deliberative democracy, there are four central reasons favoring publicity over secrecy: first, only public justifications can secure the consent of citizens, whether it be tacit or explicit; second, making reasons public contributes to the broadening of moral and political perspectives that deliberation ought to encourage; third, making reasons public fulfills the potential for mutual respect that deliberation seeks by clarifying the nature of moral disagreement; and fourth, secrecy undermines the self-correcting character of deliberation.[40]

While Gutmann and Thompson acknowledge that sometimes under narrow circumstances secrecy is necessary,[41] drawing on a distinction Kim Lane Scheppele first proposes, they suggest that certain kinds of secrets particularly damage deliberative democracy. Scheppele contrasts "shallow" secrets—those whose existence is suspected but not fully known—with "deep" secrets—those whose very existence is unknown.[42] While harmful, shallow secrets, Gutmann and Thompson suggest, at least afford citizens the chance to take up the challenge proffered by their keepers, and ultimately to decide whether the secret should be kept (at least ideally).[43] Deep secrets, on the other hand, threaten public trust and democratic governance much more significantly insofar as citizens cannot even begin to make inquiries about information because they do not know it exists.[44] As David Pozen puts it, "Deep secrets carry forward the premodern legacy of *arcane imperii*, mysteries of state the sovereign could invoke to justify his absolute authority and 'to secure domination over an immature people.'"[45]

In some instances, though—particularly when deep secrets concerning national security, having morphed into shallow secrets, are protected by courts—citizens do not have the capability to investigate and remediate even shallow secrets in the ways Gutmann and Thompson suggest. Take, for example, the recent case of *Wilner v. NSA*.[46] Attorneys for detainees held at Guantanamo Bay had submitted Freedom of Information Act requests to the National Security Agency and the Department of Justice seeking records showing whether the government had intercepted, under the Terrorist Surveillance Program (TSP), communications with their clients.[47] The TSP, once a deep secret, had been publicly acknowledged in December 2005 by President George W. Bush. When the agencies refused their requests, the attorneys sued.

The agencies, invoking the so-called *Glomar* doctrine (which created an exception to the FOIA when an agency asserts that exposing the very existence of certain classified records, if revealed, would endanger national security),[48] neither confirmed nor denied the existence of the requested records. The Second Circuit Court of Appeals upheld the validity of the government's actions, ruling that "[t]he fact that the public is aware of the program's existence does not mean that the public is entitled to have information regarding the operation of the program, its targets, the information it has yielded, or other highly sensitive national security information that the government has continued to classify." In other words, because of the FOIA's national security exception, the courts turned a shallow secret into a deep secret and produced rulings that denied the very possibility of litigation concerning TSP.

That logic has traveled well beyond FOIA. Indeed, under the ever-expanding "state secrets" doctrine, national security considerations have more and more frequently become a free-floating exemption that allows the government to frustrate access to courts themselves. The origins of the doctrine date to the 1953 case of *United States v. Reynolds.*[49] In *Reynolds*, the widows of three civilian crewmembers killed in a military airplane crash sued the government for negligence. The Air Force withheld its official accident report, claiming (falsely, as it later emerged) that releasing those reports would harm national security. The Supreme Court agreed, giving birth to the "state secrets doctrine." Under that doctrine, disclosures of information in a judicial proceeding may be prevented if there is a "reasonable danger" that such disclosure will "expose military matters which, in the interest of national security, should not be divulged."[50]

At the start, state secrets doctrine was understood to be limited, exempting from courtroom scrutiny specific items of evidence. Today it has expanded to end some cases altogether, without a trial.[51] Recently, for example, Khalid el-Masri, a German citizen, sued the United States, alleging that U.S. law had been violated when, under the mistaken belief that he was associated with Al Qaeda, the government arrested him as he traveled through Macedonia and authorized his "extraordinary rendition" to Afghanistan, where he was held for almost seven months and tortured. Once the U.S. government realized its mistake, it released him on a road in a remote area of Albania, from where he made his way back to Germany.

Although the CIA rendition program was widely known, even publicly acknowledged by the President, the Bush administration successfully asserted its privilege under the state secrets doctrine, securing the dismissal of el-Masri's suit in its entirety.[52] The general information available to the public, the Court reasoned, did not include the specific facts necessary to litigate the case; and while the courts, not the Executive Branch, determine whether the state secrets doctrine has been invoked properly, the judiciary does not "possess . . . a roving writ to ferret out and strike down executive excess. [Under Article III] we simply decide cases and controversies."[53] If the government presents a credible argument that litigation would imperil state security, then whatever the hardship on the plaintiff and whatever the injustice done, the case cannot proceed.

And yet those who secure and *publish* government secrets have not generally been prosecuted for doing so.[54] When the *New York Times* printed a story on illegal NSA surveillance in December 2005,[55] the Bush administration fulminated but ultimately did nothing. Why? According to Eric Posner, pragmatism and politics, rather than law, mandates a nonresponse. Prosecution would provide a forum for journalists to reveal information and to demand disclosure of further secrets to mount an adequate defense. Indeed, the very fact of prosecution suggests to enemies that the facts disclosed are significant, not trivial. In addition, prosecuting journalists can appear to the public to be a way of silencing critics. The result is, as Posner writes, that "statutes and constitutional precedent permit the government to prosecute journalists for publishing secrets, but politics and prudence ensure that it never does."[56] While the WikiLeaks case may prove to be a turning point,[57] it appears that in the area of national security, norms rather than law have been the most consistent and reliable guarantor of whatever transparency is achieved in governance.

Legal Secrets

The expansion of the state secrets doctrine provides a trenchant example of nontransparency imposing itself on political and legal processes otherwise committed to the principle of publicity. Criminal prosecutions are, after all, shaped by the Sixth Amendment's guarantee of a "speedy and public trial." Public trials, Thomas Cooley argued, are "for the benefit of the accused; that the public may see he is fairly dealt with and not unjustly condemned and that the presence of interested spectators may keep his triers keenly alive to a sense of their responsibility and to the importance of their functions."[58] Moreover, while audiences have sometimes been excluded from courtrooms,[59] the Supreme Court has held that under the First and Sixth Amendments, both press and public have a presumptive right to attend criminal trials.[60] As Lindsay Farmer suggests in his critique of secret trials (see below), public trials have a communicative function that promotes critical scrutiny of state officials.

Yet even in trials, arguably among the most public of legal proceedings, law operates with considerable opacity and its own, distinctive understandings of truth. Trials are opaque spaces in which knowledge is masked or excluded for reasons of both policy and efficiency. The guarantee of a public trial does not amount to a guarantee that trial proceedings transparently publicize either the "truth" of the process or the "truth" of the trial's underlying story. Trials are not mirrors of, or windows into, the social world; they are highly stylized and rule-governed proceedings.[61] Procedural rules of the sort that Edward Stein discusses below regulate what, how, and when evidence can be presented to a decision-maker, often excluding information as irrelevant or prejudicial that we might typically want and use when discussing and evaluating past events and social conflicts—gossip, general personal histories, patterns of behavior within and between social groups, and so forth. The hearsay rule (which excludes potentially unreliable evidence), rules about character evidence (which protect against false inferences), and rules guarding certain kinds of privileges meant to protect particularly important relationships (spousal, attorney-client, doctor-patient) serve to distinguish the narratives in a trial from the narratives in everyday life. They hide things from juries that jurors might want to know.[62]

Procedural rules invoked in the courtroom produce "shallow" secrets that overtly cordon off spaces from public view. For some, this casts doubt on the reliability and referentiality of legal proceedings, mistakenly elevating a cramped conception of fairness over the trial's truth-seeking function.[63] On this view, the opacities intentionally generated by procedural rules delegitimize the trial not by excluding the public but by misleading it; while the public may be allowed to scrutinize the process of judging, it cannot effectively assess the factual accuracy of the verdict. At the very least, as Bernadette Meyler, Melanie Williams, and Richard Burt suggest below, trial reports and other sorts of evidence about crime and the legal process capture only part of the truth underlying a case. Such evidence, if it is at all legible, requires readers educated enough to identify its gaps and elisions.

Perhaps of even greater concern for advocates of transparency in law, legal processes preceding (and often superseding) trials often, for the sake of efficiency, keep the scene of accusation and judgment out of the public eye. Practices such as custodial interrogation and plea bargaining can dramatically affect the way the state carries out criminal justice; yet they occur in the shadows of public adjudication.[64] Plea bargaining, for example, which "consists of the exchange of official concessions for a defendant's act of self-conviction,"[65] is conducted offstage and out of public view. Critics of the practice worry about its ease, its relaxed evidentiary standards, and its corruptibility, all of which are at least partly enabled by its relative secrecy.[66]

Concerns of this sort also arise in relation to custodial interrogation practices. Indeed the U.S. Supreme Court famously grappled in *Miranda v. Arizona* with the problematics of secrecy in interrogation, confronting and critiquing the interrogation room's power both as a policing tool and as a means of escaping public accountability. "Privacy," the majority noted, "results in secrecy and this in turn results in a gap in our knowledge as to what in fact goes on in the interrogation room."[67] The Court could fill that gap only via inference, by turning to instructional manuals intended to train the police in interrogation techniques. It found in them evidence of the ways interrogators use secrecy as a lever in order to gain psychological advantage over suspects.[68] "It is obvious," the majority noted, "that such an interrogation environment is created for no purpose other than to subjugate the individual to the will of his examiner. . . . The current practice of incommunicado interrogation is at odds with one of our Nation's most cherished principles—that the individual may not be compelled to incriminate himself."[69] Secrecy itself, it appears, enables the abrogation of fundamental rights. Moreover, as Christopher Kutz argues, it "hurts us existentially, because it deprives us of the way in which, once we are organized as a polity, law tells us who we are, by constituting our *orientation* in moral and political space—what values and acts we project into the world."[70]

And yet, if we worry that secrecy can corrupt the operations of law, it is also true that absolute transparency can disable them. The *Miranda* decision did not, in the final analysis, end the practice of custodial interrogation, let alone require that the police question suspects in public in order to maintain their accountability in a democratic society.[71] It merely interposed a verbal mechanism—a warning concerning the rights of the accused—meant to limit the worst excesses of state power. The police are able to overcome the resistance of uncooperative suspects precisely because questioning takes place in a coercive environment set outside the eyes of onlookers. Similarly, certain critical aspects of national defense—practices such as espionage, for example—succeed only through secrecy. In those contexts, complete transparency would effectively disable the state's capacity for self-preservation.

Overview of the Chapters

The Secrets of Law takes up the problematics of secrecy, transparency, and opacity from an interdisciplinary perspective. The first three chapters explore ways in which the political and legal ideal transparency is negotiated in various contexts, particularly in public discourse and in trial processes. What advantage does secrecy provide, and to whom, as it emerges in zones of contact and disputation between the state and its citizens? And what values are forwarded by an embrace of the principle of publicity? The answers to such questions are not always as straightforward as one might expect; in some instances the public—or at least parts of it—benefits from the ways the state asserts and confers the privilege of secrecy.

If our first three contributors identify certain conundrums in the *political valuation* of transparency, the second half of this volume raises questions about the very *capacity* of language and image to represent the world in a way that could achieve the ideal of transparency in the first instance. Attending carefully to representational practices in literary and filmic texts, the final three chapters suggest that opacity is an unavoidable and constitutive part of human discourse, one that can be mobilized for political purposes but that cannot be expunged entirely, even with the most radical embrace of openness in governance. Publicity, in other words, is no guarantor of transparency: even if the state were to make every document, ruling, and decision available to the public, the necessary opacity of signification processes would still mediate our relation to their meanings.

Beginning with the question of transparency in democratic processes, Alasdair Roberts argues in "Open Secrets and Dirty Hands" that while the Bush administration was conventionally understood to be the most secretive in decades, in fact such claims both overstate the president's power to maintain secrecy and, more significantly, miss the fact that many of the abuses alleged to have been committed were in fact "open secrets." A number of pressures, Roberts notes, have encouraged and enhanced transparency in governance: laws passed since the Johnson administration era; a growing ethic of dissent rather than deference; and the digitization of media coverage. Why, then, did such "open secrets" about the conduct of the war on terror persist in the face of early and repeated publicity, which Roberts documents in detail, about "secret" prisons, extraordinary rendition, and coercive interrogation?

Roberts de-emphasizes explanations involving, on the one hand, worries about imprecise knowledge and standards of proof, and, on the other, the dynamics of news media coverage and incentives for opponents of secrecy to overemphasize its existence. Rather, he argues, citizens are complicit in maintaining the appearance of secretiveness because it helps us to avoid the problem of dirty hands and the ethical dilemmas that knowledge about unlawful government actions produce. "Open secrets," he writes, "become a convenient way of dissolving our moral problems, or at least of putting them out of sight."

If the embrace of secrets has some allure for democratic subjects ambivalent about the exercise of state power, the political values expressed in already-existing legal practices such as trials can counterbalance that allure and reassert the centrality of transparency in governance. In this vein, Lindsay Farmer's "Secret Trials and Public Justice" considers the principle of public justice in the context of England's response to the war on terror. Arguing that there is an intrinsic connection between fair and public trials, Farmer offers both an historical genealogy of the development and justification for the principle of a public trial and an assessment of normative arguments in support of it.

Early English adversarial trials, Farmer argues, were open to the public for practical reasons related to the operations of juries (who actively participated in proceedings), but by the nineteenth century, the public nature of trials was less an issue of practicality than of ideology. As punishment moved behind closed doors, trials replaced the scaffold as a space for the public staging of innocence and guilt. Farmer examines this shift in the staging of justice by tracing changes in both courtroom practice and architecture. Nineteenth-century courtrooms were built to emphasize the authority of law and the efficiency and competency of the criminal justice system rather than to include the public in any meaningful way; they reduced the scope of physical space that had encouraged sociability and increased the segregation of legal officials from the public. By the early twentieth century, Farmer argues, while publicity in judicial proceedings was acknowledged as necessary (subject to certain exceptions meant to maintain security for witnesses, evidence, and reasons of state), it had no clear rationale.

Farmer takes up the task of justifying publicity in trials at a particularly critical historical moment, one in which secret tribunals are proliferating. In doing so, he rejects commonplace arguments that support a right to a public trial on grounds of, for example, encouraging the production of truth or holding judges accountable to public opinion. Instead Farmer offers a "communicative" defense of public trials. If condemnation of wrongdoing is offered in the name of the public, he argues, then surely the public has a right to know that the condemnation is justified by scrutinizing the proceedings. If it is not, then the public (at least in liberal democracies) has a corollary right to distance itself from verdicts. If properly conducted, trials can also educate the public about both right and wrong and the norms of criminal justice. At the heart of a fair trial is publicity that enables communication and scrutiny; and under this principle, secret trials are for Farmer presumptively unfair. As he suggests, "A trial in which justice is not seen to be done cannot properly be said to be just."

Trials are not, as we noted previously, fully transparent legal forms. Edward Stein's "Spousal Secrets: Same-Sex Couples and the Functional Approach to Marital Evidentiary Privileges" explores one telling example of secrecy built into the law itself: spousal evidentiary privileges. The evidentiary law of "spousal secrets" renders inadmissible in court both confidential communications between spouses and adverse testimony against one's spouse. Spousal secret doctrines (the confidential communication privilege and adverse testimonial privilege) reflect a number of policy priorities that value the protection of marriage above the legal search for truth. In most jurisdictions courts use a bright-line rule: if one is married even in ways that indicate the marriage is moribund or a sham, the rules apply; if one is not married, even if completely committed to one's partner, the rules do not apply.

Arguing that evidence law needs to accommodate the increasing legal recognition of spouselike relationships in same-sex couples (domestic partnership, civil union, and marriage), Stein carefully recounts and evaluates the history of the spousal evidentiary privilege and arguments for and against them. He favors what he calls a "sophisticated functionalist approach" over the bright-line rules currently in place. All couples invoking the privilege, whether opposite-sex or same sex, would be evaluated in a process that would take into account emotional commitment and involvement, financial commitment and entanglement, mutual reliance for personal services, the way they have conducted themselves in their personal life and held themselves out publicly, the level of intimacy between them, and the totality of the relationship as it is expressed in mutual dedication, care, and self-sacrifice. Stein argues that this functionalist approach closely hews to the justifications put forward in favor of the privilege generally—fostering strong marriages, respecting privacy, and so forth—resulting in their fairer and more equal application.

While the first three chapters examine the role of secrecy in contemporary political and legal practices, the three chapters that round out this collection explore legal, literary, and filmic *representations* of secrets in and around law, focusing in particular on the ways in which legal knowledge (knowledge, that is, about particular cases and crimes) is rendered opaque to those attempting to access and decode it. Bernadette Meyler's "Wilkie Collins' Law Books: Law, Literature, and Factual Precedent" approaches the problem of legal transparency through the lens of cultural and literary history. Meyler argues that rhetoric in democracies extolling transparency and public access to knowledge about law ought to be evaluated by examining the ways legal texts are received by readers. She turns to the popular nineteenth-century genre of the trial report, which self-consciously addressed itself to a broad audience, and examines the genre both on its own terms and as it was taken up in the literary works of Wilkie Collins.

Following Bentham, English trial reports emphasized transparency as a check on miscarriages of justice or the distortion of doctrine. These collections aimed to produce a jury pool more capable of exercising legal judgment, teaching jurors how to consider and weigh evidence and emphasizing specifically the difficulties of relying on circumstantial evidence in criminal trials. Meyler explores debates surrounding the use of such evidence in trials as a way to reflect on the problem of interpreting evidence—and particularly textual evidence—more generally. Trial reports purport to relate accurately the trials they represent; but on Meyler's reading the collections do not offer an accurate account so much as one perspective on those trials.

Wilkie Collins comes to the same conclusion in his 1875 novel *The Law and the Lady*, which charts the course of its "naïve" reader Valeria Woodville as she works to exonerate her husband from the charge of murdering his first wife after reading a trial report's rather damning account of his trial. Valeria grows increasingly sophisticated in her capacity to read elisions in legal texts; she is more and more able to reconstruct exculpatory evidence in opposition to the logic of the trial report. At the same time, Meyler suggests, Valeria's own methods of retrospective rearrangement and judgment resemble those of the report. As such, *the Law and the Lady* offers an immanent critique of the belief that law inevitably will grow more transparent or that writing will render representations of law more accurate.

Melanie Williams's "Historiographic Secrets of the Labour Contract—The Law and Literature of Lewis Jones 'Cwmardy' and 'We Live'" takes up similar questions concerning law's transparency in both legal and literary texts. But while Meyler emphasizes the problematic of reading and interpreting the law in relatively private settings, Williams focuses on the ways in which law is implicated in public struggles over structural imbalances between capital and labor. Juxtaposing legal texts explicating labor and contract law with two novels by the Welsh writer Lewis Jones, she considers the legal effacement of a significant social history arising out of brutal clashes between mine workers and owners in early-twentieth-century south Wales.

Williams argues that Jones's novels depict in rich detail an organic critique of law, the ways legal processes and actors, from the coroner to the police, subtend oppressive working conditions in the mines and the ruthlessness with which mine owners quash miner protests. She places Jones's description of police brutality against strikers, loosely based on a famous 1910–11 strike in south Wales, alongside a leading 1925 case, *Glasbrook Brothers v. Glamorgan City Council*, concerning the contract law doctrine of consideration. The question in *Glasbrook Brothers* was whether the police may demand payment if, at the request of an individual, they provide a special form of protection outside the scope of their public duty.

The House of Lords agreed that payment was due the police without nodding in any way to what she calls a secret subtext in the visible world of law: the political context of the case (owners hiring local police to break strikes) or the larger questions at stake when private individuals commandeer public power to further their own interests and coerce their workers into the effective equivalent of slavery. The secrets law keeps in its contestable accounts of history, and its elision of the lived, subjective experience of the workers, indicate a deep ideological resistance to acknowledging law's complicity with injustice. Jones's literary narrative, she argues, offers a corrective to the legal record's "truth-space," which erases the political and historical context that produces a critique of the rule of law itself.

Finally, Richard Burt's "Duly Noted or Off the Record? Sovereignty and the Secrecy of the Law in Cinema" calls into question a set of common assumptions about the transparency and legibility of legal records and evidence, and by extension what he calls the "indivisibility" both of the record-as-truth and more generally of sovereign power as it is exercised in law's capacity to know the world through writing. Focusing in particular on the trope of the note—a kind of writing whose status as evidence and/or a legal record is unstable and undecidable—Burt offers nuanced deconstructive readings of a number of films (*All the President's Men*, *JFK*, and in particular two of Fritz Lang's films, *Fury* and *The Testament of Dr. Mabuse*). In those readings he examines the role that notes, note-taking, and note-reading play in, on the one hand, the production of conspiracy theory (the illegibility of the note makes us wonder what secret the state is keeping from us) and, on the other, the failure of law to capture the meaning of notes and fulfill its enforcement role.

These films, Burt argues, offer an allegory of law's secrets, which he equates with the ultimate unreadability of notes and their incapacity to record and reconstruct the past in order to guide investigations toward justice and narrative closure. Through a close and complex reading of the films, he highlights the ways in which notes allegorize the intractable illegibility of seemingly transparent evidence, ultimately raising a larger set of questions about the ways in which secrets disturb the operations of law and signal the limits of its reach. For Burt, the way these films represent language through notes suggests that easy assumptions about transparency in governance (those, for example, underlying FOIA requests: revelation of official records will produce a true story about state actions) are at best naive, disabled by the very operations of representational processes themselves.

Taken together, the chapters in this book suggest that democracy's aspirations to transparency are always vulnerable to, and haunted by the allure of, secrecy. The opacity built into legal and governance processes can permit the unfettered exercise of state power, and can elevate certain values—national preservation, or the protection of certain kinds of relationships, or the suppression of inconvenient failures—over a general interest in publicity. To the extent that secrecy poses dilemmas that are not just political but also epistemological and interpretive, citizens invested in political and legal transparency must cultivate a capacity to read between the lines, to look for shadows cast by the unseen, to decode the illegible and, failing that, to acknowledge both the virtues and the dangers of the unknowable.

Notes

1. This description was taken off the website in October 2010. See http://wikileaks.org/wiki/WikiLeaks:About (currently unavailable).

2. http://mirror.wikileaks.info/.

3. On the Pentagon Papers controversy, see David Rudenstine, *The Day the Presses Stopped: A History of the Pentagon Papers Case* (Berkeley: University of California Press, 1996); Sanford Ungar, *The Papers and the Papers: An Account of the Legal and Political Battle over the Pentagon Papers* (New York: Columbia University Press, 1989); and Daniel Ellsberg, *Secrets: A Memoir of Vietnam and the Pentagon Papers* (New York: Viking, 2002).

4. See Jeremy Bentham, "Of Publicity," in Jeremy Bentham, *The Works of Jeremy Bentham,* vol. 2 [1843], found at http://oll.libertyfund.org/?option=com_staticxt&staticfile=show.php%3Ftitle=1921&chapter=113929&layout=html&Itemid=2. For a different perspective on transparency, see Lawrence Lessig, "Against Transparency: The Perils of Openness in Government," *New Republic* (October 9, 2009), at http://www.tnr.com/article/books-and-arts/against-transparency. As Lessig puts it, "How could anyone be against transparency? Its virtues and its utilities seem so crushingly obvious. But I have increasingly come to worry that there is an error at the core of this unquestioned goodness. We are not thinking critically enough about where and when transparency works, and where and when it may lead to confusion, or to worse. And I fear that the inevitable success of this movement—if pursued alone, without any sensitivity to the full complexity of the idea of perfect openness—will inspire not reform, but disgust. The 'naked transparency movement,' as I will call it here, is not going to inspire change. It will simply push any faith in our political system over the cliff."

5. "What does Assange want? Does he really want the free world to cringe under constant threat from al Qaeda? If we fail to defeat this threat, what does Assange think will happen? Do we have any sense that he cares? Or is it the case, frighteningly, that Assange doesn't really 'want' anything, in a programmatic, civilizational sense, and that these explosive episodes of 'gotcha' leaks are an end in themselves, a personal moral terminus, a sort of self-righteous, self-congratulatory onanism?" Tunku Varadarajan, "What Does Julien Assange Want?" The Daily Beast, 7/28/2010, http://www.thedailybeast.com/blogs-and-stories/2010-07-28/wikileaks-founder-julian-assange-is-a-criminal/2/.

6. One has remarked, "Look deeply into WikiLeaks' efforts at radical transparency and you find complete opacity; WikiLeaks wants to shine a light on the world, but only by keeping itself shrouded in secrecy." Farhad Manjoo, "The WikiLeaks Paradox," Slate, July 28, 2010, http://www.slate.com/id/2262066/.

7. For an interesting discussion of anonymous speech, see Danielle Allen, "Anonymous: On Silence and the Public Square," in Austin Sarat, ed., *Speech and Silence in American Law* (New York: Cambridge University Press, 2010).

8. The premise that candor is incompatible with disclosure has become a cornerstone of the edifice of government secrecy, and an axiom of freedom of information policy, which provides an exemption for deliberative records. It seems intuitively obvious that private discussions lend themselves to greater candor than do public ones. In private, anyone might be more willing to reveal ignorance or uncertainty, to express personal emotion, or to consider risky or improbable alternatives. For an interesting reflection on arguments about the relationship of secrecy and candor, see Eric Lane, Frederick A. O. Schwarz, Jr., and Emily Berman, "Too Big a Canon in the President's Arsenal: Another Look at United States v. Nixon," 17 *George Mason Law Review* (2010): 1737. In practice, according to the authors, secrecy may actually discourage candor. "When policy deliberations are deemed likely to remain secret, dissenters from the majority view might be more reluctant to give voice to their concerns. . . . And decision makers themselves might feel freer to silence dissenters when they do not expect their decision-making processes to be subject to scrutiny."

9. See Barbara Benedict, *Curiosity: A Cultural History of Early Modern Inquiry* (Chicago: University of Chicago Press, 2001), ch. 3.

10. For one example, see Carol Smart, "Law and the Regulation of Family Secrets," 24 *International Journal of Policy and the Family* (2010): 397.

11. Marianne Valverde, *Law's Dream of a Common Knowledge* (Princeton: Princeton University Press, 2003), 1.

12. See "Bond and Feinstein Urge Prosecution of WikiLeaks' Julian Assange," *Politico* (December 2, 2010), at http://www.politico.com/blogs/joshgerstein/1210/Bond__Feinstein_urge_prosecution_of_WikiLeaks_Julian_Assange.html.

13. Sissela Bok writes, "Awareness of the allure and the dangers of secrecy . . . is central to human experience of what is hidden and set apart. Rooted in encounters with the powerful, the sacred, and the forbidden, this experience goes far deeper than the partaking of any one secret. Efforts to guard secrets, probe them, or share them often aim for this deeper and more pervasive experience." See Bok, *Secrets: On the Ethics of Concealment and Revelation* (New York: Vintage Books, 1989), 5.

14. On the ambiguity of the sacred, see Emile Durkheim, *Elementary Forms of Religious Life*, trans. Karen E. Fields (New York: Free Press, 1995), 34–39.

15. Bok, *Secrets*, 10.

16. Ibid., 18.

17. See Georg Simmel, "The Secret and the Secret Society," in Karl Wolff, ed., *The Sociology of Georg Simmel* (New York: Free Press of Glenco, 1950), 331.

18. As Simmel describes it, "From secrecy, which shades all that is profound and significant, grows the typical error according to which everything mysterious is something important and essential. Before the unknown, man's natural impulse to idealize and his natural fearfulness cooperate toward the same goal: to intensify the unknown through

imagination, and to pay attention to it with an emphasis that is not usually accorded to patent reality." Ibid., 333.

19. Kim Scheppele, *Legal Secrets: Equality and Efficiency in the Common Law* (Chicago: University of Chicago Press, 1988), 5.

20. Bok, *Secrets,* 8, 25.

21. See, for example, Winston Smith's collapse at the hands of his brutal torturer O'Brian in George Orwell's midcentury classic *1984*. George Orwell, *1984* (New York: Harcourt Brace Jovanovich, 1949); or the moral dilemmas of the surveillance expert so sensitively rendered in the recent German film *The Lives of Others,* dir. Florian Henckel von Donnersmarck (Sony Pictures Classics, 2006).

22. Samuel B. Warren and Louis D. Brandeis, "The Right to Privacy [The Implicit Made Explicit]," 4 *Harvard Law Review,* no. 5 (December 1890): 193–220.

23. Bok, *Secrets,* 5–6. Scheppele also stresses the importance of intention in defining secrecy. Scheppele, *Legal Secrets,* 13.

24. Bok, *Secrets,* 10–11.

25. Bok argues that we require secrecy for at least four reasons: to protect identity and its sacredness; for choosing and planning, and producing creativity; to allow us to act in the world with openness; and for linking things with our identity in a property-oriented way. Ibid., 20–23.

26. Edward A. Shils, *The Torment of Secrecy: The Background and Consequences of American Security Policies* (Chicago: Ivan R. Dee, 1956), 26. See also Stanton K. Tefft, ed., *Secrecy: A Cross-Cultural Perspective* (New York: Human Sciences Press, 1980), 25–34.

27. In an important early-twentieth-century essay on secrets, for example, the sociologist Georg Simmel argues that individuals can never fully express their psychical processes ("their flaring up, their zigzag motion, the chaotic whirling of images and ideas which objectively are entirely unrelated to one another") even to themselves. "All we communicate to another individual by means of words or perhaps in another fashion—even the most subjective, impulsive, intimate matters—is a selection from that psychological-real whole whose absolutely exact report (absolutely exact in terms of content and sequence) would drive everybody into the insane asylum. . . . With an instinct automatically preventing us from doing otherwise, we show nobody the course of our psychic processes in their purely causal reality. . . . Always, we show only a section of them, stylized by selection and arrangement." For Simmel, secrecy is a part of a more general dynamic at the heart of all social relationships, which necessarily depend upon a dialectic of self-restraint and self-revelation. "Relationships being what they are," he writes, "they . . . presuppose a certain ignorance and a measure of mutual concealment." Simmel, "The Secret and the Secret Society," 311–12, 315.

28. See Burt in this volume for an example of this sort of deconstructive approach to secrecy.

29. Christopher Kutz, "Secret Law and the Value of Publicity," 22 *Ratio Juris* (2009): 202–3.

30. Jeremy Bentham, *Benthamiana; or Select Extracts from the Works of Jeremy Bentham, With an Outline of His Opinions on the Principal Subjects Discussed in His Works*, ed. John Hill Burton (Edinburgh: W. Tait, 1843), 115.

31. Alisdair Roberts, *Blacked Out: Government Secrecy in the Information Age* (Cambridge: Cambridge University Press, 2006), 10.

32. After the explosive growth of the administrative branch during the New Deal raised concerns about government transparency, for example, Congress passed the 1946 Administrative Procedures Act, which substantially increased public access to bureaucratic decision-making. Ibid.,13.

33. For a helpful overview of government secrecy in that era, see ch. 6 in Geoffrey R. Stone, *War and Liberty, An American Dilemma: 1790 to the Present* (New York: W. W. Norton, 2007), and Stone, *Perilous Times: Free Speech in Wartime, from the Sedition Act of 1798 to the War on Terrorism* (New York: W. W. Norton, 2004).

34. Freedom of Information Act (5 U.S.C. 552). See, generally, Harold Relyea and Michael Kolalowski, *CRS Report for Congress: Access to Government Information in the United States*, http://www.fas.org/sgp/crs/secrecy/97-71.pdf, accessed on January 19, 2011. The FOIA contains nine exemptions, however, that can block requests. Those exemptions cover national security information; internal personnel rules and practices; information exempt under other laws; confidential business information; inter- or intra-agency communication that is subject to deliberative process, litigation, and other privileges; personal privacy; certain law enforcement records; financial institutions; and geological information. See FOIA information at the National Security Archive, http://www.gwu.edu/~nsarchiv/nsa/foia/guide.html, accessed February 19, 2011.

35. See FOIA information at the National Security Archive, http://www.gwu.edu/~nsarchiv/nsa/foia/guide.html, accessed February 19, 2011.

36. Roberts, *Blacked Out*, 56. For a good overview of transparency theory, a critique of the assumptions embedded in an uncritical embrace of transparency in relation to open government laws, and an argument that the term "transparency" is itself opaque, see Mark Fenster, "The Opacity of Transparency," 91 *Iowa Law Review* (2006): 885–949.

37. Amy Gutmann and Dennis Thompson, *Democracy and Disagreement* (Cambridge, MA: Harvard University Press, 1996), 95. See also Joseph E. Stiglitz, "On Liberty, the Right to Know, and Public Discourse: The Role of Transparency in Public Life," in Matthew J. Gibney, ed., *Globalizing Rights: The Oxford Amnesty Lectures 1999* (Oxford: Oxford University Press, 2003), 114–56.

38. Gutmann and Thompson, *Democracy and Disagreement*, 97. As James Madison famously said, "A popular government, without popular information, or the means of acquiring it, is but a Prologue to a Farce or a Tragedy; or, perhaps both." James Madison,

"Letter to W. T. Barry" (August 4, 1822), in Gaillard Hunt, ed., *The Writings of James Madison, 1819–1836* (New York: G. P. Putnam's Sons, 1910), 103.

39. Gutmann and Thompson, *Democracy and Disagreement*, 99.

40. Ibid., 100–101. Sissela Bok puts the point more generally. In a democracy, she argues, "[s]ecrecy can diminish the sense of personal responsibility for joint decisions and facilitate all forms of skewed or careless judgment, including that exhibited in taking needless risks. It offers participants a shield against outside criticism, and can obscure the possibilities of failure—especially if the decision-makers come to think that the situation resembles a game." Bok, *Secrets*, 108.

41. Gutmann and Thompson, *Democracy and Disagreement*, 101–17.

42. Scheppele, *Legal Secrets*, 21.

43. Gutmann and Thompson, *Democracy and Disagreement*, 121.

44. David Pozen invokes former Secretary of Defense Donald Rumsfeld's definition, "[T]hings we do not know we do not know," as a gloss on deep secrecy. David E. Pozen, "Deep Secrecy," 62 *Stanford Law Review* (2009–10): 260. See also Gutmann and Thompson, *Democracy and Disagreement*, 121–23. For an epistemological exploration of the process of keeping and classifying government secrets, see Peter Galison, "Removing Knowledge," 31 *Critical Inquiry* no. 1 (Autumn 2004): 229–43.

45. Pozen, "Deep Secrecy," 288 (internal citations omitted).

46. *Wilner et al. v. NSA*, 2009 U.S.App. LEXIS 28610 (December 30, 2009), at 23.

47. On the TSA, see Jane Mayer, *The Dark Side: The Inside Story of How the War on Terror Turned into a War on American Ideals* (New York: Doubleday, 2008), 67–70; and Jack Goldsmith, *The Terror Presidency: Law and Judgment inside the Bush Administration* (New York: Norton, 2009).

48. The *Glomar* doctrine originated in *Phillippi v. CIA*, 546 F.2d 1009 (D.C. Cir. 1976).

49. *United States v. Reynolds*, 345 U.S. 1 (1953). See also Louis Fisher, *In the Name of National Security: Unchecked Presidential Power and the Reynolds* Case (Lawrence: University of Kansas Press, 2006); Michael Freedman, "Daughters of the Cold War," *Legal Affairs* (January/February 2004), http://www.legalaffairs.org/issues/January-February-2004/story_freedman_janfeb04.msp, accessed January 19, 2011.

50. *Reynolds*, at 10.

51. See, most recently, *General Dynamics Corp. v. U.S.* (case number 09-1298), oral arguments heard January 18, 2011.

52. *El-Masri v. United States*, 479 F.3d 296 (2007).

53. Ibid., at 22.

54. For opposing opinions on the subject of publishing national security secrets, see Stone, *Perilous Times* and Gabriel Schoenfeld, *Necessary Secrets: National Security, the Media, and the Rule of Law* (New York: W. W. Norton and Co., 2010).

55. James Risen and Eric Lichtblau, "Bush Lets U.S. Spy on Callers without Courts," *New York Times*, December 16, 2005, http://www.nytimes.com/2005/12/16/politics/16program.html?_r=1&scp=1&sq=december%202005%20nsa%20surveillance&st=cse (accessed January 21, 2011).

56. Eric Posner, "The Prudent and the Imprudent," *New Republic Online* (May 18, 2010), http://www.tnr.com/book/review/the-prudent-and-the-imprudent (accessed January 20, 2011).

57. Charlie Savage, "U.S. Tries to Build Case for Conspiracy by WikiLeaks," *New York Times* (December 15, 2010), http://www.nytimes.com/2010/12/16/world/16wiki.html (accessed January 21, 2011).

58. Thomas M. Cooley, *A Treatise on the Constitutional Limitations Which Rest Upon the Legislative Power of the States of the American Union*, vol. 1 (8th ed. 1927), 647. As the Court said in *Estes v. Texas*, "A fair trial is the objective, and 'public trial' is an institutional safeguard for attaining it." *Estes v. Texas*, 381 U.S. 532 (1965), at 588.

59. For example, the protection of public morality in sex crimes trials; to elicit sensitive testimony from victims (particularly children); to preserve the anonymity of undercover officers; or to maintain order in the courtroom. See Comment, "Scaling Waller: How Courts Have Eroded the Sixth Amendment Public Trial Right," 59 *Emory Law Journal* (2009): 507–9.

60. *Richmond Newspapers Inc. v. Virginia*, 467 U.S. 555 (1980); *Press Enterprise Co. v. Superior Court*, 464 U.S. 501 (1984); *Waller v. Georgia*, 467 U.S. 39 (1984).

61. See, generally, Robert Burns, *A Theory of the Trial* (Princeton: Princeton University Press, 1999), esp. chs. 2 and 3.

62. William Finnegan, "Doubt," *New Yorker* (January 31, 1994), found at http://www.newyorker.com/archive/1994/01/31/1994_01_31_048_TNY_CARDS_000367305.

63. See, for example, William Pizzi, *Trials without Truth: Why Our System of Criminal Trials Has Become an Expensive Failure and What We Need to Do to Rebuild It* (New York: New York University Press, 1999).

64. For a critique of plea bargaining, see Albert W. Altschuler, "Plea Bargaining and Its History," 79 *Columbia Law Review* no. 1 (January 1979): 1–43; and John Langbein, "Torture and Plea Bargaining," 46 *University of Chicago Law Review* no. 1 (Autumn 1978): 3–22. For a revealing look into the interrogation room, see Richard Leo, "Inside the Interrogation Room," 86 *Journal of Criminal Law and Criminology* no. 2 (1996): 266–303.

65. Altschuler, "Plea Bargaining and Its History," 3.

66. See Langbein, "Torture and Plea Bargaining," 15–19.

67. *Miranda v. Arizona*, 384 U.S. 436 (1966), 448.

68. Ibid., 449 (quoting Inbau and Reid, *Criminal Interrogation and Confessions* [1962], 1).

69. *Miranda*, 457–58.

70. Kutz, "Secret Law and the Value of Publicity," 200.

71. On the efficacy of *Miranda*, see Richard Leo, "Miranda's Revenge: Police Interrogation as a Confidence Game," 30 *Law and Society Review* (1996): 259.

Open Secrets and Dirty Hands

ALASDAIR ROBERTS

There has never been an executive branch more fetishistic about secrecy. The secrecy has been used to throw a veil over detentions, renditions, suspension of the Geneva Conventions and of habeas corpus, torture and warrantless wiretaps.

—Garry Wills, January 2007[1]

To understand the magnitude of what may have gone on in America's secret prisons, you don't need special security clearance or inside information. Anyone who wants to connect the dots can do it.

—Anne Applebaum, June 2004[2]

The conventional wisdom about the presidency of George W. Bush is that it was more secretive than any administration in decades. Indeed, critics of President Bush appeared to engage in a bidding war when it came to describing precisely how secretive his administration had been. The distinguished historian Arthur Schlesinger, Jr., opened with an offer of three decades: Bush, he said, headed "the most secretive administration since Nixon."[3] Larry Klayman, chairman of Judicial Watch, a conservative watchdog organization, upped the ante. The Bush administration, he said, was the most secretive since the inauguration of President Eisenhower in 1951.[4] John Dean, President Nixon's legal counsel, went further, claiming that the administration was the most secretive since Roosevelt.[5] Distinguished journalist Haynes Johnson said that secrecy in the Bush administration was the worst since the presidency of Herbert Hoover.[6] The Reporters' Committee for Freedom of the Press outdid them all, saying simply that the Bush administration had "embarked on an *unprecedented* path of secrecy."[7]

Complaints about secrecy were tied to a broader argument about the accretion of executive power in the five years after the attacks of September 11, 2001. Indeed, secretiveness was alleged to serve as one of the bulwarks of that expanded power. Critics feared that it allowed the president to undertake actions that would, if exposed, strike Americans as unconscionable—the lawless abduction of suspected terrorists, for example; or the indefinite detention of suspects in secret prisons; or the abuse and torture of prisoners believed to have knowledge of terrorist networks. Secrecy, it was thought, was the predicate for the persistence of these Kafka-esque policies. If only the truth came out, the abuses would stop, and administration officials would be held accountable.

This was an affirmation of Justice Louis Brandeis's claim, ninety years earlier, that transparency is the assured corrective to abuse of power. "Sunlight," said Brandeis, "is said to be the best of disinfectants."[8]

There are two broad difficulties with this line of argument. The first is that it substantially overstates the capacity of a postmillennial president to maintain secrecy. There is a disjunction between the rhetoric of executive power, which has deep roots in American political culture, and the realities of governance in an advanced liberal state. The second difficulty is that many abuses were not secret at all. The American public knew, or with reasonable effort could have known, the darker aspects of the antiterror program that the federal government had crafted for their protection. These were *open secrets*—generally known facts about which we purported to be ignorant.

Why did these open secrets persist for so many years? To put it another way, why did we persist in claiming ignorance about certain key facts? Perhaps because of our inability to overcome a deeply entrenched tradition of lamenting executive secrecy. Or perhaps because so many actors—booksellers and media outlets, advocacy groups and opposition politicians—had strong incentives to persuade us that generally known facts were actually well-kept secrets. Or perhaps because the forthright acknowledgment of these facts would lead to awkward questions about our willingness to tolerate such practices, or our complicity in their continuance. It is easier to protest against government secrecy than to address the reality of our own dirty hands.

Worse Than Nixon?

It was not hard to become outraged over the policies of the Bush administration. After 2001 it fumbled in its attempts to improve homeland security; treated immigrants and other aliens roughly; threatened the civil rights of citizens; treated Congress and the media with disdain; and launched an ill-considered war in Iraq that led to the death of more than four thousand U.S. soldiers and one hundred thousand Iraqi citizens.

The Bush administration also attempted to tighten government secrecy. It did this in many ways: by attempting to bend the interpretation of existing laws; classifying or withdrawing information that was previously in the public domain; asserting its right to withhold information in sensitive court cases; threatening public servants and journalists with leak investigations; firing officials suspected of leaking information; and prosecuting citizens who received government secrets for criminal offenses established by archaic laws.[9] A few of the administration's policies were defensible responses to the new circumstances that confronted the nation after September 11. But many of these policies were indefensible assertions of executive prerogatives that threatened to undermine public discourse, governmental accountability, and the capacity of citizens and aliens to protect their fundamental rights.

Even so, we have an obligation to maintain a sense of proportion. Indignation at the Bush administration's various attempts to restrict transparency, or at the broader effect of Bush policies, does not entitle us to exaggerate what it sought to do by way of tightening secrecy, or what it actually accomplished. The Bush administration tried to restrict openness. But it did not attempt a complete overturning of the elaborate system of rules and policies that has been constructed to ensure governmental openness; it was often unsuccessful in its attempts to increase secrecy; and it remained subject to closer scrutiny that many other presidencies of the modern era.

The reality is that the United States probably has one of the most open systems of government in existence. One way in which this transparency is ensured is through a battery of laws adopted since the Johnson administration that created obligations to disclose information, and new watchdog agencies to scrutinize government operations. The Bush administration did not attempt a frontal assault on a single one of those laws—and for good reason. In the last three decades a substantial network of nongovernmental organizations and supportive media has emerged that is capable of organizing quickly to resist direct attacks on the foundations of the U.S. transparency regime. The broad decline in trust of government over the last three decades has eased the task of mobilizing public support for such antisecrecy campaigns.[10]

Other considerations also tend toward greater openness. One is the decline of deference within public institutions and the rise in its place of an ethic of dissent, which legitimizes decisions by public servants to disclose information about governmental wrongdoing. Whistle-blowing was a concept largely unknown four decades ago; today the practice is sanctioned by law and likely to draw public approbation. Market pressures also encourage transparency, as media outlets and publishers compete for the right to publish tell-all accounts of governmental decision-making.[11] Insider knowledge has been commodified.

Technological change enhances transparency as well. Digitized information is more easily leaked, and once leaked is disseminated more rapidly. "Old media"—such as the major newspapers and broadcast television networks—no longer dominate the news business. Competition among a larger number of outlets—including Internet-based outlets and cable news networks—means that news stories will circulate much more quickly.

The combined effect of these legal, cultural, and technological changes is twofold: information is more likely to escape the grasp of government leaders, and more likely to circulate quickly—indeed, instantaneously—once it has escaped. This is a reality that provokes substantial anxiety about government leaders, who realize that their ability to control the policy agenda has substantially eroded. Policy debate is faster moving and more chaotic than ever before. Attempts to restore control over the policy agenda—by improving the capacity to impose "message discipline" within an administration, or to limit the unauthorized outflow of information—can be construed as responses to this anxiety about the loss of control, and attempts to regain mastery of the policy agenda.[12]

Thus the Bush administration's drive to increase secrecy is comprehensible, if not defensible. Nonetheless we must remember that there is a critical distinction between the desire to increase secrecy and success in attaining that goal. Throughout the first five years of President Bush's tenure, there was a Canute-like quality to the drive for secrecy. Despite its best efforts, the administration was foiled by inquiries, such as the 9/11 Commission; by leaks; by the tell-all books of former insiders; and journalistic exposes, such as the trilogy written by the *Washington Post*'s Bob Woodward. "At some point," said Tim Rutten of the *Los Angeles Times* in 2007, "George W. Bush's administration became the literary equivalent of a television reality show."[13]

The paradox of the Bush years is that we came to know an extraordinary amount about the inner workings and foibles of an administration that was, at the same time, damned for unprecedented secretiveness.

What We Knew, and When We Knew It

Largely because of these changes in the conditions of governance, it was often possible to obtain information about the behavior of government that would not have been available so readily in earlier years. And yet we continued throughout the Bush years to complain about the wall of secrecy that prevented us from comprehending how the federal government had executed its Global War on Terrorism. This complaint ought to be treated with a measure of skepticism. During the congressional investigation of the Watergate scandal, Senator Howard Baker—trying to gauge President Nixon's complicity in wrongdoing—famously asked: What did the President know, and when did he know it? It is useful to ask ourselves, with respect to the major controversies of the Bush administration: What did *we* know, and when did we know it?

Secret prisons. Consider, for example, the case of the CIA's prisons. In September 2006, President Bush conceded that a "small group of suspected terrorist leaders and operatives" had been captured and held in overseas detention centers operated by the CIA over the preceding five years.[14] This was widely reported in the U.S. media as an acknowledgment by the president that the United States had operated "secret prisons" since 2001.

But were these really *secret* prisons? As the editorialists of the *Hartford Courant* observed after the president's speech, the existence of the facilities had been an "open secret" for a considerable period of time.[15] Indeed, the *Washington Post* published an expose of the CIA's detention program in November 2005. The *Post*'s Dana Priest described "a covert prison system set up by the CIA nearly four years ago that at various times has included sites in eight countries, including Thailand, Afghanistan and several democracies in Eastern Europe ... [a] hidden global internment network [that] is a central element in the CIA's unconventional war on terrorism."[16] Priest's story appeared to be based on leaks from CIA sources who questioned the wisdom and legality of its policy. In January 2006, *New York Times* reporter James Risen also drew on CIA sources to describe the overseas prison systems run by its Counter-Terrorist Center, or CTC. About one of the largest facilities, code-named Bright Light, Risen wrote:

> CIA officers soon learned one thing for sure—prisoners sent to Bright Light and other facilities handling high-value detainees were probably never going to be released. "The word is that once you get to Bright Light, you never come back," said the CTC veteran.[17]

The credibility of these accounts was bolstered by a December 2005 report that the *Post*'s executive editor had met with President Bush before running Priest's story, to discuss "national security issues" that would be raised by its publication.[18] The CIA also notified the Justice Department that Priest's story provided evidence of an unauthorized disclosure of classified information.[19] Republican leaders in Congress urged its intelligence committees to launch their own investigation of the "egregious disclosure" of information to the *Post.* A CIA officer was fired five months later for allegedly leaking information to Priest and other journalists.[20]

At the time, the *St. Petersburg Times* called Priest's story a "revelation."[21] The *Boston Globe* said that the nation had been "shocked" by "news that the Central Intelligence Agency is running a system of secret prisons."[22]

Shocked? Even in November 2005 the existence of these "secret" prisons was widely acknowledged. The nongovernmental organization Human Rights Watch had complained in April 2004 that the United States was holding its most important detainees in undisclosed locations overseas.[23] In May 2004 the *Post* itself reported on an array of "small and secret CIA-run facilities where top al Qaeda figures are kept."[24] At the same time, *U.S. News & World Report* described

> the archipelago of prisons the United States has packed with suspected jihadists since 9/11. The Pentagon's base at Guantanamo Bay, where some 600 detainees are held, is well known, but there are a half-dozen others, all overseas, including facilities in Jordan, Afghanistan, and the U.S.-British base on Diego Garcia, in the Indian Ocean. . . . "They don't want anyone seeing what's happening to these guys," says a counterterrorism official.[25]

The *New York Times* reported in June 2003 that the government of Thailand had allowed the CIA to hold detainees within its borders "as part of a broader CIA program to take captives to 'undisclosed locations.'"[26] And in December 2002, the *Washington Post* described "a number of secret detention centers overseas where U.S. due process does not apply, according to several U.S. and European national security officials, where the CIA undertakes or manages the interrogation of suspected terrorists."[27]

In fact, the existence of secret detention centers could have been inferred from the earliest months of the War on Terrorism. It was reported in October 2001 that President Bush had given the CIA "new authority . . . for a global campaign against al Qaeda."[28] The U.S. government soon acknowledged that it had captured a number of high-profile affiliates of al Qaeda. The first two were Ibn al-Shaykh al-Libi, captured in January 2002, and Abu Zubaydah, captured in March 2002. Both were said at the time to be held at "undisclosed locations."[29] As the number of suspects known to be in U.S. custody increased, the following question naturally arose: Where were they?

Extraordinary rendition. There were other topics on which we continued to profess ignorance despite a steady supply of incriminating evidence. One of these topics was extraordinary rendition—the CIA's practice of abducting citizens from other countries and delivering them, on CIA-chartered jets, for interrogation by friendly intelligence services, or within the CIA's own detention facilities. Amnesty International complained in 2006 that the rendition program "thrives on secrecy."[30] In fall 2006, two best-selling books purported to expose the program. The authors of *Torture Taxi*, published in September, explained that rendition was "one facet of a much broader story of secrecy and imprisonment that spans the globe."[31] *Ghost Plane*, published a month later, described a "secret world of prisons, planes, and tortures cells" that is "a secret only from the public, from ordinary citizens."[32]

Secret from the public? "Credible reports" about the practice of extraordinary rendition had already been discussed by the Council of Europe's Parliamentary Assembly in April 2005.[33] Indeed, such reports were available to the public within weeks of the 9/11 attacks. The *Washington Post* reported in October 2001 that U.S. authorities had seized an al-Qaeda suspect, Jamil Qasim Saeed Mohammed, in Pakistan, "bypassed the usual extradition and deportation procedures," and flown him on a chartered Gulfstream jet to an unknown destination.[34] The *Australian* reported in February 2002 on the collection of al Qaeda suspect Muhammad Saad Iqbal in Indonesia. Citing "Indonesian and Western sources," the *Australian* said that Iqbal was also placed on a CIA-chartered Gulfstream jet, and flown to Egypt for interrogation.[35] The *Washington Post* reported on its front page in March 2002 that in the preceding six months,

> the U.S. government has secretly transported dozens of people suspected of links to terrorists to countries other than the United States, bypassing extradition procedures and legal formalities. . . . The suspects have been taken to countries, including Egypt and Jordan, whose intelligence services have close ties to the CIA and where they can

> be subjected to interrogation tactics—including torture and threats to families—that are illegal in the United States, the sources said. In some cases, U.S. intelligence agents remain closely involved in the interrogation, the sources said. "After September 11, these sorts of movements have been occurring all the time," a U.S. diplomat said. "It allows us to get information from terrorists in a way we can't do on U.S. soil."[36]

In July 2002, the *Christian Science Monitor* also reported that U.S. officials had privately confirmed the practice of seizing suspects and transporting them to countries (Egypt, Syria, and Jordan) that used torture. "These deportations," the *Monitor* observed, "are not done through official channels or according to extradition treaties."[37]

Indeed, it is difficult to abduct a large number of people and maintain secrecy about the practice. The Canadian news media knew within days that something had happened to Maher Arar, a Canadian citizen who became a "person of interest" to U.S. authorities in September 2002. "He has simply disappeared," Arar's brother told the press.[38] It was soon learned that the U.S. had delivered Arar to the Syrian intelligence service, which held him for interrogation, sometimes under torture, for a year. By February 2004 the Canadian government had established an judicial inquiry into Arar's treatment. (In September 2006 it found that Arar was innocent of any connection to terrorist groups.)[39] There were also public controversies over CIA abductions in Italy, Germany, and Sweden.

Coercive interrogation. By the end of 2006, there could be little doubt that federal authorities had used extraordinary methods while attempting to extract information from suspected terrorists. The president himself acknowledged in September 2006 that the CIA resorted to "an alternative set of procedures" when two major prisoners, Abu Zubaydah and Khalid Sheikh Mohammed, resisted questioning.[40]

Yet it was not unusual to read public professions of ignorance about what those procedures might be. In November 2006 the *New York Times* criticized the Bush administration for refusing to release a 2002 memorandum outlining permissible interrogation techniques, arguing that "Americans have a right to know what standards their president has been applying to the treatment of prisoners."[41] The editors of the *Los Angeles Times* put it more directly: "What those methods might be," they wrote in January 2007, "is anybody's guess."[42]

Anybody's guess? In truth, it was easy to discern what the standards of interrogation had been. In October 2005, for example, Senator John McCain proposed an amendment to the 2006 defense appropriations bill that prohibited federal employees from subjecting prisoners to "cruel, inhuman, or degrading treatment or punishment."[43] It was publicly reported that Vice President Cheney had lobbied senators to block the amendment or obtain an exemption for the CIA.[44] Congress compromised by adopting McCain's amendment but providing immunity if CIA employees had relied on the advice of legal counsel, and the prisoner was one whom the president has designated a suspected terrorist.[45] What inference would a reasonable person draw from these facts regarding the treatment of detainees by the CIA?

In June 2006, the Supreme Court raised the prospect of CIA liability once again, when its ruling in *Hamdan* suggested that CIA detainees could be protected by Common Article 3 of the Geneva Conventions, which prohibits not only cruelty and torture but also "outrages upon personal dignity, in particular humiliating and degrading treatment."[46] Congress responded in October 2006 by adopting legislation that raises the bar for prosecution of federal employees under U.S. law so that prosecution is possible only for "grave breaches" of the Conventions, such as cruel and inhuman punishment. It also loosened the standard for judging conduct before 2006, stating that the infliction of mental harm could not be punished if it was not prolonged.[47] Again, what inferences about the treatment of detainees would a reasonable person draw from these facts?

As the *St. Petersburg Times* said in November 2006, "[T]he fact that the Bush administration has used abusive and coercive interrogation techniques . . . is America's worst kept secret."[48] This had been clear for quite some time. In 2005 ABC News, drawing on "former and current intelligence officers," described several interrogation methods used by the CIA. These included waterboarding, in which "the prisoner is bound to an inclined board, feet raised . . . . Cellophane is wrapped over the prisoner's face and water is poured over him . . . [inducing] a terrifying fear of drowning."[49] Earlier that year, CIA director Porter J. Goss told the Senate Armed Services Committee that he was not able to say whether the agency used interrogation techniques in the aftermath of 9/11 "that are in any way against the law."[50] Documents leaked in June 2004 showed that the Justice Department had been determined, in the aftermath of the attacks, to stretch the interpretation of law to permit harsh interrogation techniques.[51]

These leaked documents were widely said to provide "revelations" about U.S. policy on interrogation. However, the *New York Times* had already reported in

March 2004 on "coercive interrogation methods . . . authorized by a set of secret rules" given to the CIA after 9/11.[52] (The methods included waterboarding and refusal of pain medication for injuries.)[53] In 2003 it was reported that recently captured al Qaeda leaders Abu Zubaydah and Khalid Sheik Mohammed were being held at a CIA center nicknamed Hotel California ("You can check out," the Eagles once sang, "but you can never leave") where, in the words of an intelligence source, "they do not worry too much about humanitarian laws."[54] Even in 2002, the *Washington Post* reported that the CIA was employing "stress and duress" techniques for interrogation. National security officials, it said, defended the use of violence against detainees as "just and necessary."[55]

Why Do Open Secrets Persist?

As the Bush administration's War on Terror escalated, Defense Secretary Donald Rumsfeld often described the epistemology upon which he relied. "There are known knowns," Rumsfeld said,

> . . . there are things we know we know. We also know there are known unknowns; that is to say we know there are some things we do not know. But there are also unknown unknowns—the ones we don't know we don't know. And if one looks throughout the history of our country and other free countries, it is the latter category that tend to be the difficult ones.[56]

However, this categorization is incomplete. It forgets the unacknowledged knowns—the things we know but profess not to know. This is the category of open secrets. This is, perhaps, the most peculiar category of all. After all, why would we insist that we do not know something when we clearly do?

One reason could be confusion about the standard to be applied in judging whether something is known. First, there is the question of *precision of knowledge*. We may have reason to believe that coercive interrogations are underway, for example, but we may be uncertain about precisely what coercive methods are employed. We may have evidence that there are CIA detention centers—but absent evidence about their precise location, may still consider them to be "secret." And so on.

At the same time there is a question about the *standard of proof*. One standard is that which is applied to everyday reasoning—which says that the reasonableness of a claim should be judged according to the weight of the evidence available to support it.[57] By this standard, I might be said to know a fact once I become aware that several usually credible sources have reported it. There are, however, more rigorous standards. I might insist that I do not know something to be a fact until a person in authority (the president, for example) explicitly acknowledges its truth. Or I might at least insist on seeing some document, authored or approved by persons in authority, that concedes the truth of some fact. We might call this the "smoking gun" standard.[58]

Critics who continued to typify the CIA's practices as "secrets" typically applied strict standards of precision and proof. Because the president had not admitted the practices, and no incriminating document had been leaked, and because we were unable to say exactly how or where the CIA had engaged in the practices, we were entitled (so the reasoning appeared to go) to consider them secret.

This way of thinking about secrets is deeply problematic. On one side, the rule about precision is unnecessarily rigorous. What precisely we need to know hinges on why we need to know it. If we are high officials in the European Union, we need to know whether the CIA's detention centers are in an EU member state, or not. Italian judges need to know whether the CIA undertook a rendition on Italian soil, and whether the Italian government cooperated in the abduction. In the United States, defense attorneys attempting to weigh the credibility of incriminating statements made by CIA prisoners need to know exactly how those statements were extracted.

For the rest of us, such details are not essential. Our main obligation arises out of our role as citizens, and has to do with our complicity in wrongdoing, and the imposition of accountability on our political leaders. The question is whether we, as citizens, are prepared to pressure our leaders to stop these practices, or whether we accept the practices as necessary evils. This question arises when we know that the practices are ongoing, even if we are ignorant of the exact details. Knowing whether a secret CIA prison is in Poland or Romania, or precisely what kind of cruel and inhumane interrogation tactic is being employed, is not crucial to the performance of our obligations as citizens.

Not only is our standard of precision sometimes unduly rigorous; our standard of proof is also unnecessarily high. We demand too much evidence before we concede that we know something. In fact, there are certain ironies at play here. Many Americans who criticized CIA practices were also deeply distrustful of President Bush and skeptical of the view, which he was said to endorse, that the Constitution established a "hierarchical, unified executive department" under his direct command.[59] However, a standard of proof that requires a statement by the president to substantiate a claim about executive branch activities implies an acceptance of the idea of a "unified executive" (on behalf of which the president speaks) and also faith that the president is being truthful when he admits or denies a fact.

On most other subjects relating to government operations we are not usually so cautious in reaching judgment. For example, most Americans concluded that the federal response to Hurricane Katrina had been badly botched even before the president acknowledged "serious problems in our response capability."[60] The media had already provided good evidence to support their beliefs about what the government had done. If we accepted this lesser standard of proof with regard to Katrina, why did we not apply it to CIA abuses as well?

None of this argument is meant to deny that there were key facts about CIA activities that remained unknown, and ought to have been revealed. But the material point is that the *essential* facts were well established very early in the War on Terrorism, by the standards of reasoning typically applied in everyday discourse. Editorialists who wrote of "open" or "badly kept" secrets were essentially conceding this point. But if that is the case, why did we persist in calling them *secrets* at all?

There may be several reasons, some of which arise of out the realities of life in an advanced liberal society. The first of these is market pressure for novelty and revelation. Stories that appear to recapitulate or elaborate upon what is generally known do not sell: they are not regarded as newsworthy or, for the trade press, as marketable.[61] Consequently there are strong incentives for media outlets and publishers to deny the significance of what is already known.

Thus St. Martin's Press, the publisher of *Ghost Plane*, was impelled to insist that the book tells "an inside story . . . for the first time" even if (as one reviewer noted) "it is essentially . . . infill material connected with sensational revelations already broadly known."[62] Similarly the *Washington Post* could not scoop other news outlets with stories about CIA detention facilities if the existence of such facilities was already widely acknowledged.

This tendency to deny the extent of what is already known is inadvertently encouraged by the network of nongovernmental organizations that is dedicated to the promotion of transparency in government—what I earlier called the transparency network. The function of this network is to defend and extend laws and policies that promote open government. To do this, the network must persuade other actors—philanthropies, journalists, legislators, citizens—to contribute scarce resources, such as money, space on the legislative agenda, and political support.

While campaigning for resources, constituents of the transparency community are unlikely to put great emphasis on evidence about advances toward more open government. They are more likely to assert that transparency is a gravely threatened value. As this community has grown, its skill in propagating concern about government secrecy has improved, likely reinforcing popular perceptions about the decline of governmental openness. In other words, there is no necessary correlation between the perception of secretiveness and actual secretiveness. We may believe we know less, even as we know more.[63]

There are, in addition, incentives for the president's political opponents to emphasize the secretiveness of government. As politicians, they hope to build as broad as base as possible; to do this they must appeal to values or concerns that are widely held. In dealing with subjects such as coercive interrogation or overseas prisons, the president's opponents must make a decision about how the debate should be framed to maximize political support.[64] One obvious approach is to condemn such practices directly. The difficulty with this approach is that there is a sizable constituency that might endorse the practices, and construe a direct attack on them as a sign of weakness in the War on Terrorism.

An oblique approach, more likely to attract broad support, is to withhold judgment on the practices themselves but to condemn the secretiveness with which they are undertaken. In essence, an opposition politician asserts that he does not know enough to judge. This is more likely to appeal to the substantial proportion of the electorate that is predisposed to condemn government secrecy even if they are broadly supportive of the administration's antiterrorism campaign. (A 2005 survey found that 70 percent of Americans said that they were concerned by government secrecy.[65] Obviously this must include a large number of Americans who were otherwise supportive of the War on Terrorism.) An effect of this oblique approach is to affirm the suspicion that key facts *are* being kept from public view, as well as the position that it is legitimate to suspend judgment until full disclosure of those key facts has been made.

Dirty Hands and Plausible Deniability

In short, many different actors have incentives to persuade us that we know less than we actually do—in other words, to enlarge the category of open secrets. However, we are not simply the victims of circumstance. Citizens themselves also have strong incentives to broaden this category. Open secrets are a useful way of dealing with the problem of dirty hands—that is, the predicament that arises when some great evil is bound to occur unless an individual permits some smaller evil.

The classic illustration of the dirty hands problem is the "ticking bomb" scenario, in which a captive terrorist is known to have information about the location of a bomb that will soon kill hundreds of innocent citizens, and torture is believed to be the only way of extracting the information before the bomb's detonation.[66] The question is whether an official decision to torture can be justified in such circumstances. It is tempting to evade the question by challenging the facts. Perhaps we do not know with certainty that there is bomb, or that there are pedestrians nearby; or that the captive has information; or that torture will be effective in extracting it. We could bundle these uncertainties together and justify a decision not to torture.

Suppose, however, that the uncertainties are small, or nonexistent. What is the right course of action? There is no easy answer. Choosing to torture a prisoner is morally offensive; but so is inaction that leads to the death of innocents. In some circumstances a leader may need to get his hands dirty (by torturing) to serve the larger public interest.

Of course, citizens themselves do not make the decision to torture or violate other ethical or legal constraints. Our leaders typically make these decisions on our behalf. But such decisions, once made by our leaders, generate conundrums for the rest of us as well. One such problem arises if a leader chooses to tell us that he has dirtied his hands for the public good. Indeed, the political theorist Michael Walzer suggests that a good leader has an obligation to tell us that he has got dirty hands, and that we have an obligation to punish him for breaking the rules. This process of disclosure and punishment is essential, Walzer suggests, so that leaders are discouraged from breaking the rules except in extraordinary cases.[67]

At this stage, the leader's problem becomes ours as well. If we take Walzer's advice, we are required to punish a leader even if we agree that he has done the right thing. Our concern is not about justice in this case, but about assuring the right amount of caution in future cases where leaders must make decisions about the violation of legal or ethical rules. This is unfair to the current leader, and therefore requires that each of us dirty our own hands. "And then," says Walzer, "we must find some way of paying the price ourselves."[68] (How do we do this? Walzer does not say. This statement is the closing sentence of his influential 1973 article on the dirty hands problem.)

In fact, our own ethical quandaries can arise without any explicit disclosure by the leader who chooses to dirty his hands. For example, a predicament would be created even when the leader himself refuses to tell us about his decisions, but we learn from other credible sources about his conduct. We still have the same obligation to punish the leader for his decisions; at the very least we have an obligation to determine whether the allegations of rule-breaking are correct. If we choose not to pursue the allegations, or decide not to punish the leader, then we are complicitous in his rule-breaking, especially if it is ongoing. And so we have dirty hands too. On the other hand, if we pursue the allegations and punish the leader, even though we think that he did the right thing overall, we have dirty hands once again.

Is there any way out of this ethical quagmire? Perhaps there is. We could profess ignorance, and persuade ourselves that we do not know about the leader's rule-breaking—or at least, that we do not know all that we need to know in order to hold the leader to account. We could accept the argument advanced by booksellers, advocacy groups, and opposition politicians: that the truth is being suppressed. The category of unacknowledged knowns—of open secrets—could be kept firmly intact. If we persuade ourselves that we are kept in ignorance, we are not obliged to punish our leaders, or contemplate the question of what we must do to atone for our own complicity in their decisions. Open secrets become a convenient way of dissolving our moral problems.

Below the Radar Screen?

Arguments have repeatedly been made by distinguished legal scholars about the virtue of institutionalizing the rough practices that seemed necessary as the nation waged its War on Terrorism. In 2002, Alan Dershowitz made a controversial case for legalizing the practice of torture in extraordinary circumstances. The thought of countenancing torture is deeply distasteful, Dershowitz conceded, but there is justification for doing it in extreme cases—and if it is to be done, the practice should respect the value of "open accountability and visibility in a democracy." Dershowitz argued:

> "Off-the-book actions below the radar screen" are antithetical to the theory and practice of democracy. Citizens cannot approve or disapprove of governmental actions of which they are unaware. . . . There may be danger in open discussion [of this subject], but there is far greater danger in actions based on secret discussion, or no discussion at all.[69]

Other scholars made similar claims about the need for transparency. Philip Heymann suggested in 2006 that there should be publicly accessible guidelines that enumerate the "highly coercive interrogation" techniques that are authorized for use by federal officials, and which acknowledge the right of the president to permit "cruel, inhuman and degrading" treatment in a moment of emergency. The publication of such guidelines, Heymann argued, would make it possible for the boundaries of coercion to be addressed "thoughtfully and publicly" and "provide a variety of forms of accountability to replace the secrecy that now hides our interrogation practices."[70]

Bruce Ackerman, meanwhile, disagreed with Dershowitz about the wisdom of authorizing torture, but agreed nonetheless that guidelines on "hard-driving interrogation tactics" should be "debated and decided in public," in part because transparency itself will restrain unjustifiably abusive practices.[71]

Kenneth Anderson made a similar case. Anderson said that the Bush administration understandably reacted to the 9/11 crisis by improvisation and the exercise of executive discretion. But when the shock of the attacks had passed, the Bush administration had an opportunity to define and entrench the rules by which its War on Terrorism would be executed. The administration, Anderson argued, failed to exploit this opportunity by developing a "long term, systematic, comprehensive, institutionalized counterterrorism policy for the United States." The lack of explicit rules on interrogation was said to be symptomatic of this larger failure to institutionalize counterterrorism policy. There should be "plain, non-euphemistic definitions and legal rules" about the boundaries of coercive interrogation, Anderson said:

> [Rules on] the specifics of interrogation and the line of torture, ought in fact to be legislated in complete detail so that the world knows what is legal and illegal and so American voters can know what tradeoffs their representatives make between liberty and safety.[72]

Note the assumption that is common to all of these arguments: *that citizens were kept in the dark* about the practices of their government throughout the War on Terrorism—and that this ignorance of actual practice made it impossible for Americans to make judgments about appropriate tradeoffs, express their approval or disapproval of U.S. policy, or wield their influence at the ballot box to sanction leaders who have overstepped the boundaries of proper conduct. This reasoning reproduces the old Progressive notion about the tonic effect of transparency. *If only we had been told*, these arguments suggest, *the abuses would have stopped.*

But we were told. Perhaps we were not told by the president, but we knew nonetheless. The U.S. government decided, in the first weeks of the War on Terrorism, to "take the gloves off" with suspected terrorists. Suspects were abducted from other countries without due process of law. They were delivered to the intelligence services of countries that were known to engage in torture, and held in U.S. facilities indefinitely, without recourse to counsel. In the course of interrogation, prisoners were subjected to humiliating and degrading treatment.

All of these facts were open secrets—which is to say, they were not secrets at all. They were easily observed expressions of government policy, continued over five years and through two national elections, tacitly endorsed by Congress, and broadly understood to be necessary measures for protecting U.S. national security. Nonetheless, we were encouraged to regard these facts as secret, and we yielded to the encouragement. We did this, in part, because the alternative path—which commenced with an open acknowledgment of complicity in these practices—was less easily traveled.

Notes

1. Garry Wills, "At Ease, Mr. President," *New York Times*, January 27, 2007, 17.
2. Anne Applebaum, "Torture: Connect the Dots," *Milwaukee Journal Sentinel*, June 17, 2004, 29A.
3. Arthur Meier Schlesinger, *War and the American Presidency* (New York: W. W. Norton, 2004), 61.

4. Alan Elsner, "Bush Expands Government Secrecy, Arouses Critics," *Reuters*, September 3, 2002. Klayman called the presidency the most secretive in his lifetime; he was born in 1951.

5. John Dean, *Worse Than Watergate* (New York: Little, Brown and Co., 2004). Similarly, a complaint that the presidency is the most secretive in his lifetime. Dean was born in 1938.

6. Haynes Johnson, *The Age of Anxiety* (Orlando, FL: Harcourt Books, 2005), 490. The same charge; Johnson was born in 1931.

7. Reporters' Committee for Freedom of the Press, *Homefront Confidential*, 4th ed. (Washington, DC: Reporters' Committee for Freedom of the Press, September, 2003), 1. Emphasis added.

8. Louis D. Brandeis, *Other People's Money: And How the Bankers Use It* (New York: F. A. Stokes, 1914).

9. I canvass some of the Bush administration's attempts to tighten secrecy in Alasdair Roberts, *Blacked Out: Government Secrecy in the Information Age* (New York: Cambridge University Press, 2006), chs. 2 and 3.

10. Ibid., ch. 2, and pages 118–19.

11. Alasdair Roberts, *The Collapse of Fortress Bush: The Crisis of Authority in American Government* (New York: New York University Press, 2008), ch. 6.

12. Roberts, *Blacked Out*, ch. 4.

13. Tim Rutten, "CIA, under Tenet's Watch," *Los Angeles Times*, April 30, 2007.

14. Executive Office of the President, *President Discusses Creation of Military Commissions to Try Suspected Terrorists* (Washington, DC: Office of the Press Secretary, September 6, 2006).

15. Hartford Courant, "The Outing of Secret Prisons," *Hartford Courant*, September 8, 2006, A8.

16. Dana Priest, "CIA Holds Terror Suspects in Secret Prisons," *Washington Post*, November 2, 2005, A1.

17. James Risen, *State of War: The Secret History of the CIA and the Bush Administration* (New York: Free Press, 2006), 31.

18. Howard Kurtz, "Bush Presses Editors on Security," *Washington Post*, December 26, 2005, C1.

19. Jonathan Weisman, "GOP Leaders Urge Probe in Prisons Leak," *Washington Post*, November 9, 2005, A1.

20. Jeffrey R. Smith, "Fired Officer Believed CIA Lied to Congress," *Washington Post*, May 14, 2006, A1.

21. "Tortured Logic," *St. Petersburg Times*, November 5, 2005, 14A.

22. "American Gulag," *Boston Globe*, November 4, 2005, A22.

23. Reed Brody, "What About the Other Secret U.S. Prisons?" *International Herald Tribune*, May 4, 2004, 8.

24. Dana Priest and Joe Stephens, "Secret World of US Interrogation," *Washington Post*, May 11, 2004, A1.

25. Mark Mazetti et al., "Inside the Iraq Prison Scandal," *U.S. News and World Report*, May 24, 2004, 18–22.

26. Raymond Bonner, "Thailand Tiptoes in Step with American Antiterror Effort," *New York Times*, June 8, 2003, 29.

27. Dana Priest and Barton Gellman, "US Decries Abuse but Defends Interrogations," *Washington Post*, December 26, 2002, A1.

28. Barton Gellman, "CIA Weighs 'Targeted Killing' Missions," *Washington Post*, October 28, 2001, A1.

29. "US Says It Now Has Custody of Top Al-Qaida Commander," *Minneapolis Star Tribune*, April 1, 2002, 3A; Philip Shenon and James Risen, "Terrorist Yields Clues to Plots, Officials Assert," *New York Times*, June 12, 2002, 1. The other high-profile prisoners were Ramzi bin al Shibh, captured in September 2002; Khalid Sheikh Mohammed, captured in March 2003; Mohamad Farik Amin, captured in June 2003; Riduan Isamuddin, captured in August 2003; and Majid Kahn, also captured by August 2003.

30. Amnesty International, *Below the Radar: CIA Rendition Flights* (London: Amnesty International, 2006), accessed January 20, 2007, available from http://www.amnesty.org/resources/flash/torture/renditions/. Similarly, an AI representative told the *Irish Times* in 2006 that the program was "shrouded in secrecy": Ruadhán MacCormaic, "'Rendition' Aircraft Used Irish Airports," *Irish Times*, April 5, 2006, 12.

31. Onnesha Roychoudhuri, *Secret CIA Prisons in Your Backyard* in *AlterNet* (2006).

32. Stephen Grey, *Ghost Plane* (New York: St. Martin's Press), 261.

33. Parliamentary Assembly, *Lawfulness of Detentions by the United States in Guantánamo Bay* (Strasbourg, France: Council of Europe, April 8, 2005); Parliamentary Assembly, *Alleged Secret Detentions in Council of Europe Member States* (Strasbourg, France: Council of Europe, January 22, 2006), 2.

34. Kamran Khan and Rajiv Chandrasekaran, "Cole Suspect Turned Over by Pakistan," *Washington Post*, October 28, 2001, A1.

35. Don Greenlees, "Love Letter Tracks Terrorist's Footsteps," *Weekend Australian*, February 23, 2002, 1.

36. Rajiv Chandrasekaran and Peter Finn, "US behind Secret Transfer of Terror Suspects," *Washington Post*, 2002, A1.

37. Faye Bowers and Philip Smucker, "US Ships Al Qaeda Suspects to Arab States," *Christian Science Monitor*, July 26, 2002, 1.

38. Levon Sevunts, "Ex-Montrealer Has 'Simply Disappeared,'" *Montreal Gazette*, October 17, 2002.

39. Arar Commission, *Report of the Events Relating to Maher Arar: Analysis and Recommendations* (Ottawa, Canada: Commission of Inquiry into the Actions of Canadian Officials in Relation to Maher Arar, September 18, 2006).

40. Executive Office of the President, *President Discusses Creation of Military Commissions to Try Suspected Terrorists.*

41. "Spin and Consequences," *New York Times*, November 15, 2006, 26.

42. "Make Them Talk," *Los Angeles Times*, January 4, 2007, 14.

43. Detainee Treatment Act, Title X of the Defense Appropriations Act of 2006, Public Law 109–148.

44. Dana Priest and Robin Wright, "Cheney Fights for Detainee Policy," *Washington Post*, November 7, 2005, A1.

45. Michael Garcia, *Interrogation of Detainees: Overview of the Mccain Amendment* (Washington, DC: Congressional Research Service, 2006), 6.

46. *Hamdan v. Rumsfeld*, 126 S.Ct. 2749 (2006).

47. Military Commissions Act, Public Law 109–366.

48. "America's Dirty Secrets," *St. Petersburg Times*, November 17, 2006, 18A.

49. Brian Ross and Richard Esposito, *CIA's Harsh Interrogation Techniques Described* (November 18, 2005), accessed January 27, 2006, available from http://abcnews.go.com/WNT/Investigation/story?id=1322866.

50. Douglas Jehl, "Questions Left by CIA on Torture Use," *New York Times*, March 18, 2005, 1.

51. Dana Priest and R. Jeffrey Smith, "Memo Offered Justification for Use of Torture," *Washington Post*, June 8, 2004, A1; Jess Bravin, "Pentagon Report Set Framework for Use of Torture," *Wall Street Journal*, June 7, 2004, A1; Neil Lewis and Eric Schmitt, "Lawyers Decided Bans on Torture Didn't Bind Bush," *New York Times*, June 8, 2004, 1.

52. James Risen, David Johnston, and Neil Lewis, "Harsh CIA Methods Cited in Top Qaeda Interrogations," *New York Times*, May 13, 2004, 1.

53. Dana Priest, "CIA Puts Harsh Tactics on Hold," *Washington Post*, June 27, 2004, A1.

54. Toby Harnden, "Top Bin Laden Aide Is a Guest of the CIA," *Chicago Sun-Times*, March 4, 2003, 3.

55. Priest and Gellman, "US Decries Abuse but Defends Interrogations."

56. Department of Defense, *DoD News Briefing—Secretary Rumsfeld and Gen. Myers* (Washington, DC: Office of the Assistant Secretary of Defense [Public Affairs], February 12, 2002).

57. Stephen Edelston Toulmin, *The Uses of Argument*, rev. ed. (New York: Cambridge University Press, 2003).

58. The term was popularized during the Watergate scandal, when congressmen referred to documents and tapes that implicated President Nixon as "smoking gun" evidence.

59. This is the so-called unitary executive theory. See Steven Calabresi and Kevin Rhodes, "The Structural Constitution: Unitary Executive, Plural Judiciary," *Harvard Law Review* 105, no. 6 (1992): 1153–1216, 1165.

60. Executive Office of the President, "President Welcomes President Talabani of Iraq to the White House," Office of the Press Secretary, Washington, DC, September 13, 2005.

61. Gaye Tuchman, *Making News: A Study in the Construction of Reality* (New York: Free Press, 1978).

62. Tim Rutten, "Torture as a Tool of Democracy," *Los Angeles Times*, October 25, 2006, E1.

63. See also Alasdair Roberts, "Dashed Expectations: Governmental Adaptation to Transparency Rules," in *Transparency*, ed. Christopher Hood and David Heald (London: Oxford University Press, 2006), 107–25.

64. Joseph Schneider, "Social Problems Theory: The Constructionist View," *Annual Review of Sociology* 11 (1985): 209–29.

65. Sunshine Week, *News Release: Survey Finds Public Concerned about Secrecy* (Washington, DC: Sunshine Week Executive Committee, March 11, 2005), accessed April 15, 2005, available from http://www.sunshineweek.org/index.cfm?id=5556.

66. Michael Walzer, "Political Action: The Problem of Dirty Hands," *Philosophy and Public Affairs* 2 (1973): 160–80, 166–67.

67. Ibid., 179–80.

68. Ibid., 180.

69. Alan Dershowitz, *Why Terrorism Works* (New York: Yale University Press, 2002), 152 and 163.

70. Philip Heymann, *Seeking Common Ground in the Fight against Terrorism: Coercive Interrogation as an Example* (Cambridge, MA: Harvard Law School, 2006), 19–20.

71. Bruce A. Ackerman, *Before the Next Attack: Preserving Civil Liberties in an Age of Terrorism* (New Haven: Yale University Press, 2006), 108–12.

72. Kenneth Anderson, "Law and Terror," *Policy Review*, no. 139 (2006): 3–24, 4 and 21.

Secret Trials and Public Justice

LINDSAY FARMER

Introduction

One of the significant legal issues raised in the ongoing "War on Terror" is that of the right to a public trial, as the governments of both the United States and the United Kingdom have sought to adopt procedures for the trial of terrorist suspects that would entail all or part of the proceedings being held in secret. In the United States, the Bush administration controversially proposed that detainees held in Camp Delta at Guantanamo Bay should be tried in closed proceedings before military commissions.[1] Likewise, the UK government has argued that hearings relating to either the imposition of "control orders" or for the deportation of terror suspects could be held in closed sessions using special procedures so as not to compromise national security.[2] Critics in both countries have argued that such measures breach the right to a fair trial, which is understood to include the requirement that trials be held in public. This, it is argued, is not only because justice should be seen to be done for the individuals concerned, but for other broader reasons. A piece by Anne-Marie Slaughter is typical in claiming that to try terrorist suspects in secret would be to hand them and their supporters a symbolic victory, for not only would the state lose the opportunity publicly to convince the public as to the necessity of these measures, but such trials would also "challenge Americans' identity as a people."[3] The argument about the fairness of the trial thus slips into a broader political and cultural claim about the public trial as an institution that is connected with a certain way of life.

While such assertions about public trial and its importance are easily made, the grounds for such claims are rarely explored, especially when, as in the context of the "War on Terror," this has become such an emotive issue.[4] It is not clear, for example, that there is a settled understanding of why a public trial matters, or why closed proceedings should be understood as automatically breaching due process protections. The fact, for instance, that the European Court of Human Rights distinguishes between the need for a public hearing and the requirement that judgments be pronounced publicly suggests that neither the content of the principle nor its justification is necessarily as clear as might be.[5] Indeed, as it is understood in the same context that publicity is not intrinsically connected with fairness, it is not clear that the European Convention on Human Rights protects a right to a public trial—and thus from a European perspective it is not properly understood as a due process protection at all.[6] Indeed, when we look at the arguments given in support of public justice we find inconsistency and contradiction, and it is far from clear that it is either coherent or sensible to claim that public justice is intrinsically connected with democratic institutions or a certain way of life.[7] At the very least this requires an examination of the development and justification for the principle of public justice.

These issues thus raise the question of the connection between the public trial and the fair trial. Why should a secret trial not be fair; or conversely why might a public trial be unfair? And how do issues of secrecy and privacy interact with principles of public justice? Is there a difference between trials held in private and those that are secret? The fear of the secret trial, moreover, is commonly linked to what is understood to be the purpose of that kind of trial, the suppression of dissent or the maintenance of an unfair or oppressive political regime, such that it is hard to discuss the problem of secret trials outwith the contexts in which they have been used. We thus need to look more closely at the relation between public and secret trials. I shall argue here that there are due process issues involved in relation to some of the suggested measures, but that in several cases this is less because of the "secrecy" of the proceedings than because of their connection with other rights. That said, however, I shall go further to claim that there is an intrinsic connection between the public trial and the fair trial, and that this should lie at the heart of our discussions over the appropriate measures to be taken in the trial of terror suspects—and indeed of anyone else accused of any crime.

These are central normative questions about the meaning of a fair trial. However, rather than moving to these issues directly I want to approach them through an examination of the genesis of the modern idea of the public trial, as this can illuminate our understanding both of the secret trial and of the normative issues at stake. What quickly becomes apparent when we look at the historical origins of the idea of a public trial is that while there has long been an opposition between openness or publicity and secrecy, the content of these terms and significance of the opposition has varied in different historical periods. It is thus important to identify and analyze the modern understanding of public justice in order to understand the precise way in which it might be undermined by the secret trial. In order to do this it is necessary first to trace the genealogy of the idea of the public trial, an idea that was formed largely in opposition to the "private"; and second, to examine the emergence of secrecy as a problem that could be framed specifically in opposition to the idea of the modern public trial. I should also note that the discussion is largely in terms of the development of ideas of public justice in the English and Scottish criminal trials. There are obviously strong parallels with the development of the American trial, but there may also be important divergences.

The Meaning of Public Trial

The origins of the Anglo-American trial lie in openness—the trial before the country, as it was termed. The early adversarial trial was open to the public, and members of the public participated actively, as witnesses, jurors, or spectators—and there were not, in any case, rigid distinctions drawn between different categories of participant. The trial had no purpose-built accommodation, being held in convenient halls or spaces, with a simple bar dividing the participants from the other business that was being conducted there.[8] The accusation was openly made, before royal justices, and the jury would listen to information from both accuser and accused, as well as drawing on information that was within their own local knowledge. A verdict would be delivered following the retiral of the jury, and the sentence and its execution would be publicly performed. This was also a system that laid great stress on the rituals and appearance of justice—from the procession that accompanied the arrival of the royal justices in the assize town, to the assize sermon, and the rituals of public execution itself. This was less because of any fixed ideas about the value of public justice as an end in itself, than for the opportunity it allowed to underscore the sources of temporal and spiritual authority, for the trial had evolved as a series of ad hoc responses to the problem of how to prove guilt in a way that allowed an accommodation between royal (or central) and local interests. Thus although English, and later American, lawyers were later to accord significance to the principle of public justice—they liked, in particular, to sing the praises of open English justice as compared with the tyrannical practices of the Inquisition in Catholic Europe—there was no political principle underlying the origins of the adversarial trial.

This is reflected in works of political theory of the early-modern period. These occasionally mention the importance of public trial, but in doing so would connect it to some particular aspect of trial proceedings rather than the trial itself. Sir John Fortescue, for example, writing in the fifteenth century, links the value of publicity specifically to the institution of the jury. Witnesses, he points out, must testify "in the presence of twelve trustworthy men of the neighbourhood in which the fact in question occurred."[9] This prevented secret or dishonest accusations, since the jurors would know and be able to judge the background and honesty of the witness. And in a trope that was to become characteristic of English writings on the public trial, he contrasted this with criminal procedure in France, where a person accused of a crime might be brought before the king or his representative directly and convicted and executed in private.[10] Sir Thomas Smith, writing in the mid-sixteenth century likewise laid stress on the fact that all proceedings except the deliberation of the jury were conducted in open court, "that all men may heare from the mouth of the depositors and witnesses what is saide."[11] And Sir Edward Coke, writing in the early seventeenth century, stressed that verdicts in criminal causes should not be given in private but in open court.[12] What links these brief discussions was the belief that a public trial could prevent dishonesty and oppression, and the conception of the jury as honest representatives of the country—a country specifically identified as England.

We find some direct recognition of the value of public justice only in the late seventeenth-century, a period that began to see the crystallization of protections for the defendant and the emergence of a new conception of the political subject.[13] The Scottish parliament passed an act "anent Advising Criminal Processes with open doors" in 1693. This was part of the constitutional settlement that followed the revolution of 1689, and was a direct response to the abuses of legal process that had occurred throughout the religious wars of the seventeenth century.[14] There was no comparable English legislation, and perhaps surprisingly, no litigation that raised the issue directly—which might be interpreted as an indication of how deeply rooted was the idea of public justice.[15] However, there was a subtle shift in the perception of role of the jury from seeing them as simple judges of the character of witnesses to being freeborn members of the public who could act as a bulwark against executive and judicial tyranny.[16] This changing view was articulated in the preface to one of the early collections of *State Trials*. Here it was pointed out that the form of the criminal trial demonstrated the excellence of the laws of England as compared with those of its neighbors. This was because the trial was held in public, not in secret, witnesses were examined in the presence of the accused in open court, the use of torture was outlawed, and executions were public:

> [It] being necessary to answer the end of Justice, that a public Example be made of Offenders in order to deter others from the like Crimes; but where the Trial and Execution are in private, it not only defeats the end of Justice, but affords an Opportunity of secretly destroying innocent Men, which must needs expose the Subject to a variety of Fears and Dangers inconsistent with the liberties of a free People.[17]

However much this might have been out of step with reality—the records of the political trials of the late seventeenth century suggest that the Crown was normally confident in its ability to bend jurors to its will—it did reflect the emerging conception of the criminal trial as a public argument, before a jury, over the meaning of testimony.[18]

This view is reinforced in Blackstone's references to public trial, which both look back to the older tradition and suggest ways in which the meaning of the term "public" is changing. His discussion of the requirement for the public and oral examination of witnesses stresses that it is more conducive to the production of truth than private or secret examination: the presence of judge and jury could provide a check on what a witness might say; witnesses could be questioned; and they could be confronted by adverse witnesses.[19] He went on to refer to the idea of public justice, but primarily in the sense of justice in matters of public wrong or criminal law.[20] He also referred to public courts, but it is clear that by this he means only those that are of general, rather than special or private, jurisdiction.[21] Finally, he rejected the idea of public as opposed to private prosecution, on the grounds that the former contributed to the oppressions of the Star Chamber.[22] He also famously defended the jury as the "palladium of liberty" and the "glory of English law," while his argument that it should be protected against public attacks and being undermined by "secret machinations" suggests an identity between the jury and the public.[23] Thus, while it is clear that there is an underlying conception of political liberty founded on the jury and the fear of the secret machinations of power, his sense of the public character of justice is primarily based on a comparison with the private—private wrongs, special jurisdictions, and private places. This comparison between public and private was to shape the development of the modern understanding of the public trial.

It is Jeremy Bentham's *Rationale of Judicial Evidence* which contains the first extended modern treatment of the subject of public justice.[24] Here Bentham incorporated the older justifications within a more systematic account of the value of public justice, laying particular emphasis on the panoptic principle: that the gaze of the public acted as a control on the actions of witnesses and officials. He thus argued that witnesses would be less likely to lie for fear that "Environed, as he sees himself, by a thousand eyes, contradiction, should he hazard a false tale, will seem ready to rise up to him from a thousand tongues."[25] Judges, equally, would be more impartial, for publicity "keeps the judge himself, while trying, under trial, with the public acting as witnesses, judges and potential executioners of the sentence."[26] He additionally noted that a collateral benefit of publicity was that it had an educative function, making the court a theater in which "the most important branches of morality are enforced by the most impressive means."[27] He went on to compare the English with the "Roman" system, in which secrecy prevailed, but in contrast to the panegyrics of those such as Blackstone or Fortescue, suggests merely that the principle of publicity makes the English system "the least bad extant, instead of being amongst the worse."[28]

While influential and important, these views still in large part reflected an understanding of the criminal justice system as dependent on private prosecution and with little information-gathering capacity of its own—and thus dependent on publicity as a means of controlling false accusations. The modern understanding of public justice, however, was decisively shaped by the reforms of the trial and of political power that took place at the beginning of the nineteenth century. The transformation in crime and punishment that took place in this period was driven in large part by the desire to make punishment more certain and effective, but it also aimed to restore the legitimacy of criminal justice, which had been challenged by the critics of the Bloody Code.[29] These critics were concerned not only that the use of capital punishment was ineffective, but also that the public display of authority that was the spectacle of the scaffold was too easily subverted, for the condemned person often refused to display the necessary degree of contrition and the behavior of crowds became increasingly difficult to manage.[30] The reformers argued that the criminal justice system resembled a lottery in which few offenders were detected, fewer still convicted, and where capital punishment was inflicted largely on those unfortunates who did not have the social resources to make a successful plea for mercy.[31] As a consequence, in the early part of the nineteenth century the system that supported the Bloody Code was dismantled and replaced by new institutions of punishment, principally the penitentiary but also the use of transportation, which offered the possibility of a more certain and measured infliction of punishment. As a consequence, punishment became a secret process, hidden behind the walls of the prison, operating on the soul or mind, rather than the body, of the condemned person.

Yet the decline of the scaffold as the symbol of criminal justice and the move to conceal the process of punishment did not mean the decline of the idea of public punishment; rather that the principle of publicity came to be expressed in a different way as the trial replaced the scaffold as the "public climax of state justice and its imaginatively defining scene."[32] McGowen has argued that the reform of the Bloody Code led to the creation of a new image of criminal justice, as reformers sought to secure wider public support for the legal system.[33] The authority of the criminal law was no longer to be based on the personal authority of the judge and the widespread use of the pardon. Justice was instead to operate through the impersonal application of predetermined (and less severe) laws, introducing distance, uniformity, and impartiality in place of the interplay of severity and mercy. The trial was central to this image as a means of displaying the legitimate consequences of a criminal act, the representation of punishment as an idea.[34]

The criminal trial was itself undergoing massive transformation in this period, and the new iconography of the trial drew on and represented these changes.[35] The main lines of this development are now well known, and need only be briefly stated.[36] During the course of the eighteenth century, lawyers began to enter the criminal trial. Beginning with the Treason Trials Act of 1696, which permitted those accused of treason to access counsel in the preparation and conduct of their defense, lawyers gradually began to be involved in the trial of more serious crimes. Although their involvement in felony trials was still formally prohibited by law, judges began to admit defense counsel in a limited capacity.[37] They were gradually allowed to cross-examine witnesses, to enforce evidentiary rules, and to advise the accused person, though not yet either to present arguments or summarize the case. The lawyers made the process more adversarial as they fought to establish their professionalism and their presence in the trial.[38] The passing of the Prisoners' Counsel Act of 1836, permitting counsel to address the jury directly in an opening speech and summing up of the case, was a formal recognition of the adversarial nature of the criminal trial.[39]

This led to the transformation of the roles of other courtroom actors. While the earlier trial had been dominated by the figure of the judge—preventing the accused from pleading guilty in order to learn something of their background, examining witnesses, and advising the jury—lawyers began to take over some of these functions. The role of the judge in the trial increasingly became that of neutral arbiter, removed from active involvement in the discovery of evidence. Equally, there is evidence to suggest that as lawyers came to control the examination of witnesses, and sought to limit the evidence that was presented to the jury, the jury itself became increasingly passive, observing rather than participating in the trial process. Langbein has argued forcefully that the entry of the lawyers led to the creation of the modern—inexperienced, taciturn, autonomous—jury.[40] A third important consequence was on accused persons themselves, as the involvement of lawyers at both pretrial and trial stages led to the silencing of the accused. While, in the absence of other forms of defense, the accused was obliged to speak to the court (though not permitted to do so on oath), lawyers advised the accused to remain silent in committal proceedings and in court so as to oblige the prosecution to prove its case.[41] Public trial did not require the participation of accused parties (though it did normally require their presence), and indeed was increasingly premised on their silence.[42]

The trial that emerged over the course of the nineteenth century was very different, then, from the public "altercation" that lay at its origins. It was no less public, but it was staged in a very different way, and this gave rise to different concerns with public justice. First, this trial was "reconstructive": that is to say that it was increasingly organized around the detailed reconstruction of the incident that founded the charge, and of the state of mind of the accused at the time of that incident.[43] The role of the court was to "witness" and judge the representation of the original incident. This process was increasingly organized and controlled by the police, who both investigated the crime and organized and presented the case for the prosecution.[44] Second, the trial was organized around the principle of the public testing by lawyers of the prosecution case.[45] It is important to note, however, that the model for this trial was that of private litigation. Sir James Fitzjames Stephen writing in 1863 remarked upon the "private character" of the English criminal trial.[46] This was to be seen primarily in the structure of prosecution, which remained (formally at least) the responsibility of private individuals, but which also meant that the parties to the litigation, as in a private dispute, controlled the trial process. The belief that the battle between advocates, as champions of the parties to the dispute, was the best means of establishing the "truth" of events shaped the understanding of the "trial" as a continuous, oral, public hearing. There was no strong conception of a public interest in the trial or of the role of the state (in policing or prosecution) as a public body.[47] Third, the changes in the form of the proceedings did not reflect any commitment to individual rights (particularly for the accused), but were driven by the desire to standardize the administration of justice. The value of publicity, then, was understood largely in instrumental terms, as a means of publicly demonstrating the efficiency of the criminal justice system, the impartiality of the judge, and the competence of criminal justice officials.[48] Fourth, the proceedings were staged for the passive jury, and by extension the public at large. However, if in the earlier trial the jury saw their role as participants in the proceedings, or as actors in a political process, the change in the form of the trial meant that they were increasingly spectators to a theatrical spectacle, assessing the quality of the performance of the actors. The general public then "consumed" the trial in the form of newspaper reports, again as spectators second-guessing the actual jurors.[49] Trials were followed with great interest, and though they demonstrated the complete impartiality of the law, they stood apart from political or public life and did not require any commitment to, or involvement in, the institutions of justice.[50]

These developments all subtly contributed to the reshaping of the idea of publicity in criminal proceedings, emphasizing certain meanings of the term, while playing down others. This point can be illustrated further by looking at changes in courtroom architecture, and at what that tells us about the public nature of the modern trial.

A recent study of English courtroom architecture identifies architectural trends that correspond in important ways to the transformations of the criminal trial described above. By the end of the nineteenth century, Graham argues,

> [t]here is a shift from multi-purpose to single-purpose buildings, from movable furnishings to fixed fittings and a greater elaboration of architectural decoration; from open access to restricted circulation and segregated accommodation; from the general and the public to the specific and the private.[51]

The broad argument is that the move to single-purpose buildings (in a way that was common to other public buildings in this period) reveals a fixing of the public meaning of law: the coming together of architecture and legal procedure to impose a new sense of order on the trial. This new order was based on restrictions on access and circulation, and on new forms of segregation and interaction (of witnesses, lawyers, judges, the accused, and the public at large).[52] This is illustrated by pointing to the contrast between eighteenth- and nineteenth-century courtrooms. The former encouraged sociability, with large public areas and spaces for the judge and jury separated only by screens, columns, and archways.[53] These courts were places for public display, where members of polite society might meet for purposes that extended beyond the simple witnessing of the actions of the court, reflecting the broader place of the assizes as a social event in the life of the community. In the latter there develops a strict contrast between the courtroom and open public areas, but more importantly within the court itself between those areas open only to lawyers and court officials and the public areas.[54] Within this there were strict forms of segregation allowing reintegration only under controlled conditions. It began to be common for there to be a passage from below the dock, through which the prisoner could be brought up into the courtroom; the lawyers' quarters (robing rooms, judges' chambers) were separated by walls and corridors from the public parts of the court, distancing them from the public and even their own clients; there were separate waiting rooms for witnesses, and corridors so that they could be taken to and from the courtroom without encountering others; and jury members were clearly segregated from the public through the use of special entrances and accommodation. These courtrooms were designed to facilitate the specialized functions of criminal justice through the efficient flow of different groups and individuals around the central space of the courtroom.

The move to specialized accommodation was a result of the feeling that the majesty of the law could be enhanced through a more dignified architectural setting, and the court buildings that were constructed during the nineteenth century accordingly sought to represent the authority of the law, primarily through the adoption of styles of architecture and ornament that projected the order and authority of the law.[55] It is in this period that we see the courtroom beginning take on its recognizably contemporary form: the vertical organization of the seating that reflected the hierarchical arrangement of participants, from judge, to clerks, to lawyers; there was also, in a significant move, dedicated space for members of the press. Significantly, however, as Taylor points out, members of the public were physically removed from the courtroom, sitting in galleries isolated from and overlooking the floor of the court, underlining the fact that their presence was for the purpose of observation rather than participation.[56]

Overall, although trials were becoming more publicly visible, this did not mean that a principle of publicity was operating freely in the organization of the trial. The model of private litigation, indeed, was understood to play down the element of spectacle and limit the accessibility of courtroom and of legal procedures to the general public. In spite of the undoubted interest of the public in capital proceedings, few steps were taken to improve access to courtrooms. When the Central Criminal Court, the Old Bailey, was reconstructed in 1907, the bar advised that public access to courtrooms should be restricted.[57] At the same time steps were being taken to ensure that journalists had prime access to the courtroom, reflecting the degree to which public access was increasingly mediated through newspapers and other literary representations of the trial.[58] The necessity of publicity was recognized, but at the same time it was acknowledged that this should be subject to limits—by not admitting too many members of the public, by attempting to reduce elements of explicit theatricality in the trial, and by excluding the public altogether when the subject matter of the trial was generating an interest that might be deemed prurient or potentially disorderly. The public face of the trial was important, but the public themselves were often considered to be something of an inconvenience.[59]

The development of the modern public trial was thus primarily concerned with the questions of how the trial should look—the management of the criminal trial so as to project a certain image of legal authority—rather than with the question of why the trial should be public.[60] This has been understood as a one-way process of conveying a particular image or understanding of the law to a public audience. The focus that this led to on the defensive aim of engendering public acceptance was also consistent with the contemporary understanding of the trial as being based on a broad conception of equality of arms—the standardization of procedure—rather than any rights or entitlements of the defendant. The fairness of the trial could be publicly demonstrated, but not at the cost of affording the accused (or any other party) the right to a public trial. It comes as little surprise that we find the problem of the management of secrecy emerging in this same period. The reshaping of the courtroom had led to the creation of private spaces and the potential for proceedings to be carried out in secret when they posed problem of management or control in relation to the public trial.

Secrecy is understood primarily in terms of potential administrative restrictions on the norm of public justice, which in its turn is articulated around an unreflective understanding of the openness of the courts. This view was formalized in the leading case of *Scott v. Scott* (1913), which was the first English case to discuss the principle of public justice directly.[61] One of the most striking features of the case, which concerned the rather mundane question of whether the record of a hearing in camera in divorce proceedings could be disclosed, was the surprise of the judges in the House of Lords at the absence of authority on public justice. This gap was filled with ringing declarations of principle. For Viscount Haldane the broad principle was "that the Courts of this country must, as between parties, administer justice in public."[62] The Earl of Halsbury declared the rule to be that "every Court of Justice is open to every subject of the King," and that this had been the case for centuries, adding bathetically that this was at least "the unquestioned rule since 1857."[63] Earl Loreburn considered this to be the "almost priceless inheritance" of the English.[64] And Lord Shaw declared himself to be "shocked" by the whole proceedings, since the proceedings marked an undermining of constitutional security such as would have "accorded with the genius and practice of despotism."[65] He went on:

> Had this occurred in France, I suppose Frenchmen would have said that the age of Louis Quatorze and the practice of *lettres de cachet* had returned.[66]

This was then subject to certain exceptions which might be allowed in order that justice be done. Although the court considered it impossible to "enumerate or anticipate all possible contingencies," it considered that there could be departures in cases involving wards of courts and lunacy, or where the confidential subject matter of the dispute would be destroyed by a hearing in open court, or in order to secure the court against disorder or tumult.[67] These exceptions did not, decisively in the context of the case, extend to the protection of public decency or the preservation of individual privacy. What we have here then is the now familiar combination of the statement of broad principle followed by the listing of exceptions. It is important also to note, however, the language of these declarations, which not only invoke the idea of constitutional guarantees but also hyperbolically link this to the English Ancient Constitution standing in opposition to alien, despotic power. Public justice stands as a way of life, as much as a rule of criminal procedure.[68]

The exceptions have subsequently been developed and formulated more systematically, particularly in relation to the theme of security.[69] This is now understood not only in the traditional sense of the protection of the physical security of the courtroom—allowing the exclusion of those who might disrupt proceedings—but also as extending to the protection of certain witnesses or certain sources of evidence. Most significant is that it now extends to allowing hearings in camera where issues of national security are concerned.[70] This is understood as allowing the exclusion of public and press, and the nonpublication of the judgment or official record of the proceedings. This common law right is, however, supplemented by numerous statutory provisions—the most significant of which is s.8(4) of the Official Secrets Act of 1920, which permits the court to take steps to prevent the disclosure of secret information in the courtroom by holding proceedings in camera.[71] Most important, there has developed the practice of the straightforward exclusion of the jurisdiction of the ordinary courts—and hence of the requirement of publicity—by the appointment of special tribunals. This practice is justified by the existence of a state of emergency, and has been developed as a response to the perceived risks of disclosure of evidence that might arise from the continuing presence of the accused and his lawyers in proceedings that take place in camera. This is the procedure which has most recently caused uproar in the UK, where terrorist suspects who have been detained without trial have had their cases heard in secret by the Special Immigrations Appeals Commission, without disclosure of the evidence, or even some of the charges, to the defendant or the defendant's legal team.[72] Although this kind of practice is consistent with other measures used by recent governments in the UK to avoid due process protections,[73] it is not a new practice and can be traced back through detention without trial in Northern Ireland and the use of emergency powers in World War II.[74] What is of greatest significance here is, on the one hand, the development and regularization of procedures of this sort which exclude the requirement of publicity, and on the other, of the formulation of an understanding of "secrecy" in relation to state security rather than the subject matter of the evidence or the control of the courtroom.

If the value of publicity was initially defined in opposition to a view of "French" or secret forms of criminal procedure, with the development of the modern criminal law, the content of the concept of "public" justice began to take on more specific meanings—often by contrast with the private. However, as we have seen, the value of publicity was not unrestricted, as it depended on an increasingly strict definition of those aspects of the trial that were to be considered "public" and those which were private, and on a strict control over the uses of publicity—the issues that have particularly shaped the understanding of the need for secrecy and security in the modern trial.

Having clarified the particular meaning of public and secret trials, we must now turn to assess the normative arguments in support of public trial.

Public Justice and the Fair Trial[75]

As we have noted, to the extent that the principle of public justice was discussed by early writers on the common law, it was in the context of the dangers of secret accusations and the importance of allowing accused persons to confront their accuser. This has led to the suggestion that the right to a public hearing has at least an affinity with the adversarial model of trial: an inquisition conducted against the defendant in secret would not enable any meaningful participation on his part. The requirement that the defendant should have the right to have access to the prosecution's case is thus linked to the right of confrontation, which requires that the defendant should have the right to confront those who make accusations against him as well as those who testify against him.

This argument provides a rationale for publicity of a kind: the content of the prosecution's case must be publicized to the defendant and evidence must be given by witnesses in the defendant's presence, to allow meaningful confrontation on his part.[76] One important aspect of the rationale for public justice is to ensure transparency to the defendant in particular, so that a proper defense can be mounted. Public justice in this sense is a challenge to the idea of trials that require minimal disclosure to the defendant of the charges brought against him and of the prosecution's case—which has implications not only for the trial but for pretrial procedure as well. However, this conception of public justice is insufficient to establish the right to a hearing which is not only publicized to the defendant but also open to the public more generally. At best, as Roberts and Zuckerman note, these arguments show that there is an affinity between the right to participate in one's own trial and the right to public justice.[77] The principle of public justice—a trial that is open to the *general* public rather than to the defendant alone—cannot be established through the right of participation, for one's right of participation might be fully guaranteed by trials which exclude the general public.

If we are to understand the basis for the principle of public justice, we must therefore consider other potential rationales. We begin with two instrumental arguments that are sometimes offered for public trials: the argument that public trials enhance the ability of trials to establish the truth; and the argument that they encourage officials to adhere to independent standards of fairness. We then offer what we shall argue is a more plausible rationale grounded in the communicative character of the trial.

The Encouragement of Truth

As we have seen, one of the principal arguments made by Bentham in favor of public justice was that it could enhance the truth-determining capacity of the trial.[78] His argument was that publicity acts as a means of discouraging witnesses from lying, as the false statement could come to the attention of other potential witnesses, who would thereby be moved to contradict its claims. Witnesses who might be tempted to perjure themselves would hesitate to do so in the eyes of the public. The fear of discovery would thus potentially act as a means of discouraging perjury or false testimony, or more generally acting as a prompt to witnesses to assist the court by adding their testimony to that already in the public domain.[79] There are thus two dimensions to this argument. First, it is said to improve the quality of evidence actually presented, either by discouraging witnesses from lying or as a stimulus for the production of more reliable evidence. Second, evidence given in public, whether true or false (but particularly if false) might encourage witnesses to come forward whose evidence would otherwise be unavailable at the trial.

These arguments are unconvincing, however. The tendency of public justice to improve the quality of evidence will vary from witness to witness: there may be witnesses who are inclined to lie in private, but who would tell the truth in public as a consequence of the greater chance of the discovery of the lie; equally, there may be those who would tend to give fuller and more truthful evidence in private, particularly if the information that they have is embarrassing or likely to cast them in a bad light. There may also be those who are intimidated by the public setting, who would be more articulate in a more private environment. This may particularly be true, for example, of complainants in sexual abuse cases or of children where there is sometimes a restriction on the requirement to be present in the court in person; but this may apply with at least some degree of force to a much larger group of witnesses.[80] There may be those who fear intimidation, or conversely those who seek publicity for themselves.

Second, public trials might hinder as well as stimulate the production of new evidence. Some witnesses, who might have been willing to give evidence in a private session, would not be willing to give evidence in open court. This is likely to be for the same set of reasons just considered. Furthermore, the fact that the public has a *right* to attend a trial does little to encourage witnesses to come forward if in fact members of the public are rarely present at trials, as is the case in reality. It should also be noted, of course, that Bentham was writing in a period before organized policing and prosecution. At that time it might have been imperative to encourage witnesses to present themselves; for us the problem is rather that of ensuring the quality or reliability of the testimony of those witnesses already located by the police or the publicizing of the crime before the trial takes place. The idea that public trials enhance their epistemic capacity is certainly difficult to defend in any uniform way across trials, and it is quite difficult to defend at all.

It has, of course, also been argued in this context that the public trial could prevent secret accusations or denunciations. However, while this rationale is, as we have noted, of historical significance (and symbolic importance) to the common law tradition, it is not clear that it enhances truth on its own (for the reasons given), or whether it is linked to a separate claim about an independent right to confrontation, regardless of whether such confrontation might enhance the epistemic capacity of the trial. Overall, then, although the argument about the encouragement of truth might have force in some cases, it cannot provide a basis for a right to public justice.

The "Court of Public Opinion"

A second type of claim, also encountered in Bentham, is that the political legitimacy of the criminal trial rests in part on its being held in public. This is often expressed in the maxim that justice should not only be done but should be seen to be done, and that ensuring the latter is a way of securing the former.

A crucial component of legitimate trials is that they are conducted in a fair and impartial manner; that decision-makers are motivated by concerns of justice and only those concerns. It is commonly argued that conducting trials in public will be a way of ensuring that decision-makers properly respect concerns of justice by making the judge accountable to the "court of public opinion."[81] In Bentham's formulation, the judge while judging is simultaneously being judged by those members of the public who are observing the proceedings, and this acts as a brake on any urge they might have to surrender to individual or political bias.[82]

On this conception, the role of public scrutiny is primarily instrumental: it will tend to ensure that independent concerns of justice will be tracked effectively by decisions in trials. As such, there may be countervailing concerns: that public pressure for a particular verdict or for particular irrelevant reasons to be taken into consideration in the decision will bear negatively on the extent to which decisions track concerns of justice.[83] In addition, there may be a public perception that "technical" rules of evidence and procedure are unfair and that the trial is not adequately aiming at the truth, putting pressure on the judge to apply those rules less stringently.[84] We should note, moreover, that the ability to create such pressure (or indeed to provide the kind of scrutiny envisaged by Bentham) does not necessarily require the actual presence of members of the public at trials, as the media (particularly newspapers and television) are increasingly central to the reporting of criminal trials. Indeed, the fact that members of the public are rarely actually present at trials increases the power of the media to represent (or misrepresent) certain issues as public concerns, and thereby to increase pressure on judge and jury to favor a particular outcome. The argument for public scrutiny, insofar as it is persuasive at all, seems to be an argument in favor of requiring impartial public observers rather than of the right to a public trial.[85]

It may, of course, be argued that public scrutiny of trials should not be seen on a trial by trial basis, but rather as a general claim of public involvement in scrutinizing the criminal justice process to ensure that it *generally* meets standards of fairness. But even then, it would need to be shown that the public conception of criminal justice that provides the standard of public scrutiny of trials enhances fairness overall, and that would be difficult to establish. Given the prevailing attitude of the mass media to criminal justice, it would be surprising if public attitudes to justice could be seen as a guarantee of enhanced justice.

Finally, it would be remiss not to recall in this context the way in which public trials have historically been used, and still are used, as a way of legitimizing the power of the state. While the most extreme and systematic examples of this took place in the Soviet Union under Stalin, it is important to note that this was neither unique to the Soviet regime nor a feature only of "political" trials.[86] Recent events, such as the trial of Saddam Hussein, show how the criminal trial might be used to seek to demonstrate the fairness or impartiality of a political order, as compared with those that preceded it, while other trials might acquire unanticipated political resonances such that the state has a particular interest in either the outcome or the procedure.[87] Such trials can only call into question the instrumental efficacy of publicity in ensuring that standards of fairness are met, as the demand for legitimacy may be driven by state demands or requirements and will depend on prevailing social conditions that will vary from place to place and time to time.[88] That trials are held in public can be as much an instrument of illegitimate public power as a disciplining mechanism to ensure fairness. The possibility of using the symbolic power of the trial to achieve unjust and coercive ends erodes the confidence that one can have in their instrumental efficacy in contributing to independent standards of fairness.

The instrumental defense of public trials, then, depends on empirical claims about the tendency of public scrutiny to ensure correctness that are difficult to verify, or on claims about legitimacy that are historically dubious and have little theoretical basis. If the right to a fair trial is to be used as a justification of public trials, we will need a more foundational moral and political theory to ground the right, one that is not simply based on the instrumental potential of the trial in achieving fairness.

A Communicative Defense of Public Trials

This brings us to a third possibility, that there is a more general communicative rationale for the criminal trial. Our argument here is that the defendant is called to answer and to account for perpetrating a public wrong. The judgment constitutes a condemnation of the defendant as a public wrongdoer, a condemnation that, at least in the institutional voice, articulates a commitment to the relevant norms of the criminal law. From this perspective it is not difficult to see why the verdict or condemnation should be public. A public wrong is a wrong that the public has an interest in prosecuting and, if a conviction is warranted, condemning. Public condemnation of this kind obviously requires public knowledge of the conviction.

This alone, however, does not make the demand for public trials apparent. In order to establish that the defendant has committed a public wrong, it is clear that the trial must be conducted by public officials who are in an important sense *representatives* of the public: individuals who can be trusted to ensure that it is only those defendants who deserve public condemnation who are convicted of crimes. But given earlier arguments that the interests of justice are not necessarily enhanced by the public having a right to be present during the trial, are there any other reasons why they should be invited to be present? Here we would return to the nature of convictions as public condemnation to argue that condemnation is justified if the trial has established knowledge of public wrongdoing by the defendant. Such condemnation purports to be in the name of the public, in the sense that it is an expression of a wrong with which the public has a proper concern. But if condemnation is in the name of the public, then surely the public has a right to ensure that the condemnation was justified. This cannot be achieved merely by knowledge of the verdict, but also requires that in any individual case the public should be able to determine (through presence in court or some other form of access to the court proceedings) both that the grounds for the verdict were adequate and that the proceedings were conducted in a fair manner.

Furthermore, although the trial is intended to be representative of the public, the public, in a liberal democracy, should have the right to distance itself from public decisions, including decisions to prosecute and convict defendants.[89] While convictions constitute public condemnation of the defendant, members of the public are entitled to express the view that any or all such convictions are "not in their name," in the sense that there is disagreement over either the content of the norms or their application in a particular case. This is only consistent with the demands of liberalism to be tolerant of dissent about the proper content, scope, and application of public wrongs. Obviously the ability to take a critical view about criminal convictions that is the foundation of this entitlement is dependent on the right to know the conditions under which the defendant is convicted. Protecting the right of citizens to distance themselves from prosecutions and convictions is a necessary condition of public condemnation properly understood. A system of condemnation that does not protect the right of the public either to affirm or deny that condemnation can hardly be called public in the proper sense.

This facilitation of public scrutiny might depend on a number of distinct elements. Jaconelli, for example, distinguishes four parts: the provision of adequate facilities for the attendance of members of the public or press; that the press can report freely on the proceedings they observe; that documents used in the trial should be freely available; and that the identities of the personnel involved in the trial should be known.[90] What is important here is that these illustrate different ways in which the requirement for public scrutiny might be implemented, and also that these seek to broaden the requirement for public justice beyond the hearing itself. However, these also point toward the larger principle that effective public scrutiny goes beyond public access to the hearing, to include access to information that is necessary to understand the nature of the proceedings.

The right to critical scrutiny of the trial, then, is not to be regarded as valuable for the benefits that it has in ensuring that the trial meets other, independent standards of justice. Rather, it is required in order to ensure that convictions have the appropriate standing as expressions of public condemnation. Trials and punishments for public wrongs require a defense of the right to public scrutiny and participation. But we should not only think about the impact that public trials might have on the public in negative terms. We should also hope that trials, properly conducted, will have an educative role.[91] Criminal trials, as we conceive them, are designed to show the proper degree of respect for those who are suspected of public wrongdoing. Trials might display to the public not only the norms of the criminal law, which is commonly regarded as an ambition of the criminal justice system, but also the norms of criminal justice. Just as criminal offenses have a communicative role in outlining what the polity holds to constitute public wrongdoing, so the rules and practices of criminal justice communicate to the public the norms according to which suspects should be treated. Trials have a symbolic role in affirming the values of citizenship that apply even to those whom we suspect of violating the most fundamental values of the state.[92]

Overall, then, the value of holding trials in public lies in the critical scrutiny of trials that this allows. We should not see this in instrumental terms, in improving the extent to which trials will track independent values of procedural and substantive justice, but in terms of the rights of citizens either to affirm verdicts or to distance themselves from them, rights that are grounded in the critical independence that liberal democracies ought to afford their citizens. In terms of the popular formulation, it is not just that justice should be seen to be done—which suggests a purely contingent relationship between justice and the public—but that a trial in which justice which is not seen to be done cannot properly said to be just. The defendant's right to a public trial is not grounded in ensuring that standards of justice are met, for those standards might be supported or hindered by holding trials in public. Rather it is grounded in the opportunity that ought to be afforded to him to have the verdict called into question by the public in whose name it purports to be delivered.

This has important consequence for the way that we think about secret trials and the other exceptions to public justice. Writers from Bentham onward have discussed the issue of exceptions to the principle of publicity, acknowledging that there may be circumstances in which public access or scrutiny should be restricted.[93] It is instructive, however, to consider the principles set out by Bentham in thinking about these issues. He argued that four principles should be observed: that the concealment should not be perpetual or indefinite; that it should not extend beyond its purpose; that there should never be a situation where there is a special tribunal reserved for secret causes; and that every courtroom should have a private chamber to which the parties might retire if necessary.[94] It follows from our own argument that it would be presumptively unfair to hold such proceedings in secret, and that the burden of showing that the restrictions are necessary and that the proceedings are fair should lie on the state in each case. To Bentham's principles we would thus add that what is crucial in such situations is that the grounds for a decision to hold the hearing in secret should be subject to scrutiny, whether by the public or an "independent" assessor acting on behalf of the public. This would require three things: that the exceptions should be clearly defined in law; that those whose cases are proposed to be heard in private should have the opportunity to have the basis for that decision reviewed; and, crucially, that members of the public or the press should be able to have this decision reviewed, even in cases where those involved might opt for secrecy.

Finally we should consider whether this requirement can properly be understood as a right to public justice.[95] Many of those who have argued against this position have done so on the basis that public justice is extrinsic to, or independent of, the understanding of the fair trial. Publicity then is seen as something that is desirable in criminal proceedings, but additionally as something that might present an obstacle to a fair hearing, and that therefore can be restricted if some other powerful interest should be at stake. Jaconelli, for example, to suggests that the right to a public trial can be understood as an element of the right to a fair trial only if "the former is invariably guaranteed as the best means of securing the latter."[96] Our argument is that there is an internal connection between a public trial and a fair trial due to the communicative process that is central to the calling to account for public wrongdoing. This means that trials have a necessarily public character and that they should be held in public and be open to public hearing. This is not a right that can be waived on the part of the accused, because of the character of public wrongs and the necessary public process of a calling to account for those wrongs. It is, however, a right that would inhere in the accused or any other member of the public either to attend a hearing in person, or to have a representative do so, or to have access to documents relating to a particular charge. It is, in this sense, comparable to freedom of information. And it is the right of an accused or other member of the public to challenge the decision to hold any particular hearing in conditions of secrecy. This public character means that trials which are held in secret are presumptively unfair, unless it can be demonstrated on the part of the state that the restrictions are necessary and that the conditions of fairness have been met.

Conclusion: Secret Trials and Public Justice

One of the things that I have attempted to show in this chapter is that neither the idea of the secret, nor that of the public, is straightforwardly grasped; indeed, they can only be properly understood in terms of their relationship with each other. While to talk of the principle of public justice might invoke some broad ideas of openness or public access, and these in turn might be connected in a symbolic way to a broader understanding of the culture of our political and legal institutions, this does not tell us much about the substance or basis of that principle. The idea of the public, indeed, can scarcely be defined without some attention to its limits: what does it mean to exclude public access, what is the scope of the private, and of course, when should something be secret notwithstanding the public nature of the subject matter of the proceedings? The chapter has attempted to analyze the interaction between these ideas in the formation of the modern concept of public justice to show how our understanding of public justice has been shaped by the separation of and enclosure of the juridical space of the courtroom, which has simultaneously opened up the possibility of new forms of enclosure. This, I would argue, opens up a more critical perspective on our understanding of the justification for public justice.

One of the most important conclusions that follows from this concerns secret trials themselves, for what is striking in this area is, in a sense, the absence of secrecy. I do not mean by this that secret trials or closed hearings do not take place, but that the state is quite open about that fact that this is what is happening. The whole question of secrecy, in fact, has been juridified, displacing the political question of the legitimate exercise of state power onto the courts and their interpretation of the law. The jurisprudence suggests a systematic regulation of the questions of which sort of proceedings might take place in secret and of the procedures that should be followed. This is true even of the practice of excluding the jurisdiction of the normal courts, which has become an accepted and even regular juridical practice; it is not an exclusion of law, but a fragmenting of the forms through which legal power is exercised. But perhaps this absence of secrecy should not surprise us, for this kind of juridification of the political is characteristic of the form of modern law. This does not mean that the issue of public justice becomes unimportant, but rather that we need to have a closer understanding of the process by which secrecy has been juridified in this area—something that has been almost completely neglected in legal scholarship. We should pay more attention, as it were, to the secret history of secret trials.

None of this, of course, should be understood as suggesting that the principle of public justice is unimportant, or that it is not regarded by the members of the judiciary and others as being of fundamental importance. My point is rather that when we look behind the grand declarations of principle we find a more complex picture—and one in which the question of the justification for the principle is too easily neglected. On the one hand, departures from open justice—the secret trials—are much more systematic and regular than is usually acknowledged. And on the other, the public justice that is being defended is one where the state seeks to present a certain image of the trial so as to legitimate its actions.[97] What is more, this is also true of the critics of state action in seeking resort to secret tribunals, who unreflectively invoke the same kind of vague statements about presenting the state and the nation in the best possible light. What should lie at the heart of the process—communication and critical scrutiny—has been lost.

Notes

I would principally like to thank my collaborators on The Trial on Trial project, Antony Duff, Sandra Marshall, and Victor Tadros for their advice and assistance. Thanks also to Rex Ferguson, Jenny Johnstone, Carl Knight and Sarah Summers.

1. See the description at http://news.bbc.co.uk/1/hi/world/americas/4422825.stm. President Obama initially opposed this process, as part of his plan to close the camp at Guantanamo Bay, but in 2011 he announced that the trials by military commission would resume: http://www.nytimes.com/2011/03/08/world/americas/08guantanamo.

html. The U.S. Supreme Court discussed the legality of the commissions in *Hamdan v. Rumsfeld* 126 SCt 2749 (2006).

2. See now Prevention of Terrorism Act 2005, which was passed following the condemnation of part IV of the Anti-Terrorism, Crime and Security Act 2001 in *A v. Secretary of State for the Home Dept.* [2004] UKHL 56.

3. A.-M. Slaughter, "Secret Trial by Military Commission Is Not Justice," November 19, 2001, *International Herald Tribune* (http://www.commondreams.org/views01/1119-01.htm).

4. One more recent exception is J. Jaconelli, *Open Justice: A Critique of the Public Trial* (Oxford: Oxford University Press, 2002), although this focuses on the application of the rule of public justice rather than on clearly articulating a basis for that principle.

5. S. Trechsel, *Human Rights in Criminal Proceedings* (Oxford: Oxford University Press, 2005), ch. 5.

6. One important difference between Europe and the United States is that the Sixth Amendment to the U.S. Constitution establishes the public and speedy trial as a distinct right, whereas in Europe it is (more problematically) included in Art. 6 of the European Convention on Human Rights (ECHR) as an element of the right to a fair trial.

7. The theoretical arguments are discussed more fully in R. A. Duff, L. Farmer, S. E. Marshall, and V. Tadros, *The Trial on Trial III: Towards a Normative Theory of the Criminal Trial* (Oxford: Hart Publishing, 2007), ch. 9. See also Jaconelli, *Open Justice*, pp. 110–16.

8. "In the towne house, or in some open or common place, there is a tribunall or place of judgement made aloft upon the highest bench," Sir Thomas Smith, *De Republica Anglorum* (c. 1565), bk. II, ch. 23 (available at http://www.constitution.org/eng/repang.htm).

9. Sir John Fortescue, *On the Laws and Governance of England* (Cambridge: Cambridge University Press, 1997), pp. 41–42.

10. Ibid., p. 51. In much of this literature the reference to France becomes shorthand for systems of tyranny or despotism.

11. Smith, *De Republica Anglorum*, bk. II, ch. 23.

12. *The Selected Writings of Sir Edward Coke* (Indianapolis, IN: Liberty Fund, 2003), vol. II, p. 729.

13. These are discussed in J. H. Langbein, *The Origins of Adversary Criminal Trial* (Oxford: Oxford University Press, 2003), ch. 1; See also B. Shapiro, *Beyond Reasonable Doubt and Probable Cause* (Berkeley: University of California Press, 1991), pp. 242–44; A. H. Shapiro, "Political Theory and the Growth of Defensive Safeguards in Criminal Procedure: The Origins of the Treason Trials Act of 1696," *Law and History Review* 11 (1993): 215.

14. *Act anent Advising Criminal Processes with open doors*, APS 1693 c.27; D. Hume,

Commentaries on the Law of Scotland Respecting Crimes (4th edn.) (Edinburgh: Bell and Bradfute, 1844), ii, p. 304. H. Arnot, *A Collection and Abridgement of Celebrated Criminal Trials in Scotland from AD 1536 to 1784* (Edinburgh: Wm. Smellie, 1785), provides an account of the religious trials of the seventeenth century.

15. See, however, Trial of Treasons Act 1696 s.2, requiring that conviction could be only on the testimony of two witnesses or where the accused confessed in open court. There was also a link to the idea that parliamentary proceedings should be public.

16. See, esp., T. A. Green, *Verdict According to Conscience: Perspectives on the English Criminal Jury Trial 1200–1800* (Chicago: University of Chicago Press, 1985), ch. 6.

17. *A Complete Collection of State Trials* (3rd edn.) (6 vols., London, 1742), pp. iii–iv. On the state trials series generally, see D. Thomas, ed., *State Trials, Vol. 1* (London: Routledge and Kegan Paul, 1972), Introduction; and A. Paterson, *Early Modern Liberalism* (Cambridge: Cambridge University Press, 1997), chs. 3 and 4.

18. See S. Kadri, *The Trial: A History from Socrates to OJ Simpson* (London: Harper Collins, 2005), p. 89.

19. W. Blackstone, *Commentaries on the Law of England* (1765–69) (reprinted by University of Chicago Press), vol. III, p. 373, following Sir Matthew Hale. See also C. Beccaria, *On Crimes and Punishments and Other Writings* [1764] (Cambridge: Cambridge University Press, 1995), chs. 14 and 15.

20. His chapter on crimes against public justice stressed the importance of the appearance of impartiality: Blackstone, *Commentaries*, vol. IV, ch. 10. See also the discussion in S. Devereaux, "The City and the Sessions Paper: 'Public Justice' in London 1770–1800," *Journal of British Studies* 35 (1996): 466 at 489.

21. Blackstone, *Commentaries*, vol. III, ch. 4 at p. 30.

22. Ibid., vol. III, pp. 303–8. This reflects the role that the Star Chamber was to play in the demonology of the English common law, as a symbol of royal, despotic power. For a defense of the Star Chamber, see T. Barnes, "Star Chamber Mythology," *American Journal of Legal History* 5 (1961): 8–10.

23. Blackstone, *Commentaries*, vol. III, p. 379; vol. IV, p. 350.

24. Jeremy Bentham, *Rationale of Judicial Evidence* (5 vols.) (London: Hunt and Clarke, 1827). See bk. II, ch. X (available at http://heinonline.org/home/content/Browse/Legal-Classics/Rationale-of-Judicial-Evidence.html).

25. Ibid., p. 522, citing his own *Draught of a New Plan for the Organization of the Judicial Establishment in France* (London: 1790).

26. Ibid., p. 523.

27. Ibid., p. 525.

28. Ibid., p. 585. It is interesting to note that he criticizes the Grand Jury for its secrecy (pp. 590–91).

29. Devereaux, "The City and the Sessions Paper," pp. 490ff, discusses the tension

between legitimacy and efficiency in disputes over public justice in late-eighteenth-century London.

30. See T. Laqueur, "Crowds, Carnival, and the State in English Executions, 1604–1868," in *The First Modern Society: Essays in Honor of Lawrence Stone*, ed. L. Beier, D. Cannadine, and J. Rosenheim (Cambridge: Cambridge University Press, 1989).

31. On the image of the lottery and the reform movement, see D. J. A. Cairns, *Advocacy and the Making of the Adversarial Criminal Trial 1800–1865* (Oxford: Oxford University Press, 1998), ch. 3. On capital punishment and the uses of mercy, see V. A. C. Gatrell, *The Hanging Tree: Execution and the English People 1770–1868* (Oxford: Oxford University Press, 1994).

32. J. H. Grossman, *The Art of Alibi: English Law Courts and the Novel* (Baltimore, MD: Johns Hopkins University Press, 2002), p. 7; F. Moretti, *Signs Taken for Wonders: Essay in the Sociology of Literary Forms* (London: Verso, 1983), p. 138.

33. R. McGowen, "The Image of Justice and Reform of the Criminal Law in Early Nineteenth-Century England," *Buffalo Law Review* 32 (1983): 89. See also Devereaux, "The City and the Sessions Paper," pp. 486–90.

34. See also K. F. Taylor, *In the Theater of Criminal Justice* (Princeton: Princeton University Press, 1993), p. 22; M. Foucault, *Discipline and Punish: The Birth of the Prison* (London: Allen Lane, 1977), p. 9. He goes on to argue that the criminal trial develops a new focus on accused persons, looking behind their acts to the pathologies of their character.

35. Even if, as Langbein points out, there was little clear design to the development. See *Origins of Adversary Criminal Trial*, p. 9.

36. See ibid.; Cairns, *Advocacy*; A. N. May, *The Bar and the Old Bailey 1750–1950* (Chapel Hill: University of North Carolina Press, 2003); J. M. Beattie, *Crime and the Courts in England 1660–1800* (Oxford: Clarendon Press, 1986).

37. Though this was in a very small number of cases until later in the century. See, for example, P. King, *Crime, Justice and Discretion in England 1740–1820* (Oxford: Oxford University Press, 2000), p. 228.

38. And often more aggressive. One barrister, William Garrow, became notorious for his hostile cross-examination technique. See J. M. Beattie, "Scales of Justice: Defense Counsel and the English Criminal Trial in the Eighteenth and Nineteenth Centuries," *Law and History Review* 9 (1991): 221.

39. On the 1836 act, see ibid.; Cairns, *Advocacy*; May, *The Bar and the Old Bailey*.

40. Langbein, *Origins of Adversary Criminal Trial*, pp. 318–31.

41. See D. Freestone and J. C. Richardson, "The Making of English Criminal Law (7). Sir John Jervis and his Acts," *Criminal Law Review* (1980): 5.

42. The passing of the Criminal Evidence Act of 1898, which could be said to end this period of development, allowed the participation of the accused (giving evidence on oath), but participation by the accused was strictly controlled by the lawyers.

43. For a fuller account of the "reconstructive trial," see Lindsay Farmer, "Criminal Responsibility and the Proof of Guilt," in *Modern Histories of Crime and Punishment*, ed. M. D. Dubber and L. Farmer (Stanford: Stanford University Press, 2007).

44. In England the involvement of the police led ultimately to the Grand Jury falling into desuetude. It was formally abolished in 1933.

45. Langbein, *Origins of Adversary Criminal Trial*, ch. 5.

46. J. F. Stephen, *A General View of the Criminal Law of England* (London: Macmillan, 1863), pp. 166–67. See also Stephen, *A History of the Criminal Law of England* (3 vols.) (London: Macmillan, 1883), vol. I, ch. XI.

47. The language of combat is specifically invoked in the *History of the Criminal Law*, pp. 425–27, 432. This also excluded aspects of pretrial procedure from the requirement of publicity, steps that were matched by the increasing restrictions on pretrial publicity. See D. Bentley, *English Criminal Justice in the Nineteenth Century* (London: Hambledon, 1998), ch. 5; J. M. Beattie, "Sir John Fielding and Public Justice: The Bow Street Magistrates' Court 1754–1780," *Law and History Review* 25 (2007): 61.

48. See S. Summers, *Fair Trials: The European Criminal Procedural Tradition and the European Court of Human Rights* (Oxford: Hart Publishing, 2007), ch. 2; S. E. Farrar, "Myths and Legends: An Examination of the Historical Role of the Accused in Traditional Legal Scholarship; A Look at the Nineteenth Century," *Oxford Journal of Legal Studies* 21 (2001): 331.

49. See L. Farmer, "'With all the impressiveness and substantial value of truth': Notable Trials and Criminal Justice," *Law and Humanities* 1 (2007): 57.

50. Hannah Arendt claimed this was the "greatest achievement of the century," *The Origins of Totalitarianism* (London: Harcourt, Brace, 1951), p. 91, commenting on the Dreyfus trial.

51. C. Graham, *Ordering Law: The Architectural and Social History of the English Law Court to 1914* (Aldershot: Ashgate, 2003), p. 29. See also L. Mulcahy, *Legal Architecture: Justice, Due Process and the Place of Law* (London: Routledge, 2010), chs. 3–5; Taylor, *In the Theater of Criminal Justice*.

52. Taylor, *In the Theater of Criminal Justice*. It is instructive to compare the plan of Winchester Great Hall in 1871 (p. 26), showing the traditional style of court design, with the plan for the redeveloped courts that were installed in the 1870s (p. 32).

53. See Graham, *Ordering Law*, ch. 3.

54. See the description of Winchester assize courts in ibid., pp. 279–84.

55. Though making little attempt to match the imposing theatricality of the rebuilt *Palais de Justice* in Paris: see ibid., p. 328. In nineteenth-century France there was a rebuilding of courthouses, principally the *Palais de Justice* in Paris, to present the trial as spectacle or theater, "reviving iconicity when its traditional subject, the ruler, had been displaced by a diffuse new subject, the public" (Taylor, *In the Theater of Criminal Justice*, p. xxi).

56. Taylor, *In the Theater of Criminal Justice*, pp. 13–14, drawing a contrast with the French courtroom, where the public occupied part of the court and participated in the proceedings.

57. See Sir Travers Humphreys, *A Book of Trials* (London: Wm. Heinemann, 1953), pp. xxi–xxiv. See also A. Crew, *The Old Bailey. History: Constitution: Functions: Notable Trials* (London: Nicholson and Watson, 1933). Graham, *Ordering Law*, pp. 297ff, points out that the amount of space provided for members of the general public was steadily reduced, distinguishing between the idly curious and those who had business in the court.

58. Often at the cost of seating for members of the general public. See, generally, J. Rowbotham and K. Stevenson, "Causing a Sensation: Media and Legal Representations of Bad Behaviour," in *Behaving Badly: Social Panic and Moral Outrage—Victorian and Modern Parallels*, ed. J. Rowbotham and K. Stevenson (Aldershot: Ashgate, 2003).

59. See, for example, Stephen, *History of the Criminal Law of England*, vol. I, p. 516, suggesting that the necessary degree of publicity could be secured by admitting members of the press only.

60. This is a distinction drawn by Summers, *Fair Trials*, pp. 38–47. See Department for Constitutional Affairs, *Broadcasting Courts*, CP 28/04 (2004), for a recent illustration of this concern in England and Wales.

61. Appeal Cases 417(1913).

62. Ibid., p. 437.

63. Ibid., p. 440, referring to the Divorce and Matrimonial Causes Act of 1857, which abolished the Ecclesiastical Courts.

64. Ibid., p. 447.

65. Ibid., pp. 476–77.

66. Ibid., p. 484.

67. Ibid., p. 446 (Earl Loreburn).

68. For the United States, see *In re Oliver* 333 U.S. 257 (1948); *Gannett Co. v. de Pasquale* 443 U.S. 368 (1979); *Richmond Newspapers v. Virginia* 448 U.S. 555 (1980).

69. Oddly, security was not one of the exceptions listed in *Scott*, a factor that Jaconelli suggests led to the enactment of the provisions in the Official Secrets Act of 1920. For a comprehensive treatment of the scope of this exception in English law, see Jaconelli, *Open Justice*, ch. 4.

70. A hearing in camera is understood as meaning the exclusion of the public; hearings in chambers are merely "private," and members of the public might be admitted at the judge's discretion. A hearing in camera must fall within one of the exceptions in *Scott*. Jaconelli, *Open Justice*, pp. 72–80.

71. Now the Official Secrets Act of 1989 s.11(4).

72. See *re MB* [2006] EWHC 1000; *Re MB* [2006] EWCA Civ 1140.

73. See A. Ashworth, "Social Control and 'Anti-Social Behaviour': The Subversion of Human Rights?" *Law Quarterly Review* 120 (2004): 263.

74. It is also interesting to note that Bentham anticipates this sort of procedure: *Rationale of Judicial Evidence*, pp. 575–76.

75. The argument of this section is developed more fully in Duff et al., *The Trial on Trial III*, ch. 9.

76. This was an important element of the reform of procedure in the nineteenth century that established the modern trial. The Prisoners' Counsel Act of 1836 required the disclosure of the depositions taken at committal proceedings to the defendant, though not necessarily the depositions of other witnesses. The defendant was not entitled to a copy of the indictment in felony trials until the passing of the Indictments Act in 1915.

77. P. Roberts and A. Zuckerman, *Criminal Evidence* (Oxford: Oxford University Press, 2004), p. 52.

78. Bentham, *Rationale of Judicial Evidence*, I, bk. II, ch. x.

79. Ibid., pp. 522–23.

80. See also Jaconelli, *Open Justice*, pp. 34–45.

81. Bentham, *Rationale of Judicial Evidence*, p. 523.

82. "Upon his moral faculties it acts as a check, restraining him from active partiality and improbity in every shape: upon his intellectual activities it acts as a spur, urging him to that habit of unremitting exertion." Ibid.

83. This is a common defense of the privacy of jury deliberations: concerns that bias will go unchecked, it is sometimes argued, are counterbalanced by the need to ensure that the jury can deliberate openly and freely without public pressure or pressure from the defendant, his friends, and family.

84. Garapon points out that press and TV offer an immediate (that is, unmediated) version of the truth that is presented as superior to that of law, which is regarded as vulnerable to the technicalities and the manipulations of lawyers. "Justice out of Court: The Dangers of Trial by Media," in *Law as Communication*, ed. D. Nelken (Aldershot: Dartmouth, 1996), p. 233.

85. See also Trechsel, *Human Rights*, p. 121.

86. For a brief review of the Stalinist show trials, see Kadri, *The Trial*, ch. 6. On political trials generally, see O. Kirchheimer, *Political Justice: The Use of Legal Procedure for Political Ends* (Princeton: Princeton University Press, 1961).

87. This was also true of the Nuremberg trials and of the trial of Adolf Eichmann. See H. Arendt, *Eichmann in Jerusalem: A Report on the Banality of Evil* (Harmondsworth: Penguin 1994); L. Douglas, *The Memory of Judgement: Making Law and History in the Trials of the Holocaust* (New Haven: Yale University Press, 2001).

88. For fuller discussion of these issues, see Duff et al., *Trial on Trial*, ch. 10.

89. See also M. Redmayne, "Rethinking the Principle against Self-Incrimination," *Oxford Journal of Legal Studies* 27 (2007): 209.

90. Jaconelli, *Open Justice,* pp. 2–3.

91. See also Bentham, *Rationale of Judicial Evidence,* p. 525. The didactic functions of trials are also explored in Douglas, *The Memory of Judgement.*

92. See also M. Hildebrandt, "Trial and 'Fair Trial': From Peer to Subject to Citizen," in *The Trial on Trial II.* This might extend more broadly still: "When the basic structure of society is publicly known to satisfy its principles for an extended period of time, those subject to these arrangements tend to develop a desire to act in accordance with these principles and to do their part in institutions which exemplify them. A conception of justice is stable when the public recognition of its realization by the social system tends to bring about a corresponding sense of justice." J. Rawls, *A Theory of Justice* (Oxford: Oxford University Press, 1972), p. 154.

93. See Bentham, *Rationale of Judicial Evidence,* pp. 537–68. He notes nine circumstances, including preserving the good order of the courtroom; preserving the reputation or tranquillity of families from unnecessary vexation; public decency; and protecting secrets of state.

94. Ibid., pp. 569–71.

95. Or in the United States the question would be what is the proper basis of the already existing right.

96. Jaconelli, *Open Justice,* p. 113.

97. Which is one reason why certain types of disorderly defendants create such a problem.

Spousal Secrets: Same-Sex Couples and the Functional Approach to Spousal Evidentiary Privileges

EDWARD STEIN

I. Introduction

Under the typical rules of evidence in jurisdictions in the United States, relevant evidence is presumptively admissible at trial.[1] However, in many states and under federal evidence law, the *confidential communication privilege* (or *marital communication privilege*) makes testimony regarding confidential communications between spouses inadmissible, and the *adverse testimonial privilege* (or *spousal testimonial privilege*) prevents a person from being compelled to testify against her[2] spouse. As a result, what one spouse tells the other in private and what one spouse knows about the other but does not want to testify about are legally sanctioned *spousal secrets*.[3] This information spouses have about each other that evidence law treats specially may not be "secret" in that it might already be known by other people (it might even be known publicly, in which case it might be an "open secret"),[4] but it is secret in the sense that it is *not meant to be known* by others.[5] While the scope, character, and the very existence of these rules regarding spousal secrets have been questioned by legal commentators for centuries, they remain in force in many jurisdictions in the United States.

This chapter considers the arguments for these spousal secrets in the context of the current revolution in family law regarding legal recognition of same-sex relationships. I argue that, insofar as the justifications for spousal secrets are persuasive, they also apply to same-sex couples. This chapter analyzes different approaches for dealing with the legal status of spousal secrets at this revolutionary moment and offers a sophisticated version of functionalism as a viable approach to spousal secrets.

At present, family law in the United States is going through what might be viewed as a third revolutionary period, as legal recognition for same-sex relationships is debated across the country in various forms. The first revolution in family law concerned the role of women in marriage. Traditionally, at common law, men had the power in marriage; for example, married women could not own property[6] and were treated differently than married men under inheritance laws.[7] Today, legally created and enforced gender asymmetries in family law have been mostly eliminated.[8]

The second revolution concerned divorce. In order to end a marriage, one spouse used to have to prove, first, that the other spouse was at fault for the irretrievable breakdown of the marriage, and, second, that he or she was innocent with respect to causing the breakdown of the marriage. A few decades ago, a shift started from this *fault-based divorce* regime to a *no-fault divorce* regime, in which the person guilty for the breakup of a relationship is no longer an issue with respect to allowing the dissolution of a marriage.[9] Today, every jurisdiction in the United States allows for at least some form of no-fault divorce.

The third revolution concerns the legal recognition of spouse-like relationships between people of the same sex.[10] Lesbians, gay men, bisexuals, and their allies have argued in courts and in legislatures that same-sex relationships deserve legal recognition.[11] Six states (Connecticut, Iowa, Massachusetts, New Hampshire, New York, and Vermont) and the District of Columbia now allow same-sex couples to marry. Five states (Delaware, Hawaii,[12] Illinois, New Jersey, and Rhode Island) have enacted laws allowing same-sex couples to enter *civil unions*, which are the legal equivalent to marriage under these respective states' laws. Eight states (California,[13] Colorado, Maine, Maryland, Nevada, Oregon, Washington,[14] and Wisconsin) and various local jurisdictions allow same-sex couples to register as *domestic partners*, which entitles them to some subset of the rights and benefits associated with marriage in each jurisdiction. The number and scope of the rights and benefits that flow from a domestic partnership vary widely; some domestic partnerships are effectively equivalent to civil unions (those in California, Washington, and Oregon, for example), while some only provide for a small number of benefits (those in Hawaii and Wisconsin, for example). In contrast, many U.S. jurisdictions have enacted laws and amended their constitutions to block some or all recognition of same-sex relationships. As of this writing, forty-one states have either passed laws or amended their constitutions (or done both) to prohibit same-sex marriages, to deny recognition of same-sex marriages from other jurisdictions, and/or to deny recognition of other types of same-sex relationships.[15] Additionally, the Defense of Marriage Act (DOMA), a federal law, defines marriage as between one man and one woman and says no state shall be required to recognize a same-sex marriage from another jurisdiction.[16] In sum, as a result of litigation, legislation, and voter initiatives, there exists in the United States a patchwork of legal recognition and nonrecognition for same-sex relationships.[17]

Due to these recent developments in the legal recognition of same-sex relationships, there has been a significant expansion regarding who can claim the spousal evidentiary privileges.[18] A good example of how the quest for marriage equality has led to this change in the law of spousal secrets is the case of Vermont. Before 1999, no state extended these privileges to same-sex couples. In 1999, in *Baker v. State*, the Vermont Supreme Court unanimously held that Vermont's constitution required that same-sex and different-sex couples be able to obtain the same benefits, rights, responsibilities, and duties associated with marriage.[19] The court held that the state's failure to provide same-sex couples the opportunity to obtain the rights, benefits, duties, and obligations of marriage was unconstitutional, and it ordered the state legislature to change its domestic relations laws.[20] In response, in 2000, the Vermont state legislature passed a law that created the *civil union*, a new legal relationship for same-sex couples that mirrored marriage under Vermont law. A same-sex couple that obtained a civil union was granted all of the same benefits, rights, obligations, and duties as a married different-sex couple in Vermont.[21] Specifically, the Vermont law said that "[p]arties to a civil union shall have all the same benefits, protections and responsibilities under law, whether they derive from statute, administrative or court rule, policy, common law or any other source of civil law, as are granted to spouses in a marriage," and, further, that a "party to a civil union shall be included in any definition or use of the terms 'spouse,' 'family,' 'immediate family,' 'dependent,' 'next of kin,' and other terms that denote the spousal relationship, as those terms are used throughout the law."[22] Since different-sex married couples in Vermont had some spousal evidentiary privileges,[23] those privileges also applied to same-sex couples who entered civil unions under the new law. Eight years after Vermont created civil unions, the state legislature decided to allow same-sex couples to marry. Now same-sex couples in Vermont may obtain the protections of the spousal evidentiary privileges in the same way that different-sex couples do—namely, by getting married.

Similarly, in other states that have granted same-sex couples some or all of the benefits, rights, and obligations of different-sex married couples, the spousal evidentiary privileges have been extended to same-sex couples as part of the "package" without any careful consideration of these privileges in particular. In Massachusetts, after the landmark case of *Goodridge v. Department of Public Health*,[24] married same-sex couples qualify for the same spousal evidentiary privileges as married different-sex couples.[25] Same-sex couples in New Jersey who obtain civil unions[26] and same-sex couples in California and Oregon who register as domestic partners are entitled to the same spousal evidentiary privileges as married different-sex couples in those states.[27]

In contrast, there have been suggestions to extend or modify spousal evidentiary privileges separately from granting full relationship equality to same-sex couples. For example, in Rhode Island, a bill was introduced that would have extended Rhode Island's confidential communication privilege and adverse testimonial privilege to domestic partners.[28] The bill defined a domestic partner as one who "shares an exclusive, intimate and committed relationship of mutual caring" and can satisfy certain criteria including, for example, financial interdependence and cohabitation for at least one year.[29] Separately, a *New York Times* op-ed piece, which offers what I will refer to as the *Conley proposal*, suggests that every person should be able to choose one person (who can be changed periodically) who gets the same evidentiary privileges as a spouse.[30] While both of these proposals have the virtue of expanding the spousal evidentiary privileges to some unmarried couples, they represent piecemeal approaches to the recognition of same-sex relationships. Further, these approaches have not been successful in actually extending spousal evidentiary privileges to same-sex couples.

Thus, while piecemeal approaches have been proposed, the extension of the spousal evidentiary privileges to same-sex couples has not resulted from specific debate (legislative or otherwise) about the significance of these privileges and their justifications; rather, these changes have been the result of the quest for marriage equality. On the one hand, this is consistent with history. For example, in 1948 when California, in *Perez v. Lippold*,[31] struck down that state's antimiscegenation law, thereby allowing different-race couples to marry, the state did not separately consider whether to extend the spousal evidentiary privileges to such different-race couples. Its failure to do so was neither a mistake nor a shortcut. On the other hand, as jurisdictions consider expanding access to the spousal evidentiary privileges—as part of piecemeal reform (as in Rhode Island) or by virtue of broad changes in marriage laws—some reflection on the privileges is warranted.[32]

This chapter reconsiders the spousal evidentiary privileges at this transitional moment in the development of family law in the United States. There are five possible approaches for dealing with the legal status of spousal secrets (generally) at this third revolutionary moment. First, the spousal evidentiary privileges could be abolished. Perhaps as the concepts of marriage and family have evolved—and as they continue to do so[33]—the justifications for these privileges have been undercut. (Alternatively, as some critics have argued, perhaps the privileges were never adequately justified in the first place.) Whatever else it would do, abolition of the privileges would afford equal treatment with respect to the evidentiary privileges to same-sex couples and different-sex couples as well as to married and unmarried couples. Second, same-sex couples could be allowed to marry, as they are in six states, or be given equal[34] access to all the state's rights, benefits, privileges, duties, and obligations that married couples have, as in states with civil unions or robust domestic partnerships. Third, short of full equality for same-sex couples, states could adopt what I call the *piecemeal approach* to the recognition of same-sex relationships, since it gives same-sex couples a subset of the privileges associated with marriage. This would involve giving the spousal evidentiary privileges to nonmarried registered couples, as the bill in Rhode Island proposed to do. While some jurisdictions have adopted the piecemeal approach in that they have created "weak" domestic partnership laws that give registered same-sex couples only a partial subset of the rights of married people, none of these jurisdictions have given the evidentiary privileges to registered same-sex couples under this approach. Fourth, courts and/or legislatures could adopt a *functional approach* to the spousal evidentiary privileges, giving the privilege to relationships that have certain "marriage-like" functional characteristics, even if such relationships are not actually marriages. Applying a functional approach, a married couple might not qualify for the spousal evidentiary privileges if their relationship was irretrievably broken or if their marriage was a sham, while an unmarried couple would qualify for these privileges if their relationship had the appropriate functional characteristics (for example, if the parties were cohabitating, were in an intimate relationship, and were financially and emotionally interdependent). This functional approach is opposed to the *traditional* or *bright-line* approach to spousal secrets, according to which there are necessary and sufficient conditions for determining whether the spousal evidentiary privileges should be applied: if a couple is married, they may invoke the privileges, while if they are not married, they may not. Finally, as a fifth approach, one might reject equality arguments with respect to spousal evidentiary privileges altogether by finding a relevant difference between same-sex couples and married different-sex couples (the *differentiation* approach).

Of these five options, the first two appear unrealistic at present. Abolishing the privileges seems unlikely: a proposal from an advisory committee appointed by the federal judiciary that was approved by the Supreme Court and would have mostly abolished the spousal evidentiary privileges at the federal level was strongly rejected by Congress.[35] Regarding the second approach, it seems unlikely that marriage equality for all same-sex couples is on the horizon. Although there may be more states that embrace marriage equality for same-sex couples in the next few years, it seems unlikely that the U.S. Supreme Court will rule that prohibitions on same-sex marriage are unconstitutional.[36] Given the hostility to same-sex relationships expressed in statutes and constitutions by more then two-thirds of the states,[37] it is doubtful that a significantly greater portion of the country will embrace legal equality for same-sex couples in the near future.

With the first two options at least currently off the table, the three remaining options are the piecemeal approach, the functional approach and the differentiation approach. This chapter evaluates these three options. Part II provides a legal and historical context for the spousal evidentiary privileges. Part III is a discussion of the arguments made for and against the privileges. Part IV provides an assessment of how relevant the arguments for and against the privileges are to same-sex relationships. This analysis results in the conclusion that only two of the five options for dealing with the legal status of spousal secrets at this third revolutionary moment remain—the piecemeal approach and functionalism. Part V examines some examples of how federal and state courts have embraced a functional approach to marriage and to the spousal evidentiary privileges. Part V also develops a sophisticated functionalist approach to the spousal evidentiary privileges that has advantages over piecemeal approaches. I am, in general, supportive of the approach adopted by those jurisdictions that have given the spousal evidentiary privileges to same-sex couples—namely, by allowing same-sex couples to marry or otherwise enter formal legal relationships. In any event, functionalism with respect to the privileges still warrants serious consideration and has virtues independent of the equality considerations that weigh in favor of recognition for same-sex relationships. Part VI evaluates functionalism about the spousal evidentiary privileges. Part VII concludes that advocates for reforming the spousal evidentiary privileges should seriously consider a sophisticated functional approach.

II. The Confidential Communication Privilege and the Adverse Testimonial Privilege

There are two commonly recognized spousal evidentiary privileges, the *confidential communication privilege* and the *adverse testimonial privilege*. The confidential communication privilege gives a spouse the right to refuse to disclose communications made during the marriage, in reliance on the confidence of the marital relationship, as well as the right to prevent his or her spouse from disclosing such communications. The adverse testimonial privilege prevents a witness-spouse from being compelled to testify against her spouse in court. Both types of spousal secrets are firmly rooted in the common law.

These two classes of spousal secrets share some characteristics, but they also differ in interesting ways. In terms of scope, the adverse testimonial privilege allows a spouse witness to refuse to testify against a spouse about anything, whereas the confidential communication privilege applies only to testimony about confidential communications made during the marriage. Each privilege looks to a different time period: the confidential communication privilege is concerned with the period *during the marriage*, while the adverse testimonial privilege looks to the relationship *at the time of testimony*. In terms of duration, the confidential communication privilege lasts forever, while the adverse testimonial privilege applies only while the couple remains married. Further, the adverse testimonial privilege applies only in proceedings in which the nonwitness spouse is a party (and in some jurisdictions, only in criminal proceedings),[38] while, in most jurisdictions, the confidential communication privilege applies in all proceedings, even those in which the spouses are not parties. Finally, in some jurisdictions, the confidential communication privilege even binds third parties from testifying about a confidential marital communication, while the adverse testimonial privilege does not have this effect.

A. The Confidential Communication Privilege

The confidential communication privilege prohibits testimony about communications made in confidence between spouses unless both spouses consent to such testimony. The communication can be spoken or nonverbal, and it must have been made in confidence—that is, not in the presence of a third party.[39] So long as the couple was married at the time of the communication, the testimony is prohibited forever, even if the couple divorces or if one of them dies. There are three major exceptions to the privilege: it does not apply to litigation between spouses or former spouses; it does not apply in a criminal case against one spouse in which the victim is the other spouse or a child; and it does not apply when the spouses collaborate in the commission of a crime.

As an illustration of how the confidential communication privilege works, consider the case of *United States v. Estes.*[40] Kenneth Estes was charged with bank robbery and making false testimony before a grand jury. His wife at the time was Lydia. After they divorced, Lydia contacted the FBI regarding Estes's role in a bank robbery. Lydia willingly testified before the grand jury and at trial that Estes returned home on the day in question carrying a bag full of money and told her that he had stolen the money. She also testified that she assisted him in counting, hiding, and "laundering" some of the money. Estes argued that all of his former wife's testimony should have been excluded as confidential marital communications. The trial court held that Lydia's testimony was admissible because the communication was part of an ongoing criminal activity involving both spouses. On appeal, the Court of the Appeals for the Second Circuit held that the trial court should *not* have permitted Lydia's testimony that her husband brought home a bag of money and told her that he had stolen it from an armored truck, but that it was correct to permit Lydia's testimony about what happened after she became his accomplice. The appellate court held that at the time that her husband confessed his crime to her, Lydia was not yet involved as an accessory, and so the privilege applied: "Lydia could not become . . . an accessory until she knew that the theft had taken place. The communication to her of that knowledge was a necessary precursor to her involvement and therefore could not have been made as part of an ongoing joint criminal activity."[41] But once Lydia became involved, she was an accessory, and the privilege no longer applied.[42] Even though Lydia was no longer married to her husband at the time of the trial, the confidential communication privilege prevented her from testifying about what he had said to her in confidence during the time they were married—until, that is, they became involved in a joint criminal activity.

B. The Adverse Testimonial Privilege

The adverse testimonial privilege prevents a witness from being compelled to testify against her current spouse. Under the Federal Rules of Evidence, as interpreted by the U.S. Supreme Court in *Trammel v. United States*,[43] and under the rules in most states, the witness spouse controls the privilege. This means that the witness spouse decides whether or not to testify; her testimony cannot be compelled. *Trammel* instituted a significant shift in control of the privilege. Under the rule in effect under federal law before *Trammel*,[44] which still is the law in a minority of states,[45] the nonwitness spouse controlled the privilege; a witness spouse could only testify if she wanted to *and* if the nonwitness spouse allowed it. This meant that the nonwitness spouse could prevent adverse testimony by his spouse. After *Trammel*, a witness spouse gets to decide whether to testify.

Unlike the confidential communication privilege, the adverse testimonial privilege requires that the couple is married at the time testimony is sought. Like the confidential communication privilege, the adverse testimonial privilege does not apply when the spouses litigate against each other or if the testimony sought concerns a crime against a spouse or an immediate family member.

The details of the *Trammel* case provide a useful illustration of various features of the adverse testimonial privilege. Otis Trammel and two others were indicted for conspiracy to import illegal drugs. Trammel's wife, Elizabeth, was arrested when she tried to bring four ounces of heroin into the United States from Thailand. After discussions with drug enforcement officials, Elizabeth, an unindicted co-conspirator, agreed to cooperate with the government in exchange for lenient treatment. At his trial, Trammel asserted his adverse testimonial privilege to prevent the government from calling Elizabeth to testify against him. At a hearing on Trammel's motion, Elizabeth testified that she and Trammel were involved in the conspiracy to distribute illegal drugs, that they were married at the time of the acts at issue, and that they were still married. The trial court held that, while Elizabeth could *not* testify about any confidential communications between her and her husband, she *could* testify about other matters, including acts that she observed during the marriage and communications made in the presence of third parties. The U.S. Supreme Court affirmed, concluding that "the witness-spouse alone has a privilege to refuse to testify adversely; the witness may be neither compelled to testify nor foreclosed from testifying."[46]

C. Historical Justifications

According to the U.S. Supreme Court, the adverse testimonial privilege

> sprang from two canons of medieval jurisprudence: first, the rule that an accused was not permitted to testify in his own behalf because of his interest in the proceeding; second, the concept that husband and wife were one, and that since the woman had no recognized separate legal existence, the husband was that one. From those two now long-abandoned doctrines, it followed that what was inadmissible from the lips of the defendant-husband was also inadmissible from his wife.[47]

The idea that a married couple is a single legal entity, which was part of the original justification for the adverse testimonial privilege, was also used to support the idea that a person cannot bring a tort action against his or her spouse.[48] Most jurisdictions have, however, abolished this common law idea.[49] The single legal entity idea also was an important basis for the doctrine of spousal incompetency, according to which spouses cannot be called as witnesses for or against each other in any context. This doctrine was abolished by the Supreme Court in 1933.[50] The fact that legal concepts based on the idea that spouses form a single legal entity have been rejected casts doubt on the legitimacy of the adverse testimonial privilege. Yet even while the original justifications for the adverse testimonial privilege have been significantly undermined, the privilege itself has remained as part of the common law.

Regarding the confidential communication privilege, prior to 1933, the Supreme Court had not articulated the common law principle that confidential communications between spouses are privileged; the rule prohibiting spouses from testifying for or against each other *at all* effectively prohibited them from testifying about their confidential communications. After holding in 1933 that spouses *could* be called as witnesses for or against each other, in 1934 the Court recognized the continued vitality of the confidential communication privilege.[51] Once spouses were allowed to testify, the question of whether they could testify about confidential communications emerged, and the Court was forced to justify this common law privilege as distinct from the principle of the identity of husband and wife as a single unit. I turn to the contemporary justifications of the confidential communication privilege and the adverse testimonial privilege below.

III. Contemporary Arguments for and against the Privileges

In discussing the adverse testimonial privilege, the U.S. Supreme Court in 1839 summarized the basis for many of the arguments in favor of the privilege as follows:

> Can the wife ... either voluntarily, be permitted or, by force of authority, be compelled to state facts in evidence, which render infamous the character of her husband. We think, most clearly, that she cannot be. Public policy and established principles forbid it. This rule is founded upon the deepest and soundest principles of our nature. Principles which have grown out of those domestic relations, that constitute the basis of civil society; and which are essential to the enjoyment of that confidence which should subsist between those who are connected by the nearest and dearest relations of life. To break down or impair the great principles which protect the sanctities of husband and wife, would be to destroy the best solace of human existence.[52]

This sentiment animates the arguments for and against the spousal evidentiary privileges that I survey below.

A. Arguments for the Confidential Communication Privilege

Various interrelated arguments exist in favor of the confidential communication privilege: it encourages free and open communication between spouses; it provides a safe haven for spouses; it helps to preserve the institution of marriage and strengthen individual marriages; and it is supported by our ethical intuitions and ideas about privacy.

There are two distinct empirical claims behind the argument that the confidential communication privilege fosters free and open communication between spouses: (1) marriages will be stronger and more stable if married couples communicate freely and openly,[53] and (2) if spouses cannot be forced to testify against each other, then they are more likely to communicate. The first claim is a normative psychological claim about what factors makes for good, stable, long-lasting marriages.[54] The second is a descriptive psychological claim that the privilege encourages married couples to communicate more freely. Together, the normative and the descriptive claims suggest a public policy conclusion: insofar as a state has the goal of encouraging and supporting good, stable, and long-lasting marriages, the state should give married couples the confidential communication privilege.

A related argument is that the confidential communication privilege provides a safe haven or refuge for married people. Perhaps marriage fosters open communication partly because marriage provides an important refuge. As one court put it, "[We] have sought to preserve inviolable some small island of privacy as a refuge for the human spirit where government may not intrude."[55] The idea is that having a confidant is both good for a person psychologically—providing support, a friendly ear, and the like—and good for society, because the confidant provides a second opinion that can act as a check on the confider's thoughts and plans. Further, the idea is that it is better, both for individuals and for society, for people to confide in the context of long-lasting and reliable relationships. For instance, rather than having to regularly seek out a new confidant and explain to him or her the context surrounding an idea or secret, a long-standing relationship provides continuity, stability, and a more easily accessible and user-friendly refuge where one can reflect on things and get support, comments, and criticism. Therefore, it makes sense to associate this privilege with marriage since marriages at least strive to be stable and long-lasting, and the legal framework of marriage is supposed to foster these qualities. The virtue of the confidential communication privilege is, according to this line of thought, that it enables spouses to be each other's legally protected long-term confidants.

The open-communication argument and the refuge argument both connect to the channeling function of marriage. In a classic article, Carl Schneider argued that one of the purposes of family law, in general, and the legal status and structure of marriage, in particular, is to "create [and] . . . support social institutions which are thought to serve desirable ends."[56] Creating the legal institution of marriage, providing certain rights, benefits, duties, and responsibilities that go along with it, and offering various other incentives to enter into marriages encourage and socialize people to get married in order to help people and improve the state. Marriage and family law are, on this view, justified as benevolent social engineering.

A related argument in favor of the confidential communication privilege is that it strengthens individual marriages and preserves the institution of marriage. The Supreme Court in 1934 embraced the idea that the privilege helps sustain marriage, saying that "[t]he basis of the immunity given to communications between husband and wife is . . . so essential to the preservation of the marriage relationship as to outweigh the disadvantages to the administration of justice which the privilege entails."[57] This argument relates to the preceding arguments; two of the reasons why the confidential communication privilege strengthens marriages and preserves the institution of marriage are that it encourages spouses to communicate openly and creates a refuge for them.

Another argument for the privilege is that spouses simply should not be forced to reveal marital secrets because doing so seems ethically wrong. As a leading legal treatise put it, "All of us have a feeling of indelicacy and want of decorum in prying into the secrets of husband and wife."[58] The idea is that it is a basic and core value of our society that intimate secrets like those between spouses should not be forced to come out at trial.

Some have tried to buttress this ethical argument by connecting the confidential communication privilege to the constitutional right to privacy.[59] Although the U.S. Constitution, unlike some state constitutions,[60] does not explicitly mention a right to privacy, over the past forty years, the Supreme Court has interpreted the Constitution to include such a right. This started in 1965 with *Griswold v. Connecticut*,[61] which overturned a law prohibiting the use of birth control devices because it violated the right to privacy of married couples. Eight years later, in *Roe v. Wade*, the Court more definitively located the right to privacy in "the Fourteenth Amendment's concept of personal liberty and restrictions on state action."[62] In 1986, in *Bowers v. Hardwick*, which upheld Georgia's sodomy law, the Supreme Court limited the scope of the right to privacy to cases involving "family, marriage or procreation."[63] Although *Bowers* has been explicitly overruled,[64] even its more cabined notion of privacy could arguably support the idea that constitutional privacy considerations undergird the confidential communication privilege. Intuitively, the idea is that to force someone to testify about confidential marital communications invades the "sacred precincts of marital bedrooms."[65]

To summarize, the arguments for the confidential communication privilege are that the privilege encourages open communication between spouses, it provides a confidant for spouses, it preserves individual marriages and the institution of marriage, and granting the privilege fits with our ethical intuitions and is supported by privacy considerations.

B. Arguments for the Adverse Testimonial Privilege

Many of the arguments in support of the adverse testimonial privilege parallel those in support of the confidential communication privilege. Similar to the "feeling of indelicacy" argument for confidential communications is Chief Justice Warren's argument for the adverse testimonial privilege that there is "a natural repugnance in every fair-minded person to compelling a wife or husband to be the means of the other's condemnation, and to compelling the culprit to the humiliation of being condemned by the words of his intimate life-partner."[66] Just as it is unseemly to make marital confidences public, it is unseemly to compel a person to testify against her spouse and perhaps to provide testimony that leads to her husband's conviction. This argument also potentially implicates the right to privacy: to allow a person to be forced to testify against her spouse undermines the idea of privacy, perhaps even the constitutional right to privacy.[67] In the context of the adverse testimonial privilege, it is not that privacy is undercut because marital confidences are being revealed; rather, it is the inviolable relationship of the married couple, a relationship that privacy protects, that is threatened.

A more distinctive argument in favor of the adverse testimonial privilege is that it fosters marital harmony and prevents marital conflict. In the words of an early treatise, to allow a spouse to testify against the other could "cause . . . implacable discord and dissention between [them]."[68] The adverse testimonial privilege protects a married person from having to testify against her spouse. As the U.S. Supreme Court put it:

> The basic reason the law has refused to pit wife against husband . . . in a trial where life or liberty is at stake was a belief that such a policy was necessary to foster family peace, not only for the benefit of husband, wife and children, but for the benefit of

> the public as well. . . . Adverse testimony given in criminal proceedings would, we think, be likely to destroy almost any marriage.[69]

Put another way, the adverse testimonial privilege prevents the state from driving a wedge between the spouses by forcing one to testify against the other. Without the adverse testimonial privilege, the state could potentially create discord in a marriage by trying to compel someone to testify against her spouse with the threat of contempt of court.[70]

This argument is evident in the reasoning of Judge Learned Hand in *United States v. Walker*. Walker seduced three different women, convinced each to marry him, and tricked each into lending or giving him money. At his trial for crimes relating to his taking money from the second woman, the first woman—from whom Walker was estranged but to whom he was still legally married (his marriages to the other two women were void because of his first marriage)—testified against Walker and, specifically, testified about confidential communications between them. Walker objected to the admission of his wife's testimony against him. Judge Hand held that Walker could claim the adverse testimonial privilege (the pre-*Trammel* version) and, in so doing, said:

> [Al]though it is not very usual for [the need to invoke the adverse testimonial privilege] to arise unless the spouses are estranged, not all estrangements are final, and nothing could more dispose the privileged spouse to treasure enmity and to repulse any overtures of reconciliation than the memory of what will ordinarily rankle as treachery. Nor is it either practicable or desirable to make the decision dependent upon the judge's conclusion that in the instance before him the marriage has already been so far wrecked that there is nothing to save. That was true, no doubt, here; but we must look beyond the case before us.[71]

Judge Hand's point is that even estranged spouses have a chance of reconciliation that would be undermined if one spouse is allowed to testify against the other. If the future marital harmony that might be achieved by estranged spouses who later reconcile warrants applying the privilege to prevent an estranged spouse from testifying, then surely the marital harmony of a nonestranged couple warrants application of the privilege.

C. Arguments against the Privileges

I turn now to a discussion of various replies to the arguments for the spousal evidentiary privileges. My discussion is not meant to be definitive but to provide a sense of the strength of the central arguments for the spousal evidentiary privileges.

Advocates of both spousal evidentiary privileges appeal to the basic intuition that there is something indecent or repugnant about revealing spousal secrets, either by forcing spouses to testify against each other or to testify about marital confidences. A leading evidence scholar, John Henry Wigmore, responded to this type of argument as follows:

> [The] natural repugnance in every fair-minded person to compelling a wife or husband to be the means of the other's condemnation, and to compelling the culprit of the humiliation of being condemned by the words of his intimate life-partner. . . is a natural [feeling]. But does it suffice as a reason for the rule? . . . [It] is not more than a sentiment. It does not posit any direct and practical consequences of evil.[72]

To put Wigmore's point slightly differently, there are a lot of repugnant and indecent things that the law sometimes needs to authorize. It is repugnant to take children away from their parents, but sometimes it is necessary. It is repugnant to evict people from their homes, but sometimes it is necessary. The mere fact that the spousal evidentiary privileges seem intuitively appealing is not a strong argument for them.

Turning next to the idea that the spousal evidentiary privileges are grounded in constitutional privacy, first consider whether the constitutional right to privacy is a strong argument for the adverse testimonial privilege. One commentator noted:

> [W]hat remains is testimony about nonconfidential matters, the knowledge of which did not necessarily arise from the marital relationship. There is no legitimate expectation that marriage immunizes one spouse from testimony by the other spouse concerning matters that are neither confidential nor private.[73]

The intuition is that adverse spousal testimony does not per se violate the right to privacy; when confidential communications are not at issue, requiring adverse spousal testimony does not invade "the sacred precincts of the marital bedroom."

Looking at confidential marital communications, does requiring testimony about such confidences violate the constitutional right to privacy? It has been argued,

> The state does not concern itself with the vast majority of confidential communications within a family. It seeks only that information necessary to meet its obligation of ascertaining the truth in legal proceedings, an action which would affect a comparatively small number of families. When balanced against the compelling state interest in just adjudication, the threat to the right to make family decisions is not "sufficiently grievous . . . to establish a constitutional violation."[74]

The idea is that the right to privacy probably protects against the state listening in on marital communications (at least without probable cause) or invading the private realm of the marital bedroom (or perhaps the home generally), but the constitutional right to privacy is not so broad as to require that spouses will be protected from having to testify about confidential communications. In fact, when courts have been presented with the argument that the constitutional right to privacy supports the spousal evidentiary privileges, they have universally rejected it.[75]

A general reply to the arguments for the spousal evidentiary privileges is that spouses will behave in ways that the privileges are meant to encourage even without the privileges. For example, spouses will communicate with each other openly because they love each other, trust each other, and feel loyal to each other, not because of the confidential communication privilege.[76] While acknowledging that married couples should communicate freely and openly with each other, this reply denies that the existence of the confidential communication privilege encourages spouses to communicate more or in a better manner. There is no empirical or psychological evidence to establish the connection between the privilege and better marital communication. Similarly, there is no evidence that those jurisdictions that have abolished the spousal evidentiary privileges have more contentious marriages and/or higher divorce rates.[77] On the other hand, such empirical evidence would be very hard to obtain.

Two criticisms can be made of the "safe haven" or "refuge" justification for the confidential communication privilege. First, if everyone needs and deserves a confidant, why only give the confidential communication privilege to married people? Instead, perhaps we should allow everyone to have one person—if married, then your spouse; if not married, then your mother (or your best friend)—with whom confidential communications are privileged.[78] Given the high percentage of marriages that end in divorce, a person's relationship with her mother or her best friend may be more long-lasting and stable than her relationship with her husband. Making confidential communications between spouses privileged but not giving this privilege to other relationships does not accomplish the goal of providing everyone with a refuge.

A different criticism of the "refuge" argument cuts in the opposite direction, saying that the confidential communication privilege actually encourages crimes by giving every married person a testimony-proof collaborator. Jeremy Bentham famously made the following sarcastic assertion:

> Let us . . . grant to every man a license to commit all sorts of wickedness, in the presence and with the assistance of his wife[;] . . . let us make every man's house his castle; and, as far as depends upon us, let us convert that castle into a den of thieves.[79]

Although the exception to the privilege for when spouses are partners in crime takes away some of the sting of Bentham's criticism, the confidential communication privilege does create potential for abuse—namely, spouses may use the privilege to keep bad acts secret.

One response to the marital harmony argument for the adverse testimonial privilege is that there is just as much reason to think that a person will not blame his spouse for being compelled to testify against him, but will instead blame the prosecutor or the legal system or himself. Further, similar appeals to marital harmony have been rejected in other legal contexts. For example, in addition to the now-outdated justification that a married couple is a single legal entity, most jurisdictions used to prohibit spouses from suing each other for torts on the ground that such suits would undermine marital harmony.[80] Today, almost every jurisdiction has rejected spousal tort immunity, in part because the marital harmony argument has been discredited.[81]

Further, even with the adverse testimonial privilege in place and even after *Trammel* held that the witness-spouse controls the privilege, spouses may still effectively be compelled to testify. In fact, this is precisely what happened in *Trammel*. Although the Court held that Elizabeth Trammel controlled the privilege and could decide whether or not to testify, because she was involved in the conspiracy to distribute illegal drugs, the government was able to "convince" her to testify against her husband by offering her leniency. As Richard Lempert persuasively argued:

> [T]he testimony in *Trammel* is . . . not voluntary in any pure sense of the word. It is the product of a plea bargain. To obtain Ms. Trammel's testimony against her husband the government gave her immunity for her testimony and advised her that if she cooperated with the government she might be charged only with a misdemeanor and receive probation. Ms. Trammel may have testified willingly in a certain sense, for the facts give us every reason to believe she preferred her husband in prison to being there herself. [I] would [not, however,] call [her] testimony voluntary.[82]

Thus, spouses can still be pitted against each other, perhaps more effectively than before *Trammel.*

The final argument against the spousal evidentiary privileges, which applies to both of the privileges, is that they hinder the primary goal of the Federal Rules of Evidence—the ascertainment of the truth.[83] The spousal evidentiary privileges get in the way of the truth, especially in important contexts. Returning to the *Estes* case, Linda wanted to testify that, on the day in question, her former husband told her he had just stolen some money. Her testimony to that effect was important for convicting him. In the absence of some especially strong argument for the confidential communication privilege, perhaps truth and justice are more important values. In this spirit, Wigmore called the confidential communication privilege "an indefensible obstruction to truth."[84] Although the central purpose of the Federal Rules of Evidence is to get at the truth, learning the truth does not always trump all other policies; there are exceptions in the Rules to truth-tropic principles when there are other important policies at stake.[85] Defenders of the spousal evidentiary privileges argue that, even if the privileges undercut the search for truth, they constitute important policy exceptions.

D. Conclusions and Pragmatic Considerations

While none of the arguments for the spousal evidentiary privileges considered here are overwhelmingly strong, not all of the considerations in favor of them have been completely undermined. In particular, although the argument based on the constitutional right to privacy seems weak, there remains an intuitive argument for the privileges based on privacy considerations, albeit without the constitutional basis. This argument supports the confidential communication privilege more than it supports the adverse testimonial privilege, because confidential communications between a couple are typically private in a way that most other information that a spouse knows about another is not. This comparative assessment is buttressed by the fact that more states have abolished the adverse testimonial privilege than have abolished the confidential communication privilege.[86]

This privacy rationale supports a qualified or conditional privilege, rather than an absolute privilege. If there is a qualified confidential communication privilege, a trial judge would allow testimony about confidential communications on a finding "that the evidence of the communication is required in the due administration of justice."[87] The judge could protect the marital confidence "where there is a need for otherwise unobtainable evidence critical to the ascertainment of significant legal rights."[88]

Practically speaking, it seems unlikely that the confidential communication privilege will be qualified or that the adverse testimonial privilege will be abolished in jurisdictions that presently have this privilege; it seems especially unlikely that there will be any such changes in the Federal Rules of Evidence. In 1972, an Advisory Committee to the Committee on Rules of Practice and Procedure of the Judicial Conference, established by the U.S. Supreme Court, proposed various changes to the then existing Federal Rules of Evidence. The Advisory Committee recommended abolishing the confidential communication privilege and limiting the adverse testimonial privilege to criminal proceedings against a spouse.[89] Although the Supreme Court supported this rule change, Congress, after holding extensive hearings, decided not to approve the change (as well as other proposed changes relating to privileges). Instead, Congress adopted the current Federal Rule of Evidence 501, which reads, in part:

> Except as otherwise required by the Constitution of the United States or provided by Act of Congress or in rules prescribed by the Supreme Court pursuant to statutory authority, the privilege of a witness, person, government, State, or political subdivision thereof shall be governed by the principles of the common law as they may be interpreted by the courts of the United States in the light of reason and experience.[90]

One commentator described the reaction of Congress to the proposed—but then withdrawn—changes to the spousal evidentiary rules as follows: "The [proposed] testimonial privilege rules in the Proposed Rules of Evidence . . . almost doomed the total project [of updating the Federal Rules of Evidence]. The presence of [changes to the spousal privilege] rules became a rallying point for general opposition to the entire proposal [of updating the Rules]."[91] Further, in the current political atmosphere in many states and in the U.S. Congress, in which "defending marriage" is a rallying cry for preventing any changes to existing marriage laws that would make them more "liberal," it seems unlikely that either spousal evidentiary privilege will be abolished.

The spousal evidential privileges have been around for centuries; so too have many of the criticisms of them. Although some of these criticisms have merit, it seems unlikely that the privileges will be abolished anytime soon, even though the form of the privileges has evolved somewhat, and some U.S. jurisdictions have abolished the adverse testimonial privilege. Against this background, I turn to how the law of spousal secrets is affected by the increased attention to relationships between people of the same sex and their legal recognition.

IV. The Privileges Applied to Relationships between People of the Same Sex

To examine how the current revolutionary moment in family law interacts with the various arguments for and against the privilege, I begin by considering whether the arguments for the spousal evidentiary privileges also apply to cohabitating and mutually interdependent same-sex couples. In so doing, I am, for the sake of argument and despite the objections to the spousal evidentiary privileges surveyed in the previous Part, accepting some arguments for the privileges.

Consider an unmarried cohabitating same-sex couple in a close, long-term relationship characterized by emotional and economic interdependence who are:

> suitable standard bearers for the cause of same-sex marriage [in that] [t]heir lives reflect hard work, professional achievement, religious faith and a willingness to stand up for their beliefs, [t]hey are law-abiding, taxpaying model citizens, . . . [and] [t]hey well know what it means to make a commitment and to honor it.[92]

Keeping in mind this couple, I now turn to whether the arguments for the confidential communication privilege and the adverse testimonial privilege apply to giving the privileges to a committed same-sex couple, such as the one described above.

A. The Confidential Communication Privilege Applied to Same-Sex Couples

Extending at least some of the arguments for the confidential communication privilege to such a same-sex couple seems straightforward. Unmarried same-sex couples should be encouraged to freely and openly communicate as much as married couples. A person in a same-sex nonmarital relationship would benefit from a refuge and a confidant as much as a married person would. If their communications were treated as confidential, then their relationship would be strengthened as much as a marriage is strengthened by the confidential communication privilege. Further, it would be as indecent to reveal their secrets as it would be to reveal those of a married couple. Also, if general considerations of privacy undergird the confidential communication privilege for married couples, then so too would such considerations undergird a confidential communication privilege for such same-sex couples.

A few arguments for the confidential communication privilege are not so simply extended to such same-sex couples. First, there is the argument that this privilege preserves the institution of marriage. Admittedly, it is not clear how granting same-sex couples the confidential communication privilege would preserve marriage. This is, however, the wrong inquiry. There are clearly people in such same-sex relationships who flourish in them. If these couples could claim the confidential communication privilege, then their having that privilege will arguably preserve both their relationship and the legal institution that grants them the privilege, at least as much as the privilege preserves particular marriages and the institution of marriage. Extending the privilege to same-sex couples in no way undermines the privilege and the role that it plays in preserving the institution of marriage as well as individual marriages.

The argument that same-sex couples should not have the confidential communication privilege because they are not married (and therefore granting them the privilege would not strengthen the institution of marriage) might have more force if there was a plausible argument against the legal recognition of same-sex relationships that was related to the spousal evidentiary privileges. The two most plausible arguments offered in defense of laws prohibiting same-sex couples from marrying involve procreation and child rearing—not the spousal evidentiary privileges.

In considering constitutional challenges to their state's domestic relations laws that deny recognition to relationships between same-sex couples, the highest courts of New York and Washington applied rational review to their states' different-sex-couples-only marriage laws. Traditionally, the requirement that a statute or state action be rational is very weak and highly deferential; almost any justification is enough to establish rationality.[93] The majority opinions in both state courts cited two justifications that a state legislature might have for prohibiting same-sex couples from marrying that would satisfy rational review. The courts said that it is rational for a legislator to believe that it is better for children to be raised by two parents of different sexes (that is, to be raised by one man and one woman) than it is to be raised by two parents of the same sex.[94] This argument is similar to another possible rational basis embraced by some courts that considered challenges to the state marriage laws that prohibit same-sex couples from marrying—namely, that a legislator could rationally believe that marriage laws are meant to encourage procreation.[95]

I am not convinced that this argument or the argument related to it suffices to show a rational basis for laws limiting marriage to different-sex couples. Simply put, there is no evidence that same-sex couples are less good parents than different-sex couples,[96] and, further, no state requires that couples intend to procreate or be able to procreate in order to marry.[97] But even if these are good arguments for not allowing same-sex couples to marry, these arguments have nothing to do with the spousal testimonial privileges: children and procreation have nothing to do with spousal evidentiary privileges. The fact that few if any courts have found a privilege for confidential communications between parents and children or for a privilege preventing parents from having to give adverse testimony against their children (or vice versa),[98] and only a handful of states have child-parent privilege,[99] suggests that there is no plausible connection between parenting and the spousal evidentiary privileges.

The highest courts of New York and Washington embraced another argument—of recent vintage—for preventing same-sex couples from marrying. This argument, which I call the *accidental procreation argument*, seems, on its face, deeply problematic, but it has at least the potential to justify giving the spousal evidentiary privileges to different-sex couples but not same-sex couples. This argument focuses on a difference between same-sex couples and different-sex couples: the former but not the latter can (in theory) accidentally produce children through sexual intercourse between the coupled individuals. According to an Indiana appellate court that also embraced this argument, in light of this difference between same-sex and different-sex couples,

> [t]he State . . . may legitimately create the institution of opposite-sex marriage, and all the benefits accruing to it, in order to encourage male-female couples to procreate within the legitimacy and stability of a state-sanctioned relationship and to discourage unplanned, out-of-wedlock births resulting from "casual" intercourse.[100]

This accidental procreation argument, if it works, might justify giving the spousal evidentiary privileges to different-sex couples but not to same-sex couples in the following fashion. Different-sex couples need incentives to stay together to raise the children that they might produce through accidental procreation. Without such incentives, men will abandon the women with whom they have had what turns out to be unintentionally procreative sex, leaving these women with accidentally produced children. A legislature could reasonable believe that such children will turn out worse than children born to parents who are married. The spousal evidentiary privileges are among the incentives that a legislature might rationally give to a different-sex couple to encourage marriage.

The accidental procreation argument, however, simply does not work because whether or not same-sex couples marry does not affect the incentive for different-sex couples. As the dissent in the New York same-sex marriage case pointed out:

> [W]hile encouraging opposite-sex couples to marry before they have children is certainly a legitimate interest of the State, the *exclusion* of gay men and lesbians from marriage in no way furthers this interest. There are enough marriage licenses to go around for everyone.[101]

The state can still incentivize marriage for couples at risk of accidentally procreating even if it allows same-sex couples to marry or to obtain the spousal evidentiary privileges. The incentives for potential accidental procreators to marry are the same whether or not same-sex couples can marry or otherwise obtain some or all of the benefits of marriage used as incentives to convince heterosexuals to marry.

Further, the contrasting picture of the irresponsibility of heterosexuals, especially heterosexual men, in sexual relationships compared with the unquestioned altruism of gay men and lesbians who want to be parents and the rock-solid strength of their relationships is so bizarre and removed from reality as to reveal that the accidental procreation argument must have been developed for the very purpose of justifying marriage for different-sex but not same-sex couples. Simply put, the accidental procreation argument does not support a distinction between different-sex couples and same-sex couples that warrants giving the spousal evidentiary privileges to some of the former but none of the latter.[102]

Another argument for the confidential communication privilege that might not simply extend to same-sex couples concerns a specific version of the argument based on privacy. I have already suggested that the spousal evidentiary privileges do not flow from the constitutional right to privacy. That argument aside, one might still argue that the constitutional right to privacy line of cases is limited, as it was by the U.S. Supreme Court in *Bowers v. Hardwick*, to "family, marriage, or procreation," and thereby try to distinguish giving the confidential communication privilege to same-sex couples from giving it to married couples. However, such a view of privacy has been rejected by the Supreme Court.

First, the Supreme Court's decision in *Lawrence v. Texas* undercut the "family, marriage, or procreation" limitation on the privacy line of cases. In *Lawrence v. Texas*, the Supreme Court held unconstitutional a Texas criminal law prohibiting sodomy between persons of the same sex.[103] Justice Kennedy, writing for the majority, found that the Texas sodomy law was unconstitutional on privacy grounds and overruled *Bowers v. Hardwick*. He began his opinion as follows:

> Liberty protects the person from unwarranted government intrusions into a dwelling or other private places. In our tradition the State is not omnipresent in the home. And there are other spheres of our lives and existence, outside the home, where the State should not be a dominant presence. Freedom extends beyond spatial bounds. Liberty presumes an autonomy of self that includes freedom of thought, belief, expression, and certain intimate conduct. The instant case involves liberty of the person both in its spatial and more transcendent dimensions.[104]

Toward the end of the opinion, Justice Kennedy concluded:

> [This] case . . . involve[s] two adults who, with full and mutual consent from each other, engaged in sexual practices common to a homosexual lifestyle. The petitioners are entitled to respect for their private lives. The State cannot demean their existence or control their destiny by making their private sexual conduct a crime. Their right to liberty under the Due Process Clause gives them the full right to engage in their

> conduct without intervention of the government.... The Texas statute furthers no legitimate state interest, which can justify its intrusion into the personal and private life of the individual.[105]

In overturning *Bowers*, *Lawrence* displaced *Bowers*'s narrow view of the right to privacy as limited to "family, marriage, or procreation," arguably broadening it into a "right to intimate association."[106]

Second, in *Eisenstadt v. Baird*,[107] an early and important constitutional privacy case, the Supreme Court held that, just as it violates the right to privacy to make contraception illegal for married couples (this was the holding of *Griswold*), it also violates privacy to make contraception illegal for single people. The Court said in *Eisenstadt*:

> If the right of privacy means anything, it is the right of the individual, married or single, to be free from unwarranted governmental intrusion into matters so fundamentally affecting a person as the decision whether to bear or begat a child.[108]

The reasoning of *Eisenstadt* undercuts the attempt to use the right to privacy argument to distinguish same-sex couples from married couples for purposes of the confidential communication privilege. Having shown that all of the arguments supporting the confidential communication privilege for married couples also support extending this privilege to same-sex couples, I turn to the arguments supporting the adverse testimonial privilege.

B. The Adverse Testimonial Privilege Applied to Same-Sex Couples

Insofar as the adverse testimonial privilege fosters harmony and prevents conflicts in a marriage, so too will the privilege foster harmony and prevent conflict in a same-sex relationship. Similarly, to the extent that the adverse testimonial privilege prevents the state from driving a wedge between spouses, so too will it prevent the state from driving a wedge between same-sex partners. If there is a "natural repugnance" to compelling a person to testify against a spouse, there is also the same repugnance in forcing a person to testify against his or her same-sex partner. And, finally, the same analysis discussed above regarding privacy considerations with respect to the confidential communication privilege applies here: in light of *Lawrence* and *Eisenstadt*, the constitutional right to privacy does not justify distinguishing between some same-sex couples and married couples with respect to the adverse testimonial privilege.

Therefore, insofar as any arguments for either of the spousal evidentiary privileges are successful, they also justify giving same-sex couples these privileges.

C. Other Considerations Regarding Applying the Privileges to Same-Sex Couples

One possible reply to this general argument is that it proves too much. The very same arguments that I have just made about why the spousal evidentiary privileges should be extended to same-sex couples could also be made with respect to unmarried cohabitating different-sex couples. Courts have, however, consistently resisted extending the evidentiary privileges to such cohabitants.[109] As the argument just laid out for extending the spousal evidentiary privileges to same-sex couples also applies to extending them to cohabitating different-sex couples and since cohabitating different-sex couples should not get these privileges, according to this reply, same-sex couples should not get these privileges either. In other words, embracing my argument that the spousal evidentiary privileges should be extended to same-sex couples entails a conclusion that courts have been unwilling to accept—namely, that the spousal evidentiary privileges should be extended to unmarried different-sex couples, who are clearly not spouses.

There are two possible counters to this reply. First, show that, in jurisdictions that do *not* allow for the legal recognition of same-sex couples, there is a significant distinction between same-sex couples and unmarried different-sex couples. Second, argue that, contra the approach that courts have taken, some unmarried different-sex couples *should* get the privilege. I turn to the first counter now and to the second in Part V.

Several courts have determined that an unmarried different-sex couple and an unmarried same-sex couple are not similarly situated in relevant respects in jurisdictions where different-sex couples have the option of getting married while same-sex couples do not.[110] In *Foray v. Bell Atlantic*, a male employee who lived with a female domestic partner sued his employer, which provided domestic partner benefits only to the same-sex partners of its employees. Foray argued, inter alia, that his employer was engaging in prohibited discrimination based on sex under Title VII of the Civil Rights Act of 1964. In rejecting Foray's claim, the court reasoned that Foray and his female domestic partner were differently situated than an employee with a same-sex domestic partner because Foray and his female partner were able to marry, while a same-sex couple was not.[111] In a similar case, *Irizarry v. Board of Education of the City of Chicago*, an unmarried female employee sued her employer, which provided health benefits to same-sex domestic partners of its employees, for its refusal to provide health benefits to her male domestic partner. Judge Richard Posner, writing for a unanimous court, reached the same conclusion as in *Foray*, finding that it is "rational for the board to [extend benefits to same-sex domestic partners but] refuse to extend domestic-partnership benefits to persons who can if they wish marry."[112] These cases show that unmarried same-sex couples and unmarried different-sex couples are not similarly situated. This shows that the main argument of this Part—that insofar as some different-sex couples get the spousal evidentiary privileges, so too should some different-sex couples—does *not* prove too much. My argument need not entail that unmarried different-sex couples might also get the spousal evidentiary privileges because unmarried different-sex couples and unmarried same-sex couples are *not* similarly situated.

V. Functional Approaches to the Evidentiary Privileges

In the previous Part, I argued that, if there are good arguments for giving the spousal evidentiary privileges to married couples, then the privileges should also be given to some same-sex couples. All of the states that have given same-sex couples the spousal evidentiary privileges have done so in virtue of giving them all (or most) of the benefits, rights, duties, and obligations associated with marriage in the respective jurisdiction. In doing so, these jurisdictions have adopted the traditional or bright-line approach to the spousal evidentiary privileges according to which all and only married couples—or those in civil unions or robust domestic partnerships—qualify for the privileges. In this Part, I consider an alternative to this traditional approach—namely, the *functional* approach to the privileges. Under this functional approach, the privileges are not extended to all and only married couples; rather, this approach would look at the qualities of a particular relationship to determine whether the evidentiary privileges should apply. For example, if the confidential communication privilege is adequately justified by the goal of encouraging free and open communications between couples that cohabitate and are emotionally and economically interdependent, then the functional approach to the privilege would look to whether a couple is cohabitating and is emotionally and economically interdependent to determine whether they qualify for the privilege.

A. Functional Approaches in Family Law

Functional approaches are not unheard of in family law. In general, marriage law has certain functional aspects to it. Ten states[113] and the District of Columbia recognize *common law marriages*, legally valid marriages that have not been solemnized in the usual ceremonial manner but instead come into existence when two people capable of marrying (a) cohabitate, (b) intend and agree to be married, and (c) hold themselves out to their community as married.[114] Part of the contemporary justification for recognizing common law marriages is that such marriages share many of the functional attributes of standard (ceremonial) marriages. Another functional aspect of marriage law is evident in the *sham marriage doctrine*. This doctrine says that even though a couple has gone through all the formal requirements of a marriage, such as filing the appropriate documents with the state and having a ceremony, their marriage is void if the couple has no intention of living together as husband and wife, but rather is getting married only for health benefits, the legitimization of children, immigration or naturalization purposes, or some other limited purpose.[115]

Common law marriage and the sham marriage doctrine exhibit, respectively, what I call *positive* and *negative functional factors*. A *positive* functional factor is one that counts in favor of some particular thing belonging to a category even though that particular thing fails to meet the traditional or bright-line account of belonging to that category. For example, common law marriage involves a positive functional factor because if a couple has certain functional characteristics—they hold themselves out as married, they intend to be married, and so forth—then they are counted as married even though they were not married in the standard ceremonial manner. A *negative* functional factor is one that counts against some particular thing belonging to a category even though it satisfies the traditional account of belonging to that category. For example, the sham marriage doctrine involves a negative functional factor because, if a couple that was otherwise capable of marriage got married in the standard ceremonial manner but did not have certain functional characteristics—if they were marrying only so one of them could get a green card—then they would be disqualified from counting as married.

The functional approach has played a role in family law generally, as well as a limited role in the context of spousal evidentiary privileges. First, consider two family law cases in which functional approaches played a role. Miguel Braschi was living in a rent-controlled New York City apartment with his male partner, to whom the apartment was leased. After his partner died, the landlord informed Braschi that he was going to be evicted. Under the city's rent-control law, a landlord may not evict the surviving spouse or another family member of the deceased tenant if that person had been living with the tenant for a specified time period. Adopting a functional definition of family and rejecting the traditional bright-line view of family as people related by blood, marriage, or adoption, the New York Court of Appeals held that Braschi should be treated as Blanchard's "family member" and thus allowed to retain the apartment. The Court of Appeals reached this conclusion by looking to the following factors:

> the exclusivity and longevity of the relationship, the level of emotional and financial commitment, the manner in which the parties have conducted their everyday lives and held themselves out to society, and the reliance placed on one another for daily family services . . . [and especially to] the totality of the relationship as evidenced by the dedication, caring, and self-sacrifice of the parties.[116]

A functional account of family also plays a role in various Ohio courts' application of that state's domestic violence law, which says that "no person shall knowingly cause or attempt to cause physical harm to a family or household member."[117] The law defines "family or household member" in part as "[a] spouse, a person living as a spouse, or a former spouse"[118] and defines "living as a spouse" as "a person who is living or has lived with [a person] in a common law marital relationship, who otherwise is cohabiting with [him or her], or who otherwise has cohabited with [him or her] within one year."[119] In *State v. Yaden*, shortly before the incident in question, Joe Fields had been living together in a same-sex relationship for four years with Ronnie Yaden, who was (and continued to be) married to a woman for several years. Yaden allegedly committed acts of violence against Fields and was charged under Ohio domestic violence law. Against Yaden's argument that a same-sex couple could not satisfy the statutory language of "living as a spouse," the court took a functional approach to "living as a spouse" that focused on "financial support and consortium." Specifically, to assess degree of financial support, the court looked to "shelter, food, clothing, utilities, and perhaps co-mingled assets." To assess consortium, the court looked to "mutual respect, fidelity, emotional support, affection, society, cooperation, solace, comfort, aid of each other, friendship, conjugal relations and companionship."[120] The court in *Yaden* viewed the relationship between Yaden and Fields functionally: even though they were not married to each other—and despite the fact that Yaden was, throughout his relationship with Fields, married to someone else—the court viewed the relationship as "spousal" and applied the state's domestic violence law.

B. Functional Approaches to the Spousal Evidentiary Privileges

The functional approach has also played a role, although a limited one, in the context of spousal evidentiary privileges. Various courts have refused to allow a married couple to invoke one or both of the privileges because their marriage lacked certain functional characteristics. In many of these cases, courts have found that the spousal evidentiary privileges were inapplicable to couples who were still married but were permanently separated or living separately with no chance of reconciliation.[121] Other courts have refused to apply a spousal evidentiary privilege because the marriage at issue was a sham marriage.[122] When a court determines that a marriage is *moribund* or a sham, it is invoking negative functional factors: even though the marriage at issue satisfies the bright-line test for marriage, the couple does not qualify for the spousal evidentiary privileges because their marriage lacks certain functional characteristics.

Not all courts have taken this functional approach to the spousal evidentiary privileges when dealing with moribund or sham marriages. Some courts have instead embraced the bright-line test for marriage and rejected any role for negative functional factors. For example, in *United States v. Sims*, the prosecutor argued that a husband and wife should not be able to invoke the confidential communication privilege because of their history of serious fights and extramarital affairs. The court, however, rejected the prosecutor's argument, saying:

> We do not believe that courts can or should assess the social worthiness of particular marriages or the need of particular marriages for the protection of the privilege. We, therefore, reject the contention that appellant's marital problems support [not applying the privilege].[123]

An even more dramatic illustration of this is *People v. Fields*. In this case, William and Alice Fields, although still married, had not been living together for six months and William had been living with another woman. After shooting two people, William called Alice, told her about the shootings, and said he wanted to come to her home. When he arrived, he suggested he was going to kill Alice as well, but he then fell asleep. While William slept, Alice wisely went to the police. At his trial, when the prosecution asked Alice what William told her when he called her that day, William tried to invoke the adverse testimonial privilege. The prosecutor argued that the court should take a functional approach to the privilege because there was no marriage left to preserve, as evidenced by the couple's separation and by the facts that William was cohabitating with another woman and was planning to murder Alice. The majority refused to take this functional approach, holding firm to the bright-line test and finding it impractical for the trial court to determine whether a marriage is viable or whether reconciliation is possible.[124]

There is, thus, a split among courts about whether married couples who fail to exhibit some functional characteristics of marriage still can claim the spousal evidentiary privileges. In contrast, however, there are no cases where courts apply *positive* functional factors to give the spousal evidentiary privileges to an unmarried couple, even if that couple exhibits marriage-like characteristics.[125] Although a handful of courts have expressed sympathy for the idea of granting spousal evidentiary privileges to certain unmarried couples,[126] all of the reported cases have refused to do so. A typical example is the case of *United States v. Lustig*. Michael Lustig and Callie Newton had been living together for seven years, had two children, held themselves out as husband and wife, and mistakenly believed they were common law married (they lived in a state that does not allow common law marriages). Rejecting a functional approach to their relationship, the Ninth Circuit held that the communication between Lustig and Newton was not privileged.[127]

While some courts adopt functionalism when it comes to *denying* married couples the benefits of the spousal evidentiary privileges, these same courts resist functionalism when it comes to *giving* the privileges to unmarried couples whose relationships are marriage-like. This use of negative functional factors is not inconsistent with the refusal to use positive functional factors. To see this, consider *Braschi*. Before and after *Braschi*, a married person living with his or her spouse who was the tenant of record in a rent-controlled apartment qualified for eviction protection after his or her spouse died. (The same was true for other relatives by blood, marriage, or adoption.) No negative functional factors were involved; so long as the couple was married and living together, the surviving spouse got to remain in the rent-controlled apartment. After *Braschi*, unmarried cohabitating same-sex couples also qualified for eviction protection so long as they satisfied certain functional tests. Positive functional factors thus played a role. Setting aside for now whether this approach is wise or fair, it is not inconsistent to look at positive functional factors but not negative functional factors, nor is it inconsistent to look at negative functional factors but not positive ones.

C. The Rhode Island Proposed Bill and the Conley Proposal

I turn now to a discussion of the Rhode Island bill mentioned above as an example of a functional approach to the spousal evidentiary privileges. In 2007, a group of activists who support allowing same-sex couples to marry in Rhode Island and who oppose a civil union bill, proposed six bills that would each provide same-sex couples with some right or benefit of marriage.[128] In addition to the evidentiary privilege bill, other proposed bills concerned funeral arrangements and family leave for unmarried couples. Like the evidentiary privileges bill, these other bills created a legal status of domestic partner that is defined functionally. This bill did not require that a couple register for a domestic partnership to get the benefit or that a couple be of the same sex. Rather, the bill defined "domestic partner" as one who is in "an exclusive, intimate and committed relationship of mutual caring," and required that the couple prove, inter alia, that they have cohabitated for at least one year, and are "financially interdependent" (based on specific kinds of evidence).[129]

Among the virtues of the Rhode Island bill is that it would have allowed some same-sex couples to obtain the spousal evidentiary privileges even though Rhode Island does not allow same-sex couples to marry. It also would be a step, albeit a small one, toward equal benefits for same-sex couples. Some advocates of lesbian, gay, and bisexual rights favor a gradualist approach to obtaining full marriage equality. Such an approach might start by trying to obtain domestic partnerships for same-sex couples that give a subset of the rights and benefits of marriage, then trying to obtain civil unions that give all the rights and benefits associated with marriage, and, finally, trying to legalize marriages for same-sex couples. (This is roughly what happened in Connecticut and New Hampshire, for example.)

There are, however, problems with the proposed bill. First, if the bill were to become law, the requirements for getting the evidentiary privileges would be different for married couples and domestic partners. Married couples qualify for the privileges the day they get married, while domestic partners would have to wait for a year after they start cohabitating. Married couples do not have to be financially interdependent, while domestic partners not only have to be financially interdependent, they have to be able to prove their financial interdependence using a specified and limited number of methods. A low-income unmarried couple, for example, might find it difficult or too expensive to prove financial interdependence under the Rhode Island bill, while a low-income married couple would not have to offer such proof. Second, the Rhode Island bill does not adopt a functional approach to the evidentiary privileges for married couples: couples in moribund marriages, for example, would still qualify for the privileges, while couples in moribund domestic partnerships would not (because they would no longer satisfy the functional definition for being a domestic partner). Third, and most significantly for my argument, the functional characteristics required for being a domestic partner under the Rhode Island bill do not fit well with the policy arguments that might plausibly justify the spousal evidentiary privileges. If, for example, the privileges are justified because they protect the privacy of emotionally interdependent, intimate, and romantic relationships, then the Rhode Island bill would be *underinclusive*, because it requires *financial* interdependence and relationship duration of more than one year.

In contrast, the Conley proposal that every person gets to pick one other person who cannot be forced to testify against him and with whom communications are confidential[130] is *overinclusive*. In the name of equal treatment for all, such a proposal ignores the justifications for legal protections for spousal secrets (with the possible exception of providing a refuge). If a person can pick anyone to be his confidant, regardless of the nature of their relationship, then this proposal does seem, to use Bentham's words, to be granting everyone "license to commit all sorts of wickedness in the presence and with the assistance of"[131] one person. In fact, this worry is greater in the case of the Conley proposal than in marriage, because Conley's proposal allows one to claim a narrow set of the benefits of marriage—that is, the spousal evidentiary privileges—without taking on the various duties and obligations of marriage, not to mention the other rights and benefits of marriage. This decoupling of the evidentiary privileges from marriage or marriage-like relationships creates great potential for abuse.

A somewhat similar proposal, what I call the *registration* proposal, that avoids this specific problem as well as some of the problems with the Rhode Island bill, is to create a domestic partner registry and give the spousal evidentiary privileges to those couples who register as domestic partners. Depending on what duties and obligations flow from being domestic partners, and depending on the requirements for becoming domestic partners, this proposal may prevent a person from picking just anyone to be his or her domestic partner in order to obtain the evidentiary privileges. This would somewhat mitigate the problem of the Conley proposal, but the registration proposal remains overinclusive and perhaps underinclusive. The proposal is overinclusive because it will allow for sham domestic partnerships—namely, it will give the evidentiary privileges to those partners who register for the limited purpose of getting such privileges. Further, the registration proposal is arguably underinclusive because some couples who satisfy the goals of giving the privileges will not get the privileges because they did not register as domestic partners. For example, if the privileges are meant to encourage free and open communication between couples in interdependent intimate relationships, couples who are not registered but who are in interdependent intimate relationships will not get the privileges and open communications between them will not be encouraged. In defense of the registration proposal, one might argue that it is not truly underinclusive. Couples who could have obtained the privilege simply by registering (or marrying) should not, one might argue, be able to claim the privilege when they did not in fact register (or marry). In the *Lustig* case, the two people in question had been living together for seven years, were co-parenting, and had been holding themselves out as spouses. They argued that they should be allowed to claim the evidentiary privileges, but the court held that they could not because they were not married. In effect, the court was saying that the couple in *Lustig* could have gotten married and thereby been able to claim the privileges, but because they failed to do so, they could not claim the privileges.

One might contrast the *Lustig* case with the hypothetical example of a couple who had been cohabiting, co-parenting, engaged for an extended period of time, and was on their way to their wedding. One might reasonably argue that a confidential communication between such fiancés should be privileged and that the registration proposal is underinclusive because it fails to grant them the evidentiary privileges. While some courts have been willing to give some of the benefits of marriage to fiancés,[132] none have given such couples the spousal evidentiary privileges. A defender of the registration proposal might defend not including fiancés by noting that most laws have to draw boundaries somewhere, and that in doing so, some people are going to feel they are treated unjustly.[133] In sum, advocates of the registration proposal have a plausible answer to the charge of underinclusiveness—namely, that their proposal is not underinclusive insofar as it does not give the spousal evidentiary privileges to couples who could have registered and thereby obtained the privileges but simply did not bother to register.

D. The Sophisticated Functional Approach

The version of functionalism that I favor combines the approaches taken in *Braschi* and *Yaden* with the registration proposal. Under this sophisticated functionalism, to determine whether a relationship between two people qualifies for the evidentiary privileges, a court will look to the couple's emotional commitment and involvement; their financial commitment and entanglement; their mutual reliance for personal services including shelter, food, clothing, utilities, health care, and so on; the way that they have conducted themselves in their personal life and held themselves out to the society; the level of intimacy between them; and the totality of the relationship as evidenced by the dedication, caring, and self-sacrifice of the parties. The presence or absence of one or more of these factors is not alone determinative of whether a couple can or cannot claim the privileges. Rather, the question is whether the character of the couple's intimate relationship is, on the whole and all things considered, deserving of the spousal evidentiary privileges.[134] If so, then a court should grant them the privileges.

Under this sophisticated functionalism, the burden is on the unmarried couple to establish that their relationship has the relevant functional attributes. The fiancés on their way to their wedding could still be granted the privileges, but they would have the burden of establishing that they have these functional characteristics. Further, under this sophisticated functionalism, a married couple or a couple who has registered as domestic partners has a strong, but rebuttable, presumption that they can claim the privilege. This presumption can be rebutted if their relationship was a sham or is now moribund, but the burden of rebutting the presumption is on the party who thinks that the married or registered couple does not deserve the privilege.

This sophisticated functionalism is not overinclusive: only couples who have the appropriate functional characteristics get the privileges; couples in sham or moribund marriages do not qualify for the privileges, even if they are in fact married. Further, sophisticated functionalism is not underinclusive: couples who have the appropriate functional characteristics can claim the privilege even if they are not married.

VI. Evaluating Sophisticated Functionalism about the Spousal Evidentiary Privileges

The sophisticated functional approach (sophisticated functionalism, for short) to spousal evidentiary privileges sketched above incorporates both negative functional factors and positive functional factors. If an unmarried couple exhibits certain functional attributes, then the couple would qualify for the spousal evidentiary privileges. On the other hand, if a married couple fails to exhibit these functional attributes, then the couple would not qualify for the privileges.

A central virtue of this approach is that the functional attributes that determine whether a couple qualifies for the privileges closely match the various justifications for the spousal evidentiary privileges. For example, consider the justification for the confidential communication privilege that it encourages open communication and provides a refuge. Couples who have the *Braschi-Yaden* functional characteristics described above are in fact likely to communicate openly and provide each other with a refuge, while those couples who do not satisfy these characteristics are unlikely to, and thus would not qualify for the privilege. This fits with how some courts have handled sham marriages and moribund marriages. As those cases seem correctly decided, this is a virtue of the sophisticated functional approach.

This virtue also connects to an additional advantage of the sophisticated functional approach. Recall the idea that the state gives benefits to people who marry in order to channel people into certain relationships. When viewed as a package deal—that is, when all the rights, benefits, duties, and obligations associated with marriage[135] are viewed as bundled together—the effect of the spousal evidentiary privileges will seem insignificant to most people.[136] The sophisticated functional approach allows the privileges to be decoupled from the other benefits of marriage and, as such, it can incentivize the very behaviors, effects, and the like that the privileges are supposed to encourage.

Another virtue of the sophisticated functional approach to the privileges is that treats what seem like similarly situated relationships equally. Under this approach, some unmarried same-sex couples receive the same evidentiary privileges that most married couples do. Further, some unmarried different-sex couples receive the same evidentiary privileges that some unmarried same-sex couples do.

Recall the arguments for and against the two spousal evidentiary privileges discussed in Part III. For the purposes of the primary claims of this chapter, deciding whether the arguments for either of these privileges are successful is not necessary. Either one (or more) of the arguments for one or both of the spousal evidentiary privileges succeeds or none of them do. If none of them succeed, then the spousal evidentiary privileges should be abolished. If, however, one of these arguments succeeds, then the very same argument also works for giving the spousal evidentiary privileges to some same-sex couples. There are two alternative ways of doing this: *inclusion* (giving same-sex couples the spousal evidentiary privileges) and sophisticated functionalism (as described above). Whether we opt for inclusion or sophisticated functionalism determines the fate of unmarried different-sex couples. Inclusion excludes unmarried different-sex couples while sophisticated functionalism includes at least some unmarried different-sex couples. Inclusion can be accomplished by giving same-sex couples the same rights and benefits associated with marriage (either by allowing same-sex couples to marry or by creating civil unions) or—as with the registration proposal or the Rhode Island proposal—by creating a legal status that gives same-sex couples the opportunity to get the spousal evidentiary privileges but not the other benefits, rights, duties, and obligations associated with marriage (the *piecemeal approach*).

In Part IV, I showed that any plausible argument for the spousal evidentiary privileges also applies to extending the spousal evidentiary privileges to same-sex couples. I then considered a reply to this argument—namely, that it proved too much, because it necessarily also entailed that the spousal evidentiary privileges should be extended to some unmarried different-sex couples, a conclusion that no U.S. court has accepted. I then considered one possible counter-reply—namely, that same-sex couples and different-sex couples are not similarly situated. Sophisticated functionalism about the spousal evidentiary privileges provides another counter-reply. Rather than say that same-sex couples and unmarried different-sex couples are not similarly situated, the version of functionalism described here allows that some unmarried different-sex couples—those that exhibit certain marriage-like functional characteristics—should also get the spousal evidentiary privileges for the very same reasons that some same-sex couples should. This version of functionalism is a somewhat revisionist approach to the spousal evidentiary privileges. Although it embraces some of the policies that underlie spousal secrets, sophisticated functionalism suggests that the boundaries of who can and cannot claim the spousal evidentiary privileges should be changed. As such, functionalism is in tension with the results of cases like *Lustig* in which unmarried different-sex couples do not get the spousal evidentiary privileges despite having the functional characteristics that fit with the justifications for such privileges.

A. Potential Problems with a Sophisticated Functional Approach to the Spousal Evidentiary Privileges

There are, however, various problems facing a sophisticated functional approach to the spousal evidentiary privileges. First, there is an ease of application problem. As there is no clear line determining which relationships get the privileges, courts need to assess the characteristics of each relationship whenever one of the parties wants to invoke the privilege. Many courts have explicitly resisted the functional approach to the privileges for precisely this reason. Some of them have even resisted taking the functional approach to moribund marriages and sham marriages in determining whether the spousal evidentiary privileges apply.[137] Applying the bright-line approach is much easier: to determine whether a couple gets the privileges, a court just has to ask for a marriage license. When it comes to same-sex couples in jurisdictions that have given such couples the benefits associated with marriage, the inclusion approach is similarly much easier to apply than the functional approach: couples who are in civil unions or in registered domestic partnerships get the privileges, while those who are not, do not get them.

Although it will be harder for courts to apply the sophisticated functional approach than it is to apply the bright-line approach, functionalism is not as difficult to apply as this criticism suggests. First, some courts already engage in functionalism insofar as they apply negative functional factors in the context of sham marriages and moribund marriages. Second, courts now have experience applying the functional approach to families in various contexts such as rent control law, domestic violence law, and even in the context of child custody and visitation determinations. The concept of a *de facto* or *psychological parent*—a nonbiological, nonadoptive parent who, because of an ongoing parenting relationship with a child, may get custody or visitation of that child—is now common in family law.[138] Although courts were initially concerned about the difficulties of applying these functional concepts, many jurisdictions now regularly make use of functional approaches in family law. There is every reason to think that courts could similarly learn to use the functional approach to determine when to allow the invocation of the spousal evidentiary privileges. Finally, the particular version of functionalism described herein, because of the way it assigns the burdens associated with invoking the privileges, is particularly easy and efficient for courts to apply.

Another argument against the functionalist approach to the spousal evidentiary privileges is a "slippery slope" argument. The concern is that if same-sex couples are allowed to claim the spousal evidentiary privileges, then many others will too—mere roommates, people involved in polygamous relationships, people involved in incestuous relationships, and the like. This argument is not strong: the slope is not so slippery. Insofar as a characteristic is important to determining whether a couple should be able to claim the privileges, this characterization can be included among the functional characteristics that determine whether a couple qualifies for the privileges. For example, if it is important for the policy that underlies the privileges that they be limited to two people only, then exclusivity can be included among the functional characteristics required to qualify for the privileges, as it is in various jurisdictions with domestic partnership laws.[139] As applied to roommates or siblings, the appropriate reply to this argument may be to bite the bullet—namely, to say that two siblings or two roommates who meet the functional characteristics appropriate to granting the privilege should be able to claim the privilege. Given the functional characteristics involved in sophisticated functionalism, it seems that few roommates will qualify for the privilege.

A serious practical objection to sophisticated functionalism applied to the spousal evidentiary privileges is that no state in the United States is a plausible candidate for adopting this approach. Those states that are friendly to same-sex relationships have allowed or will soon allow same-sex couples to marry or obtain civil unions or domestic partnerships. Such states will not need to adopt functionalism about the spousal evidentiary privileges because same-sex couples in those states are (or will soon be) able to obtain the privileges by marrying or otherwise registering their relationships. The remaining states have passed laws or amendments to their respective state constitutions explicitly refusing to recognize same-sex relationships or to give any of the rights or benefits associated with marriage to same-sex couples. These states will not adopt functionalism about the spousal evidentiary privileges because of their laws prohibiting giving recognition to same-sex relationships. Therefore, according to this objection, functionalism is not going to be adopted by any state. This is a potentially serious objection to functionalism with respect to the spousal evidentiary privileges, since my functionalist proposal is motivated by explicitly pragmatic concerns—specifically, the realization that the spousal evidentiary privileges will not be abolished anytime soon and that full marriage equality throughout the entire United States is not imminent. However, a full appreciation of the actual provisions involved in the patchwork of recognition and nonrecognition of same-sex relationships in the United States and the details of the version of functionalism advocated here shows that this objection is not a strong one.

First, I acknowledge that sophisticated functionalism applied to the spousal evidentiary privileges does not provide the full marriage equality for same-sex couples obtained in the six states and the District of Columbia. Functionalism with respect to the spousal evidentiary privileges is just a piecemeal response to the equality arguments for the recognition of same-sex relationships. In jurisdictions that provide full equality to same-sex couples, sophisticated functionalism is, however, a serious proposal for revising the spousal evidentiary privileges for all couples—namely, functionalism justifies not giving the spousal evidentiary privileges to couples (same-sex and different-sex) in sham marriages and moribund marriages, and it justifies giving the spousal evidentiary privileges to certain (same-sex and different-sex) unmarried (and nonregistered) couples who exhibit certain functional characteristics.

Second, and more responsive to this objection, the relevant provisions in states that do not allow or recognize same-sex marriages vary widely.[140] Some states simply prohibit same-sex couples from marrying in that state, but do not say anything about prohibiting same-sex couples from obtaining the rights and benefits that married couples receive. For example, California and Hawaii have either a law or a constitutional amendment prohibiting same-sex marriage,[141] but both provide some legal recognition to same-sex relationships. Some states prohibit same-sex marriages within the state and will view as void a marriage between people of the same sex who establish residence in the state as well as a marriage between state residents of the same sex who go outside the state to get married and then return to the state and ask for recognition.[142] Other states, in addition to prohibiting marriages between people of the same sex in the state, also withhold recognition for marriages between people of the same sex contracted outside the state.[143] Nothing in any of these three types of provisions prevents the recognition of other forms of legal recognition for same-sex couples besides marriage (namely, civil unions, domestic partnerships, reciprocal beneficiaries, or functional spouses), and some of the states with more limited nonrecognition policies do in fact recognize such nonmarital relationships between people of the same sex. Other states, like Virginia and Arkansas, have, however, gone further and passed provisions that prohibit the recognition of relationships "similar to" marriages.[144] Such provisions are so broad that they may well be unconstitutional.[145] They may, for example, prohibit two people from entering private cohabitation contracts, putting one's same-sex partner in one's will, and the like.[146] But even if they are not found unconstitutional, these provisions are most likely not in tension with a sophisticated functional approach to the spousal evidentiary privileges. If a state adopts the sophisticated functional approach, not all married couples will be able to claim the spousal evidentiary privileges (namely, people in sham marriages and moribund marriages, although still married, will not be able to claim the privileges), and thus it is not clear that the privileges will be, under this regime, a benefit of marriage.

Rather, the spousal evidentiary privileges will be a benefit of having a relationship with certain functional characteristics. Thus, allowing some same-sex couples to claim such privileges would not be in tension with such broad anti-same-sex-marriage provisions.

Another argument against the functional approach is that expanding the privilege to include unmarried couples will further hinder the quest for truth, the primary goal of the rules of evidence, because it will increase the number of people who can prevent testimony about certain of their confidential communications and about certain things they know about their partners. There are two replies to this argument. First, because some married couples will not be able to claim the privilege under the sophisticated functional approach (for example, because their marriages are moribund), the sophisticated functional approach, by giving the privilege to some same-sex couples, will not necessarily lead to less truth being discovered under the rules. In other words, the amount of truth "lost" by allowing some same-sex couples to claim the privilege might be somewhat "offset" by not allowing some married couples to claim the privilege. Second, an assumption behind the spousal evidentiary privileges is that some policy considerations justify constraints on the quest for truth. It may be that the arguments for having the spousal evidentiary privileges are weak and the privileges should be abolished (or qualified). If, however, one or more of the arguments for the privileges is strong, then the quest for truth should be constrained. A properly crafted sophisticated functional approach will constrain the quest for truth no more than it needs to be constrained in order to accomplish the public policy goals behind the argument(s) for the privileges.

Another problem with functionalism about the spousal evidentiary privileges is that the different burdens associated with claiming the privileges for married (or otherwise registered) and unmarried couples will make it harder for same-sex couples to claim the privilege in jurisdictions that do not have civil unions, domestic partnerships, or another legal structure for the recognition of same-sex relationships. Recall that the burden is on unmarried, non-registered couples to establish that they have the functional characteristics that warrant giving them the spousal evidentiary privileges, while married or otherwise registered couples are presumed to be able to claim the privilege and the burden is on the opposing party to show such couples lack the appropriate functional characteristics. In jurisdictions that have no legal recognition for same-sex couples, it is much harder for same-sex couples to get the privileges than it is for different-sex couples. Given that trial judges have a strong preference in favor of admitting evidence and for narrowly construing the various evidentiary privileges, it will probably be hard for unmarried, nonregistered couples to meet the burden for claiming the privileges. However, while it may be hard, it will not be *impossible* for same-sex couples to claim the spousal evidentiary privileges as it currently is in the majority of jurisdictions.

Finally, given the historical connection between sexual minorities and secrecy,[147] one might worry that linking the legal recognition of same-sex relationship to spousal secrets will reinforce the role that secrecy and the closet play in the lives of lesbian, gay men, and bisexuals. This worry is unfounded. Allowing same-sex couples to have legally sanctioned spousal secrets like married couples actually creates an incentive for them to be open about their relationships. The most straightforward way for same-sex couples to be able to claim the spousal evidentiary privileges will be for them to register their relationships (by marrying or entering a civil union, domestic partnership, or other such legal arrangement). Further, an important (although not required) characteristic for showing that an unmarried, nonregistered couple deserves the privileges is how they hold themselves out to the public. Lastly, a same-sex couple that tries to obtain the privileges by showing that they meet the appropriate functional characteristics will need to offer evidence in court of their relationship. Sophisticated functionalism does not reinforce the pressure to keep homosexuality and same-sex relationships secret; rather, it creates incentives for same-sex couples to be open.

VII. Conclusion

Early in this chapter, I considered various arguments for the confidential communication privilege and the adverse testimonial privilege. If none of these arguments are successful, then the privileges should be abolished. Abolishing the privileges would not only be a dramatic change in the law of evidence, it would also have the effect of achieving equality for same-sex couples in the context of the spousal evidentiary privileges. This way of achieving equality by abolition has occurred in the context of family law when some gender asymmetries in the law of domestic relations were eliminated. Typically, when a law that gave husbands but not wives a benefit (or a right) was revised to eliminate the gender asymmetries, wives were also given the benefit (or right) that only husbands previously had; sometimes, however, equality was achieved by taking away the benefit or right from husbands.

If, however, the spousal evidentiary privileges are retained—either because of the strength of the arguments for them or because it is politically infeasible to abolish the privileges—then, as I argued in Part IV above, same-sex couples should also get the privileges. Thus far, every jurisdiction that has given same-sex couples the spousal evidentiary privileges has done so as part of giving same-sex couples all (or most) of the benefits, rights, duties, and obligations associated with marriage. It seems almost certain, however, that for some years to come, various jurisdictions will continue to prohibit same-sex couples from marrying. In those jurisdictions, there are two approaches for arguing that same-sex couples should have the privileges. The first approach is the piecemeal approach, whereby legislation could be introduced that would give registered domestic partners some small subset of the benefits of marriage. As proposed in Rhode Island, the spousal evidentiary privileges might be included in that subset of benefits. The second approach, and the approach that this chapter argues should be given greater consideration, is functionalism. The sophisticated functional approach to the spousal evidentiary privileges sketched in this chapter has various advantages, including the potential for an especially close fit with the various arguments in favor of the privileges. Advocates of equality for same-sex couples, as well as those interested in maintaining consistency and fairness in the rules of evidence and the law of domestic relations, should seriously consider sophisticated functionalism when considering reforms to the spousal evidentiary privileges.

Notes

Vice Dean, Professor of Law, and Director of the Program in Family Law, Policy, and Bioethics, Benjamin N. Cardozo School of Law. This chapter has benefited from comments given to me at a Faculty Development Lunch at Cardozo School of Law, a presentation at the New York Area LGBT Law Professors Workshop, and a seminar for the Department of Law, Jurisprudence and Social Thought at Amherst College. I received numerous helpful suggestions from various participants in these colloquia, especially from Paris Baldacci, Elizabeth Emens, Hilary Kornblith, Melanie Leslie, Austin Sarat,

Stewart Sterk, and Peter Tillers. Thanks also to Josh Andrix and Eva Stein for research and related assistance and to Steve Lin for various suggestions and support throughout this project. For a related discussion of some of the issues discussed herein, see Edward Stein, "A Functional Approach to the Spousal Evidentiary Privileges," *Episteme* 5 (2008): 374–87.

1. See, for example, Fed. R. Evid. 402 ("All relevant evidence is admissible, except as otherwise provided by the Constitution of the United States, by Act of Congress, by these rules, or by other rules prescribed by the Supreme Court pursuant to statutory authority").

2. Following Richard Lempert, "A Right to Every Woman's Evidence," *Iowa Law Review* 66 (1981): 727–28, I typically do not use gender neutral pronouns for the witness spouse, since in the majority of cases it is the wife's testimony that is being sought.

3. I use the term "spousal secrets" for facts that spouses know about each other and their interactions that the law specifically enables them to keep secret.

4. For an interesting discussion of open secrets related to the topic of this chapter, see Michael Musto, "Hiding in Plain Sight," *Out* (May 2007): 50 (discussing the phenomenon of the "glass closet," namely of celebrities who are apparently gay or lesbian and widely believed to be gay or lesbian but who are not explicitly open about their sexual orientation in public).

5. There are at least two senses of the word "secret": (1) not known by others and (2) not meant to be known by others. See, for example, the *Oxford American College Dictionary* (New York: G. P. Putnam's Sons, 2002): 1235 (listing the first definition of the word "secret" as "not known or seen or not meant to be known or seen by others").

6. See, for example, Marylynn Salmon, *Women and the Law of Property in Early America* (Chapel Hill: University of North Carolina Press, 1986).

7. See, for example, Carole Shammas et al., *Inheritance in America: From Colonial Times to the Present* (New Brunswick, NJ: Rutgers University Press, 1987).

8. See, for example, *Kirchberg v. Feenstra,* 450 U.S. 455 (1981) (holding that a state law that allowed a husband to unilaterally alienate community property of the marriage violated equal protection because it constituted sex discrimination); *Orr v. Orr,* 440 U.S. 268 (1979) (holding that a state law under which husbands but not wives may be required to pay alimony similarly violated equal protection). But compare *Nguyen v. INS,* 533 U.S. 53 (2001) (holding that different requirements for citizenship based on whether the citizen parent was the citizenship-applicant's mother or father did not violate equal protection).

9. See, for example, Nancy Cott, *Public Vows: A History of Marriage and the Nation* (Cambridge, MA: Harvard University Press, 2000): 79; and J. Herbie DiFonzo, *Beneath the Fault Line: The Popular and Legal Culture of Divorce in Twentieth Century America* (Charlottesville: University Press of Virginia, 1997).

10. There are other revolutionary moments in family law, involving, most notably, the role of race in family law—see, for example, *Perez v. Lippold,* 198 P.2d 17, 27 (Cal. 1948) (finding prohibition on interracial marriage unconstitutional); *Loving v. Virginia,* 388 U.S. 1 (1967) (same)—and the willingness of the state to intervene to prevent violence within the family—see, for example, *People v. Liberta,* 474 N.E. 2d 567 (N.Y. 1984) (abolishing the marital rape exception); *State v. Kelly,* 478 A.2d 264 (N.J. 1984) (recognizing the importance of battered women's syndrome).

11. Among the most important court cases are *Varnum v. Brien,* 763 N.W.2d 862 (Iowa 2009); *In re Marriage Cases,* 183 P.3d 384 (Cal. 2008); *Kerrigan v. Comm'r of Pub. Health,* 957 A.2d 407 (Conn. 2008); *Conaway v. Deane,* 932 A.2d 571 (Md. 2007); *Lewis v. Harris,* 908 A.2d 196 (N.J. 2006); *Andersen v. King County,* 138 P.3d 963 (Wash. 2006); *Hernandez v. Robles,* 855 N.E.2d 1 (N.Y. 2006); *Goodridge v. Dep't of Pub. Health,* 798 N.E.2d 941 (Mass. 2003); *Brause v. Dep't of Health & Soc. Servs.,* 21 P.3d 357 (Alaska 2001); *Baker v. State,* 744 A.2d 864 (Vt. 1999); *Dean v. Dist. of Columbia,* 653 A.2d 307 (D.C. 1995); *Baehr v. Lewin,* 852 P.2d 44 (Haw. 1993); *Singer v. Hara,* 522 P.2d 1187 (Wash. Ct. App. 1974); *Jones v. Hallahan,* 501 S.W.2d 588 (Ky. 1973); and *Baker v. Nelson,* 191 N.W.2d 185 (Minn. 1971).

12. Before January 1, 2012, Hawaii allowed same-sex couples to register as *reciprocal beneficiaries,* a limited version of domestic partnership. This form of relationship recognition was eclipsed by the availability of civil unions in 2012.

13. California's relationship recognition laws have undergone many changes in recent years. In 1999, California first passed a limited domestic partnership law. See A.B. 26, 1999–2000 Reg. Sess. (Cal. 1999). After several years of domestic partnerships, in 2008 the California Supreme Court held that failing to allow same-sex couples the right to marry violates the fundamental right to marry. *In re* Marriage Cases, 183 P.3d 384 (Cal. 2008), *superseded by constitutional amendment,* CAL. CONST. art. I, §7.5. After the 2008 decision, from June through November 2008, same-sex couples could marry in California, and over eighteen thousand same-sex couples did. See *Perry v. Schwarzenegger,* 704 F. Supp. 2d 921, 928 (N.D. Cal. 2010). In November 2008, a majority of California voters supported Proposition 8, which amended the state constitution to define marriage as between one man and one woman. In *Perry,* two same-sex couples challenged the constitutionality of this amendment in federal district court. The district court held that Proposition 8 violated the U.S. Constitution. 704 F. Supp. 2d 921. On February 7, 2012, the Ninth Circuit affirmed the district court, holding that the ban on same-sex marriage violated the Equal Protection Clause of the U.S. Constitution. *Perry v. Brown,* No. 10-16696 (9th Cir. Feb. 7, 2012), available at www.ca9.uscourts.gov/datastore/opinions/2012/02/10/10-16696.pdf. Supporters of Proposition 8 may ask for a larger panel of the 9th Circuit to hear the case or may decide to appeal directly to the U.S. Supreme Court.

14. The governor of Washington signed the state's same-sex marriage bill, S.B. 6239, into law on February 13, 2012. The law is supposed to take effect June 7, 2012. However, opponents filed a referendum shortly after the bill was signed; if more than 120,577 valid voter signatures are collected by June 6, 2012, the law will be delayed pending the outcome of a November vote. Under the new law, domestic partnerships will remain available only to couples in which at least one person is sixty-two years of age or older. S.B. 6239, 62nd Leg., Reg. Sess., 2012 Wash. Sess. Laws Ch. 3. Same-sex couples currently in domestic partnerships—in which neither person is sixty-two years old or older—may convert their domestic partnerships to marriages by getting married. If they do not marry, their domestic partnerships will automatically be converted into marriages on June 30, 2014.

15. The states that do not have such laws are Connecticut, Iowa, Massachusetts, New Hampshire, New Jersey, New York, New Mexico, Rhode Island, and Vermont. For discussion of the issues underlying such laws and amendments, see, for example, Andrew Koppelman, *Same Sex, Different States: When Same-Sex Marriages Cross State Lines* (New Haven: Yale University Press, 2006). Various federal constitutional amendments that would prohibit same-sex marriage have also been proposed. See, for example, Edward Stein, "Past and Present Proposed Amendments to the United States Constitution Regarding Marriage," *Washington University Law Quarterly* 82 (2004): 613 n.1 and accompanying text.

16. Pub. L. No. 104–199, 110 Stat. 2419 (1996) (codified at 1 U.S.C. §7 and 28 U.S.C. §1738C).

17. For a more extensive discussion of the variety of forms of relationship recognition that have emerged over the last decade or so, see Edward Stein, "The Topography of Legal Recognition of Same-Sex Relationships," *Family Court Review* (forthcoming 2012).

18. A court in Maryland allowed a woman in a same-sex marriage to claim the spousal testimonial privilege even though Maryland does not allow same-sex couples to marry. The couple had been married in Washington, DC. In this criminal case, the court accepted the argument by the defendant's spouse that Maryland should recognize the out-of-state same-sex marriage under the common principle of comity. *Maryland v. Snowden,* No. 21-K-11-45589 (Wash. Cty. Cir. Ct., June 23, 2011).

19. *Baker v. State,* 744 A.2d 864 (Vt. 1999).

20. Ibid. at 886.

21. 15 V.S.A. §1201 (2007).

22. Ibid.

23. Vermont has the confidential communication privilege, but not the adverse testimonial privilege. See Vt. R. Evid. §504 (2006); and Vt. Stat. Ann. tit. 12, §1605 (2007).

24. *Goodridge v. Dep't of Public Health,* 798 N.E.2d 941 (Mass. 2003).

25. Mass. Gen. Laws Ann. Ch 233, §20 (2006).

26. 2006 N.J. Laws ch. 103 (civil unions); N.J. Stat. Ann. §2A: 84A-22, Rule 28 (2006) (confidential communication privilege); N.J. Stat. Ann. §2A 84-17, Rule 23(2)(2006) (adverse testimonial privilege).

27. Cal. Fam. Code §297.5 (2007) (domestic partnership); Cal. Evid. Code §§980 (2006) (confidential communication privilege); Cal. Evid. Code §§970-72 (2007) (adverse testimonial privilege). H.B. 2007, 74th Leg. Assem. (Or. 2007) (enacted May 9, 2007); Or. Rev. Stat. §40.255 (2005) (confidential communication and adverse testimonial privileges).

28. S. 151, 2009 Gen. Assem., Jan. Sess. (R.I. 2009). This bill was first introduced in 2007. S. 777, 2007 Gen. Assem., Jan. Sess. (R.I. 2007).

29. Ibid.

30. Dalton Conley, "Spread the Wealth of Spousal Rights," *New York Times* (May 20, 2007): A13.

31. *Perez v. Lippold,* 198 P.2d 17, 27 (Cal. 1948).

32. Only a handful of previous articles have discussed extending the spousal evidentiary privileges to same-sex couples. See Elizabeth Penfil, "In the Light of Reason and Experience: Should Federal Evidence Law Protect Confidential Communication between Same-sex Partners?" *Marquette Law Review* 88 (2005): 815 (arguing that federal courts, under Fed. R. Evid. 501, should extend the spousal evidentiary privileges to same-sex couples); Peter Nicolas, "'They Say He's Gay': The Admissibility of Evidence of Sexual Orientation," *Georgia Law Review* 37 (2003): 869–75 (arguing that "there is no reason" why the policies that underlie spousal evidentiary privileges "would not support similar privileges for same-sex couples"); and Jennifer Brannen, "Unmarried with Privileges? Extending the Evidentiary Privilege to Same-Sex Couples," *Review of Litigation* 17 (1998): 311 (arguing that the spousal evidentiary privileges should be extended to same-sex couples, even those whose relationships are not legally recognized). Of these, the approach adopted in Brannen's article has the most in common with the functionalist account offered in this chapter.

33. On the suppleness of the institution of marriage over time, see Hendrik Hartog, *Man and Wife in America: A History* (Cambridge, Mass.: Harvard University Press, 2000): 242–86; Cott, *Public Vows,* 205–7; Glenda Riley, *Divorce: An American Tradition* (New York: Oxford University Press, 1991): 161–68; Lynne Carol Halem, *Divorce Reform: Changing Legal and Social Perspectives* (New York: Free Press, 1980): 234–87.

34. Various courts have discussed whether civil unions truly give same-sex couples full equality or whether such separate legal institutions are a sign of second-class citizenship. Compare, for example, *In re Opinions of the Justices to the Senate,* 802 N.E.2d 565 (Mass. 2004) ("[A civil union scheme] maintains an unconstitutional, inferior, and discriminatory status for same-sex couples"), and *Lewis v. Harris,* 908 A.2d 196, 224 (Poritz, C. J. dissenting) ("By excluding same-sex couples from civil marriage, the State declares that it is legitimate to differentiate between their commitments and the commitments

of heterosexual couples [saying] . . . that what same-sex couples have is not as important or as significant as 'real' marriage"), with *Kerrigan v. State*, 909 A.2d 89 (Conn. 2006) ("reject[ing] the argument that the *rhetorical* separation of marriage vs. civil union is enough to invoke an equal protection or due process analysis"), and Lewis, 908 A.2d 196, 221 ("Under our equal protection jurisprudence, . . . plaintiffs' claimed right to the name of marriage is surely not the same now that equal rights and benefits must be conferred on committed same-sex couples"), and *In re Opinions of the Justices to the Senate*, 802 N.E.2d at 572 (Mass. 2004) (Sosman, J., dissenting) (opining that whether the legal relationship between a same-sex couple is called a marriage or a civil union is "not . . . a dispute of any constitutional dimension whatsoever").

35. See below text accompanying notes 89–91.

36. Although the U.S. Supreme Court held sodomy laws to be unconstitutional, the majority and concurring opinions specifically denied that the case at issue had anything to do with same-sex marriage. See *Lawrence v. Texas*, 539 U.S. 558, 578 (2003) ("The present case . . . does not involve whether the government must give formal recognition to any relationship that homosexual persons seek to enter"); see also ibid. at 585 (O'Connor, J., concurring) (contrasting the constitutionality of Texas's sodomy law, for which there is no state interest beyond the illegitimate "moral disproval of same-sex relations," with marriage laws, for which there are legitimate state interests "beyond mere disapproval of an excluded group," including "preserving the traditional institution of marriage"). The dissent, in contrast, insisted that *Lawrence* had a great deal to do with marriage and that the case was wrongly decided because of the implications that the majority's approach had for that subject. Ibid. at 605 (Scalia, J. dissenting) ("This case 'does not involve' the issue of homosexual marriage only if one entertains the belief that principle and logic have nothing to do with the decisions of this Court"). In sum, no member of the *Lawrence* court said anything explicit in support of a federal constitutional argument for the recognition of same-sex relationships, and the court has become more conservative on such social issues since that case was decided. See, for example, Linda Greenhouse, "In Steps Big and Small, Supreme Court Moved Right," *New York Times* (July 1, 2007): A1.

37. See above, notes 15–17 and accompanying text, and below, notes 141–46 and accompanying text.

38. See, for example, Mass. Gen. Laws Ch. 233 §20 (2007).

39. Some jurisdictions have extended the confidential communications privilege to include "private marital acts," typically, sex acts. See, for example, *Rubio v. Superior Court*, 249 Cal. Rptr. 419, 421 (Cal. App. 1988) (holding that videotape of married couple having sex is a confidential communication subject to the confidential communication privilege).

40. *United States v. Estes*, 793 F.2d 465 (2d Cir. 1986).

41. Ibid. at 466 (citations omitted).

42. Ibid. at 467 (citations and quotation omitted).

43. *Trammel v. United States,* 445 U.S. 40 (1980).

44. See *Hawkins v. United States,* 358 U.S. 74 (1958).

45. See, for example, Colo. Rev. Stat. §13-90-107(1)(a)(I) (2006).

46. *Trammel,* 445 U.S. at 53.

47. Ibid. at 44.

48. See, for example, William Blackstone, *Commentaries on the Laws of England,* 3rd ed., vol. 1, ed. Thomas Cooley (Chicago: Callaghan, 1884): 445.

49. See, for example, *Brown v. Brown,* 409 N.E. 2d 717 (Mass. 1980) (abolishing spousal tort immunity); *Klein v. Klein,* 376 P.2d 70 (Cal. 1963) (same).

50. *Funk v. United States,* 290 U.S. 371 (1933).

51. *Wolfle v. United States,* 291 U.S. 7, 14 (1934).

52. *Stein v. Bowman,* 38 U.S. 209, 223 (1839).

53. David Louisell, "Confidentiality, Conformity and Confusion: Privileges in Federal Court Today," *Tulane Law Review* 31 (1956): 113 ("[F]reedom of marital communication from all government supervision, constraint, control, or observation ... [is] a psychological necessity for the perfect fulfillment of the marriage").

54. Mark Reutlinger, "Policy, Privacy, and Prerogatives: A Critical Examination of the Proposed Federal Rules of Evidence as They Affect Marital Privilege," *California Law Review* 61 (1973): 1371 n. 82, cites some social scientific studies to support the claim that open communications are good for a marriage.

55. *United States v. Neal,* 532 F. Supp. 942, 946 (D. Colo. 1982).

56. Carl Schneider, "The Channeling Function in Family Law," *Hofstra Law Review* 20 (1992): 498.

57. *Wolfle v. United States,* 291 U.S. 7, 14 (1934).

58. Charles McCormick, *Handbook of the Law of Evidence* (St. Paul, MN: West, 1954): 179.

59. See, for example, Charles Black, "The Marital and Physician Privilege—A Reprint of a Letter to a Congressman," *Duke Law Journal* 1975: 48–49; Reutlinger, "Policy, Privacy, and Prerogatives," 1370; Thomas Krattenmaker, "Interspousal Testimonial Privileges under the Federal Rules of Evidence: A Suggested Approach," *Georgetown Law Journal* 64 (1976): 613.

60. See, for example, Cal. Const. art. I, §1; Fla. Const. art. I, §23.

61. *Griswold v. Connecticut,* 381 U.S. 479 (1965).

62. *Roe v. Wade,* 410 U.S. 113, 153 (1973) (finding a woman's right to chose to have an abortion to be constitutionally protected on privacy grounds).

63. *Bowers v. Hardwick,* 478 U.S. 186, 191 (1986).

64. *Lawrence v. Texas,* 539 U.S. 558, 578 (2003).

65. *Griswold,* 381 U.S. at 485.

66. *Wyatt v. United States,* 362 U.S. 525, 535 (1960) (Warren, C. J., dissenting) (quoting John Henry Wigmore, *A Treatise on the Anglo-American System of Evidence in Trials at Common Law,* vol. 8, 3rd ed. [Boston: Little Brown, 1940]): §2228, 227.

67. See "Developments in the Law: Privileged Communications," *Harvard Law Review* 98 (1985): 1584–85.

68. Edward Coke, *The First Part of the Institutes of the Law of England, or A Commentaries upon Littleton,* 1628 ed. (New York: Garland, 1979): §6b.

69. *Hawkins v. United States,* 359 U.S. 74, 77–78 (1958).

70. See, generally, Lempert, "A Right to Every Woman's Evidence," 727–28.

71. *United States v. Walker,* 176 F.2d 564, 568 (2d Cir. 1949).

72. Wigmore, A Treatise on the Anglo-American System, 2nd ed. (Boston: Little Brown, 1923): §2228, 756.

73. David Medine, "The Adverse Testimony Privilege: Time to Dispose of a 'Sentimental Relic,'" *Oregon Law Review* 67 (1988): 552.

74. Deborah Ausburn, "Circling the Wagons: Informational Privacy and Family Testimonial Privileges," *Georgia Law Review* 20 (1988): 199 (quoting *Whalen v. Roe,* 429 U.S. 589, 600 [1977]).

75. See, for example, *LaRoche v. Wainwright,* 599 F.2d 722, 726 (5th Cir. 1979) ("[We] see no persuasive reason to extend the right of privacy, based as it is on 'penumbras and emanations' of other more explicit constitutional rights, to evidentiary matters protecting marital relationships, long thought to be uniquely within the regulatory province of the individual states"); *Port v. Heard,* 764 F.2d 423, 430 (5th Cir. 1985) (rejecting constitutional right to privacy argument for adverse testimonial *parent-child* privilege on the grounds that "the marital privilege has never been placed on a constitutional footing"); *United States v. Lefkowitz,* 618 F.2d 1313, 1319 (9th Cir. 1980) (rejecting defendant's argument that the spousal evidentiary privileges "are somehow grounded in various constitutional amendments and implement a constitutionally-protected right of marital privacy").

76. McCormick, *Handbook of the Law of Evidence,* 2nd ed. (St. Paul, MN: West, 1972): 173.

77. Medine, "The Adverse Testimony Privilege," 545; Maurice Rosenberg, "The New Looks in Law," *Marquette Law Review* 52 (1969–70): 540–42.

78. Sanford Levinson, "Testimonial Privileges and the Preferences of Friendship," *Duke Law Journal* 1984 (1984): 654–56 (offering hypothetical of giving every person a "privilege ticket" that could be given to another person in order to make privileged communications between the person giving the ticket and the person receiving it).

79. Jeremy Bentham, *Rationale of Judicial Evidence,* vol. 5 (London: Hunt and Clarke, 1827): 340.

80. See, for example, *Thompson v. Thompson,* 218 U.S. 611 (1910); *Rubalcava v. Gisseman,* 384 P.2d 389 (Utah 1963).

81. See, for example, Homer Clark, *The Law of Domestic Relations in the United States,* 2nd ed. (St. Paul, MN: West, 1988): §10.1 at 371.

82. Lempert, "A Right to Every Woman's Evidence," 734.

83. Fed. R. Evid. 102 ("These rules shall be construed to secure fairness in administration, elimination of unjustifiable expense and delay, and promotion of growth and development of the law of evidence to the end that the truth may be ascertained and proceedings justly determined").

84. Wigmore, *A Treatise on the Anglo-American System,* §2228, 761.

85. The attorney-client privilege—see Fed. R. Evid. 501 and *Fisher v. United States,* 425 U.S. 391 (1976)—is one such example.

86. See, for example, Pamela Haun, "The Marital Privilege in the Twenty-First Century," *University of Memphis Law Review* 32 (2001): 158–61.

87. McCormick, *Handbook of the Law of Evidence,* 2nd ed. (St. Paul, MN: West, 1907), §86, 174.

88. Charles McCormick, *McCormick on Evidence,* 6th ed. (St. Paul, MN: Thompson/West, 2006): §86, 133.

89. Proposed Rules of Evidence for United States Courts and Magistrates, Proposed Rule 505, 56 F.R.D. 183, 244 (1972) ("An accused in a criminal proceeding has a privilege to prevent his spouse from testifying against him").

90. Fed. R. Evid. 501. The rejection of Proposed Rule 505 and other proposed privilege rules and the substitution of Rule 501 is discussed in detail in Krattenmaker, "Interspousal Testimonial Privileges," 635–46.

91. Kenneth S. Broun, "Giving Codification a Second Chance—Testimonial Privileges and the Federal Rules of Evidence," *Hastings Law Journal* 54 (2002): 769.

92. *Andersen v. King County,* No. 04-2-04964-4-SEA, 2004 WL 1738447, at *12 (Wash. Super. Ct., August 4, 2004), *rev'd Andersen v. King County,* 138 P.3d 963 (Wash. 2006) (discussing the plaintiff couples in a case challenging laws prohibiting same-sex couples from marrying).

93. See, for example, *Heller v. Doe,* 509 U.S. 312, 319 (1993) (describing rational review standard as highly deferential); *Washington v. Glucksberg,* 521 U.S. 702 (1997) (applying rational review to a ban on physician-assisted suicide).

94. *Andersen v. King County,* 138 P.3d 963, 983 (Wash. 2006); *Hernandez v. Robles,* 855 N.E.2d 1, 7 (N.Y. 2006). See also *Goodridge v. Dep't of Pub. Health,* 798 N.E.2d 941, 998-1003 (Mass. 2003) (Cordy, J., dissenting).

95. *Andersen,* 138 P.3d at 983; *Goodridge,* 798 N.E.2d at 998–1003 (Cordy, J., dissenting).

96. *Goodridge,* 798 N.E.2d at 963–64; *Hernandez,* 855 N.E.2d at 31–32 (Kaye, C. J., dissenting).

97. *Goodridge,* 798 N.E.2d at 961–64; *Hernandez,* 855 N.E.2d at 31–32 (Kaye, C. J., dissenting). See also *Lawrence v. Texas,* 539 U.S. 558, 605 (Scalia, J., dissenting) (noting that

the "encouragement of procreation" cannot be a reason for denying same-sex couples the benefits of marriage).

98. See, for example, *In re Grand Jury—Impounded,* 103 F.3d 1140 (3d Cir. 1997) (failing to recognize parent-child confidential communication privilege); *Port v. Heard,* 764 F.2d 423, 428–432 (5th Cir. 1985) (compelling parents to testify against child charged with murder).

99. Idaho Code 9-203(7) (2006) (protecting confidential communications by a child to a parent); Minn. Stat. 595.02(1)(j) (2006) (same); Mass. Ann. Laws, ch 233, §20 (2007) (disqualifying minor children who live with their parents from testifying against their parents in a criminal proceeding).

100. *Morrison v. Sandler,* 821 N.E.2d 15, 24 (Ind. App. 2005). See also *Hernandez,* 855 N.E.2d at 7 ("The Legislature could . . . choose to offer an inducement—in the form of marriage and its attendant benefits—to opposite-sex couples who make a solemn, long-term commitment to each other"); *Andersen,* 138 P.3d at 1002 (Johnson, J., concurring) ("Unlike same-sex couples, only opposite-sex couples may experience unintentional or unplanned procreation. State sanctioned marriage as a union of one man and one woman encourages couples to enter into a stable relationship prior to having children and to remain committed to one another in the relationship for the raising of children, planned or otherwise"); and *Citizens for Equal Protection v. Bruning,* 455 F.3d 859, 867–869 (8th Cir. 2006).

101. *Hernandez,* 855 N.E.2d at 30 (Kaye, C. J. dissenting). See also *Andersen* 138 P.3d 963, 1018 (Faircloth, J., dissenting) ("[D]enying same-sex couples the right to marry . . . will not encourage couples who have children to marry or stay married for the benefit of the children").

102. See Edward Stein, "The 'Accidental Procreation' Argument for Withholding Legal Recognition for Same-Sex Relationship," *Chicago-Kent Law Review* 84 (2009): 403–35; Kerry Abrams and Peter Brooks, "Marriage as a Message: Same-Sex Couples and the Rhetoric of Accidental Procreation," *Yale Journal of Law and Humanities* 21(2009): 1–35.

103. *Lawrence v. Texas,* 539 U.S. 558 (2003) (finding unconstitutional Tex. 2003 Penal Code Ann. §21.06(a) [Vernon 2003]).

104. *Lawrence,* 539 U.S. at 562.

105. Ibid. at 525–26.

106. See, for example, Kenneth Karst, "The Freedom of Intimate Association," *Yale Law Journal* 89 (1980): 624.

107. *Eisenstadt v. Baird,* 405 U.S. 438 (1972).

108. Ibid. at 453.

109. See, for example, *United States v. Acker,* 52 F.3d 509, 514 (4th Cir. 1995) (no privilege for cohabiting different-sex couple living together for twenty-five years); *State v. Watkins,* 614 P.2d 835 (Ariz. 1980) (no privilege for cohabiting different-sex couple); *Peo-*

ple v. Delph, 156 Cal. Rptr. 422 (Cal. App. 1979) (same); *State v. Lard*, 519 P.2d 307 (N.M. App. 1974) (same).

110. See, for example, *Irizarry v. Bd. of Educ. of the City of Chicago*, 251 F.3d 604 (7th Cir. 2001); *Foray v. Bell Atl.*, 56 F. Supp. 2d 327 (S.D.N.Y. 1999); *Cleaves v. Chicago*, 68 F. Supp. 2d 963 (N.D. Ill. 1999).

111. *Foray*, 56 F. Supp. 2d at 330.

112. *Irizarry*, 251 F.3d at 610.

113. Alabama, Colorado, Iowa, Kansas, Montana, Oklahoma, Rhode Island, South Carolina, Texas, and Utah recognize common law marriages.

114. See, for example, *In re Marriage of Winegard*, 278 N.W.2d 505 (Iowa 1979).

115. See, for example, *United States v. Rubenstein*, 151 F.2d 915 (2d Cir. 1945) (finding a sham marriage void); *Garcia-Jaramillo v. INS*, 604 F.2d 1236 (9th Cir. 1979) (same); *United States v. Mathias*, 559 F.2d 295 (5th Cir. 1977) (finding no evidentiary privilege because marriage was a sham).

116. *Braschi v. Stahl Assoc.*, 543 N.E. 2d 49, 55 (N.Y. 1989).

117. Ohio Rev. Code Ann. §2919.25 (A).

118. Ibid. at §2919.25 (F)(1).

119. Ibid. at §2919.25 (F)(2).

120. *State v. Yaden*, 692 N.E.2d 1097, 1101 (Ohio App. 1997). Sometime after *Yaden* was decided, Ohio amended its state constitution to define marriage as between one man and one woman and to prohibit the creation or recognition of a legal status for relationships of unmarried individuals that "intends to approximate the design, qualities, significance or effect of marriage." Ohio Const. art. XV, §11 (2006). After some Ohio appellate courts have held that this amendment made unconstitutional the functional approach taken in *Yaden* and other Ohio cases—see, for example, *State v. Schaffer*, 2006 Ohio 2662 (2006)—the Ohio Supreme Court, in *State v. Carswell*, 871 N.E.2d 547 (Ohio 2007), held that the functional approach taken by some Ohio courts was not unconstitutional because it did not create or recognize a legal status approximating marriage.

121. *United States v. Singleton*, 260 F.3d 1295 (11th Cir. 2001); *United States v. Murphy*, 65 F.3d 758 (9th Cir. 1995); *United States v. Porter*, 986 F.2d 1014 (6th Cir. 1993); *United States v. Roberson*, 859 F.2d 1376, 1380–82 (9th Cir. 1988); *United States v. Falk*, 816 F.2d 1202, 1205 (7th Cir. 1987); *United States v. Byrd*, 750 F.2d 585 (7th Cir. 1984).

122. *Lutvak v. United States*, 344 U.S. 604, 614–15 (1953) (no privilege because the couple got married for immigration purposes); *United States v. Mathias*, 559 F.2d 294 (5th Cir. 1977) (no privilege because defendant had coerced witness into remarrying him so that he could claim spousal privilege); *United States v. Apodaca*, 522 F.2d 568, 571 (10th Cir. 1975) (no privilege because defendant married witness just three days before trial, circumstances indicating a "fraudulent, spurious marriage that was not entered into in good faith").

123. *United States v. Sims*, 755 F.2d 1239, 1243 n.3 (6th 1985) (quotation and citation

omitted). See also *In the Matter of Grand Jury (Malfitano)*, 633 F.2d 276, 279 (3d Cir. 1980) ("[We] are not confident that courts can assess the social worthiness of particular marriages or the need of particular marriages for the protection of the privilege"); *Coleman v. State*, 380 A.2d 49 (Md. 1977) (privilege applicable to communication made after husband had been served with divorce suit); *Muetze v. State*, 243 N.W.2d 393 (Wis. 1976) ("The status of the particular marital relationship has no bearing on whether a privilege exists for marital communications"); *United States v. Walker*, 176 F.2d 564 (2d Cir. 1949).

124. *People v. Fields*, 328 N.Y.S.2d 542, 545 (N.Y. App. Div. 1972) *affirmed by* 289 N.E.2d 557 (N.Y. 1972).

125. See, for example, *Greenwald v. H & P 29th Assocs.*, 659 NYS 2d 473, 474 (N.Y. App. Div. 1997) (rejecting privilege for cohabitating same-sex couple); *United States v. Acker*, 52 F.3d 509, 514 (4th Cir. 1995) (no privilege for cohabiting different-sex couple living together for twenty-five years); *People v. Delph*, 156 Cal. Rptr. 422 (Cal. App. 1979); *State v. Lard*, 519 P.2d 307 (N.M. App. 1974); *State v. Watkins*, 614 P.2d 835 (Ariz. 1980).

126. See, for example, *In re Grand Jury Proceedings (Witness Ms. X)*, 562 F. Supp. 486, 487 (N.D. Cal. 1983) ("[T]he Court believes that in some instances it might be appropriate to allow [a person who has been cohabitating with a defendant for over six years, raising four children together, and 'liv(ing) together as a family'] to invoke the marital privilege"); *People v. Stanford*, 242 N.W.2d 56, 58 (Mich. App. 1976) (finding "cogent" the suggestion that the court "not rigidly apply the requirement of a legal marriage but, instead, look to the relationship of the parties to determine whether the incidents of that relationship are those which the statute was intended to protect").

127. *United States v. Lustig*, 555 F.2d 737, 747–48 (9th Cir. 1977).

128. Ray Henry, "Gay Marriage Advocates Promises Step-by-Step Fight in Rhode Island," Associated Press (February 14, 2007).

129. "For purposes of this section 'domestic partner' shall mean a person who shares an exclusive, intimate and committed relationship of mutual caring with the respondent and can demonstrate that the respondent and domestic partner: (1) are at least eighteen years of age and mentally competent to contract; (2) are not married to anyone else; (3) are not related by blood to a degree what would prohibit marriage in the state of Rhode Island; (4) reside together and have resided together for at least one year; and are financially interdependent as evidence by at least two of the following: (i) domestic partnership agreement or relationship contract; (ii) joint mortgage or joint ownership of primary residence; (iii) two of (1) joint ownership of a motor vehicle; (2) joint checking account; (3) joint credit account (4) joint lease; and/or (iv) the domestic partner has been designated as a beneficiary for the respondent's will, retirement contract, or life insurance." S. 151, 2009 Gen. Assem., January Sess. (R.I. 2009).

130. Conley, "Spread the Wealth of Spousal Rights." See also Levinson, "Testimonial Privileges and the Preferences of Friendship."

131. Bentham, *Rationale of Judicial Evidence*, 340.

132. See, for example, *Dunphy v. Gregor*, 642 A.2d 372 (N.J. 1994) (finding that fiancée who witnessed car accident that killed her husband-to-be may be entitled to damages from alleged tortfeasor based on bystander liability theory traditionally limited to spouses or those in an intimate familial relationship).

133. A classic case about line drawing is *United States v. Locke*, 471 U.S. 84 (1985). A statute required a filing "*prior to* December 31" (emphasis added), but the plaintiffs filed their claim *on* December 31. The Supreme Court held that the plaintiffs simply filed too late; for statutes to have any meaning, such clear statement rules must be strictly followed.

134. The language of the past three sentences draws on, without quotation, the language of the *Braschi* and *Yaden* cases. See notes 116–20 and accompanying text.

135. See, for example, Rep. No 97–16 (January 31, 1997), at http://www.gao.gov/archive/1997/og97016.pdf (identifying just over one thousand federal laws in which marital status is a factor), updated by Rep. No. 04-353R (January 4, 2004), at http://www.gao.gov/new.items/d04353r.pdf. Empire State Pride Agenda and New York City Bar Association, 1324 Reasons for Marriage Equality in New York State (June 8, 2007), at http://www.nycbar.org/pdf/report/marriage_v7d21.pdf (identifying 1,324 legal rights and duties that are conferred on married individuals under New York statutes and regulations).

136. For the most part, no single benefit of marriage encourages people to marry, but the entire package of benefits, rights, duties, and obligations may encourage some people to marry, although many people marry for emotional, romantic, social, and religious reasons, not, it seems, for the legal benefits of marriage.

137. See notes 121–22, above.

138. See, for example, *V. C. v. M. J. B.*, 748 A.2d 539 (N.J. 2000) (granting visitation rights to de facto parent).

139. The Washington domestic partner statute, for example, is available only to couples, specifically to two people of the same sex or two people at least one of whom is sixty-two years of age or older. Wash. Rev. Code of §26.60.010. For information on Washington's same-sex marriage legislation and its effect, if it is enacted, on the state's domestic partner statute, see note 14, above.

140. See, generally, Stein, "The Topography of Legal Recognition of Same-Sex Relationships."

141. Cal. Fam. Code §308.5 (2007) ("Only marriage between a man and a woman is valid or recognized in California"); Haw. Const. art. I, §23 ("The legislature shall have the power to reserve marriage to opposite-sex couples").

142. See, for example, Me. Rev. Stat. Ann. tit. 19-A §701 (2007) ("[1] When residents of this State, with intent to evade this section and to return and reside here, go into another state or country to have their marriage solemnized there and afterwards return and reside here, that marriage is void in this State. [2] Any marriage performed

in another state that would violate any provision of subsections 2 to 5 [which include prohibiting marriages between people of the same sex] if performed in this state is not recognized in this State and is considered void if the parties take up residence in this State").

143. See, for example, Miss. Const. art. 14, §263A ("Marriage may take place and may be valid under the laws of this state only between a man and a woman. A marriage in another state or foreign jurisdiction between persons of the same gender, regardless of when the marriage took place, may not be recognized in this state and is void and unenforceable under the laws of this state"); Colo. Rev. Stat. §14-2-104 (2007) ("[A]ny marriage contracted . . . outside this state that does not satisfy paragraph [b] of subsection [1] of this section [which includes that marriages must be "between one man and one woman"] shall not be recognized as valid in this state").

144. See, for example, Ark. Const. amend. 83 §2 (2006) ("Marriage consists only of the union of one man and one woman. Legal status for unmarried persons which is identical or substantially similar to marital status shall not be valid or recognized in Arkansas"); Va. Const. art. 1, §15-A (2007) ("[O]nly a union between one man and one woman may be a marriage valid in or recognized by this Commonwealth. . . . This Commonwealth . . . shall not create or recognize a legal status for relationships of unmarried individuals that intends to approximate the design, qualities, significance, or effects of marriage. Nor shall this Commonwealth or its political subdivisions create or recognize another union, partnership, or other legal status to which is assigned the rights, benefits, obligations, qualities, or effects of marriage").

145. See, for example, Koppelman, *Same Sex, Different States*, 142–48 (arguing that statutes that deny "contractual rights" arising from same-sex marriages or that simply refuse to give any recognition whatsoever to another state's same-sex marriages violate the U.S. Constitution).

146. Ibid. at 144 (discussing Virginia's provision).

147. See, for example, Edward Stein, "Queers Anonymous: Lesbians, Gay Men, Free Speech, and Cyberspace," *Harvard Civil Rights-Civil Liberties Law Review* 38 (2003): 159; Richard Mohr, *Gay Ideas: Outing and Other Controversies* (New York: Columbia University Press, 1992): 11–49; Larry Gross, *Contested Closets: The Politics and Ethics of Outing* (Minneapolis: University of Minnesota Press, 1993); Eve Kosofsky Sedgwick, *Epistemology of the Closet* (Berkeley: University of California Press, 1990).

Wilkie Collins's Law Books: Law, Literature, and Factual Precedent

BERNADETTE MEYLER

The rhetoric of democracy often promotes an ever-increasing transparency of political and legal institutions, relying on the visibility of the mechanisms of power and law to obviate any of their adverse effects. This mantra of transparency is invoked throughout the pages of eminent law reviews: "If opacity frustrates and misleads outsiders [to the American criminal justice system], transparency and fuller disclosure can alleviate these problems";[1] "Transparency is a core good governance attribute: Open procedures contribute to virtually all of the foundations of legitimacy";[2] and "[T]ransparency in recent years has developed from a buzzword into a substantive policy tool, particularly in efforts to make transnational actors more socially and environmentally responsible."[3] Although some do question the transformative potential of transparency,[4] its grip on the geopolitical imagination remains firm. Nor is the goal of transparency all that new. Since at least the seventeenth century, law reformers have urged mechanisms for increasing transparency in the Anglo-American legal system.

Both historically and today, law reform efforts aimed at increasing transparency often focus on the possibilities of public access to knowledge about the law.[5] One mode of achieving such access may be textual, through the dissemination of law reports, the publication of treatises explaining legal principles, and the production of volumes containing statutory enactments. Those attempting to promote transparency by generating a proliferation of texts tend, however, to neglect both what happens to these texts after they are produced and how they are received.

Through exploring a moment in the nineteenth century when reports of particular trials and collections of cases were both becoming common and self-consciously addressing a lay audience, this article examines the efforts of both law and literature to educate the naive reader. What emerges is not an individual who can penetrate all the secrets of law, but rather one who reads with an awareness of the limits of the text's or the trial's ability to convey an unmediated truth, and who therefore retains a certain skepticism about the very possibility of complete transparency.

Acts of Reading Law and Literature

In the fall of 1882, a letter arrived from London for Albany prosecutor Nathaniel Moak, a trial lawyer responsible for the conviction of a number of notorious nineteenth-century criminals.[6] Postmarked August 21 of that year, the missive had been penned by English crime novelist Wilkie Collins and thanked the prosecutor for sending Collins a copy of a volume containing documents related to the trial of Jesse Billings for the murder of his wife. This was a case on which government resources had been heaped and which had resulted in not only one, but two, successive trials. The book Collins received had included Moak's closing argument for the prosecution in the case, dated Monday, October 7, 1878, as well as the judge's charge to the jury. These had been reported by Noel C. Andrews, Esq., and were followed by an odd document from a series called "Contributions to Medical Jurisprudence," which contained a doctor's 1881 review of the medical testimony from Billings's second trial.[7] The precise nature of Moak's connection with Collins does not emerge from the correspondence, but it is possible that the prosecutor had heard the novelist present his work to a parlor audience in Albany on his 1873 reading tour of America.[8]

Collins's letter addressed Moak as follows:

> My Dear Sir,
>
> I can only trust to this kindness which has presented me with an interesting addition to my little library to excuse this late expression of my thanks. When the "Argument" reached me, I waited to write, in the hope of finding a fit opportunity to become one of your readers without much delay. But my literary labours proved to be obstacles in the way—and these at an end, my doctor prescribed a long holiday.[9] I accepted an invitation to cruise in a friend's yacht[10]—and here I am on shore again, reading your pages with the greatest interest, to say nothing of the "agreeable surprise" of finding "The Moonstone" borrowed by a favourable allusion, in a Court of Justice. The mental capacity which can make itself acquainted with an immense accumulation of facts—present them one after another in their proper order, and draw from them the [crucial] inferences, all

steadily forming in one and the same direction—is simply a matter of wonder to *me*. I ask myself all sorts of simple questions relating to *you*. Were you assailed by nervous misgivings—especially on the first day? Did you never feel some little mental confusion here and there? Did the appearance of the jury—their looks and ways—now and then discourage you? And in the intervals of this "argument" could you sleep when you went to bed—and eat and drink *and* digest, before going to bed? These queer inquiries occur to a novelist—and they are followed by a novelist's complaint. You seize on my interest—and you don't tell me how the terrible tale of guilt ended. I look on to the last pages and see a judge's charge, and a medical writer's "Views" when I want to know *whether he was found guilty and hanged*. The case was mentioned in our newspapers—but the end has slipped from my memory.

With renewed thanks—and in the hope that I may be excused,

Vy truly yours
Wilkie Collins[11]

On first glance, this letter seems to stage the difference between literary and legal perspectives. Underlining "me" and "you," Collins opposes himself and Moak in their respective capacities as novelist and prosecutor. Whereas Moak's lengthy argument focused on constructing a plausible narrative of the crime from the range of available circumstantial evidence, and the succeeding medical analysis of the testimony—including elaborate charts and meticulous drawings of a skull with a bullet hole—concentrated on detailed evaluation of the "facts," Collins's novelistic approach attends to the plot and its ending, or, in other words, the question of whether Billings "was found guilty and hanged."[12] Whereas the report of Moak's argument depicted an elaborate process of ratiocination, expressing "[t]he mental capacity which can make itself acquainted with an immense accumulation of facts," Collins wishes instead to know what emotions lay behind this virtuosic display of reason, or what fissures might have rested beneath the eloquent surface of the argument, inquiring about the confusion, nervousness, and even sleep patterns of the prosecutor. On holiday from novel writing, Collins simultaneously becomes a novelistic reader of the report Moak sent him, supplementing the text as it was produced with questions characteristic of his fictional preoccupations. One of the burgeoning cadre of nineteenth-century "travel readers,"[13] Collins thus replaces his work of fiction writing with the work of legal reading.

On second perusal, however, the letter opens onto a number of correlations between legal and literary endeavors. As Collins notes, Moak referred at length in his argument to the novelist's work *The Moonstone*, often deemed the first detective novel.[14] Defense counsel had already drawn the jury's attention to a number of works of fiction broadly conceived, including *Oedipus* and the *Arabian Nights*. Critiquing the precedent provided by these texts, Moak insisted that the *Arabian Nights* might, in fact, be applicable, but only because of its framing conceit—the idea that the teller of the tales was spinning them out regardless of truth or falsity in order to save her own life. To provide a counterexample to these literary precedents, Moak instead invoked *The Moonstone* and its representation of inductive analysis. According to the prosecutor:

> We may safely study fiction provided we discreetly apply it, for when properly applied it is intended to faithfully represent humanity. In the story of the Moonstone, a jewel had been stolen; detectives had been sent for to ascertain who was the guilty party; a door of the room from which the moonstone had been taken had been newly painted; upon the jamb of the door was discovered a small spot from which the paint had been brushed by a passing garment; the local detectives—or in the language of my learned friend, the "wolves and hyenas" of the locality—had all passed it as of no importance; the city detective, with the experience of a life-time, regarded it as an important circumstance. I cannot better give you his idea of it than by reading it, for it is an illustration by one skilled in human character, of the importance of a trifling circumstance . . . . [Moak then quotes at length from *The Moonstone*.] That is a circumstance related in a work of fiction, but said to have been founded on fact—on the experience of an eminent detective. . . . It is these small circumstances which lead as unerringly to the guilty party, as if the finger of Providence had pointed directly to him.[15]

Moak thus insisted that, rather than being specific to his own line of work, the mustering of circumstantial evidence into a coherent story pointing to the guilt of the defendant was a technique that none other than Collins himself had previously employed. The language of Collins's novel best encapsulated, he believed, the process of reasoning from a small clue to the guilt of the party accused.

Just as Moak relied on Collins to provide a literary precedent for his own legal argument, Collins deployed the reports of actual trials in service of his novelistic work. As many critics have remarked, Collins frequently used legal motifs ripped from the headlines; the figure of aptly named female poisoner Lydia Gwilt in *Armadale* thus recalls the reader to the stories of comparable real-life antiheroines Sarah Chesham and Constance Wilson, who had been executed in 1851 and 1862, respectively.[16] Collins did not remain content, however, with newspaper sources, and instead, in some works, made extensive use of the genre of trial reports. The novella *John Jago's Ghost*, published in installments during 1873 and 1874, played upon an American trial report,[17] and Collins acknowledged having found the plot of *The Woman in White*, among other works, in a collection of French trials entitled *Recueil des Causes Célèbres, et des Arrêts qui les Ont Décidées* that he had encountered in Paris when wandering there with Charles Dickens.[18] Not only did law mimic the work of fiction, but art also imitated the law's representation of life.

Finally, the kinds of questions that Collins raises about Moak's mental state—including his anxiety, and his relation to the jury—are questions similar to those that Moak himself asked about the motivations and feelings of the protagonists in his criminal narrative. The principal difference consists simply in perspective. Moak attempted to create a story of the case from which he was disentangled and in which he would function as a neutral observer, resisting, in the process, the other side's imputations as to his motivations, including the defense attorney's claims that Moak desired to wrest a conviction from the case simply in order to rise up in the world. Collins insists instead that the prosecutor is bound up in the tale, and that Moak's own character must be further developed beyond the surface of how he wished to represent himself.

Analysis of these distinctions reveals that the crucial differentiation between Moak's and Collins's perspectives is not that between lawyer and literary figure but rather that between author and reader—with Moak in this context assuming the guise of the former and Collins that of the latter. Collins, whose "little library" mentioned in the letter seems to have contained many law books,[19] and who also extracted legal updates from the newspapers and trial reports to which he refers, constructed *critical readings* of law and its documentation. A number of Collins's novels contain, as Sue Lonoff has argued, "counterparts or doubles for his readers in the text, characters whose activities correspond or intersect with those of the audience."[20] Interpreting the activities of the novels' legal readers may lead to a conclusion somewhat distinct from D. A. Miller's claims about *The Moonstone*. According to Miller, the form of *The Moonstone* itself, although seeming to liberate the reader by presenting a series of narratives from different points of view, actually renders him complicit in a disciplinary apparatus by "promot[ing] a single perception of power," which leads everyone inexorably to render the same judgment.[21] By reading legal texts in ways that call these texts' own judgments into question, some of the readers that Collins represents instead suggest that the vantage point of legal institutions may not be authoritative. Nor does the perspective of the novel, which Collins on occasion renders as itself partial, simply replace the legal one.

Some of the critical readings in Collins's work involve documents that, like Moak's argument, emanate from trial practice; the associated genre to which Collins most often returns is that of the trial report.[22] In his 1875 novel *The Law and the Lady*, Collins furnishes an exemplary reading of a trial report that answers the questions he himself had asked of Moak about the Billings trial. The novel therefore frames the trial in such a way as to render the legal advocates and decision-makers themselves a subject of inquiry. The novel also rehearses one of the principal preoccupations of Moak's own argument in the Billings trial—the accuracy and desirability of proof by circumstantial evidence. Whereas Moak had deployed Collins's *Moonstone* in support of the merits of this variety of legal induction, Collins himself in *The Law and the Lady* demonstrates the possibility and occasional desirability of a revisionist account of the evidence adduced at trial, and, thereby, the difficulties with "reading" circumstantial evidence itself. In the context of *The Law and the Lady*, the trial report as a document may not transcribe reliably, and this unreliability is symptomatic of the interpretive quandaries presented more generally by circumstantial evidence.

Causes Célèbres Transplanted

The nineteenth century brought with it a proliferation of printed sources, among them newspapers, periodicals serializing works of fiction, and even a wealth of trial pamphlets, some quite dramatically illustrated. Increasingly, private libraries began to contain not only reports of English and American trials but even accounts of historical "French trials." These latter included many stories of doubled or mistaken identity, such as "The Return of Martin Guerre," several following along the lines of the mirroring of Anne Catherick and Laura Fairlie in Collins's own *Woman in White*.[23] Such tales, although legal in substrate, presented an exterior that resembled fiction, and seemed targeted at gratifying the reader's literary sensibilities more than at accurately depicting the developments in a particular case. They derived ultimately from the extremely popular twenty-volume French collection entitled *Causes Célèbres et Intéressantes*, first published in 1734 by Lyons lawyer Francois Gayot de Pitaval.[24] As Sarah Maza has explained in *Private Lives and Public Affairs*, the work was "designed not just to satisfy the curiosity of readers"—a group that included "members of the Bar, members of society (*les gens du monde*), and even the ladies"—but also to "instruct their minds in the rules of Jurisprudence."[25] This collection quickly went through a number of editions and spawned a variety of successors, some of which were present in Collins's library.[26]

The status of the French trial, in Collins's representation, accorded in many respects with that of the French novel. The latter served the role of transporting the reader beyond the mundane confines of daily life; on the first night of his visit to American relatives in order to obtain some rest, the English lawyer-narrator of *John Jago's Ghost* explains that he "lit the candles, and took from [his] portmanteau what [he] firmly believed to have been the first French novel ever produced at Morwick Farm. It was one of the masterly and charming stories of Dumas the elder. In five minutes I was in a new world, and my melancholy room was full of the liveliest French company."[27] The French trial also functioned to absorb the reader and remove quotidian concerns; as the individual nicknamed "the Cur" in *The Guilty River* recounts in his diary or confession, "The bookseller has found a second-hand copy of the French Trials, and has sent them to me (as he expresses it) 'on approval.' 'I more than approve—I admire; and I more than admire—I imitate. These criminal stories are told with a dramatic power, which has impelled me to try if I can rival the clever French narrative. . . . I cannot remember having read any novel with a tenth part of the interest that absorbed me, in constructing my imaginary train of circumstances.'"[28] If the French novel worked to enhance sentimental distraction, the French trial instead increased morbid obsession.

English adaptations of the framework of, or cases from, the French *Causes Célèbres* demonstrated a similar suspicion of the French mode of narration yet attempted to reclaim the didactic purpose that Pitaval had articulated. These English trial reports purported to represent what had actually happened in a certain courtroom yet simultaneously refrained from simply transcribing the events that took place—some of which were recounted centuries after the fact. George Henry Borrow's *Celebrated Trials and Remarkable Cases of Criminal Jurisprudence, from the Earliest Records to the Year 1825*, which could be found in

Collins's library, proclaimed itself as the first work in the English tradition to be inspired by the French *Causes Célèbres*.[29] The 1840 volume that announced more explicitly that it constituted the *English Causes Célèbres or Reports of Remarkable Trials* was edited and illustrated by George L. Craik. Both collections' prefaces emphasized the distinctive style of the French *Causes Célèbres*, commenting on their tendency toward the sensational and their verbosity. The English versions, each insisted, would rely more faithfully on the actual material of the underlying trials, and reduce the wordiness of the French accounts. According to the preface to Borrow's *Celebrated Trials*:

> [M]ore persons praise [the French *Causes Célèbres*] than have read it; for it is altogether Gallic—light, frothy, prolix, and sentimental—and in no way adapted to the chastened taste and matter-of-fact curiosity of English readers. It is a series of novels in manner, while the editors are restrained in their fancy, by a shew of respect to the facts of each case. The articles are therefore romances in style, without those flights of imagination which render romantic compositions fascinating. . . . The best cases in that celebrated work have nevertheless been transferred to these volumes; but to adapt them to English reading, they have been stript of all their verbosity.[30]

Despite including some trials from the French *Causes Célèbres* among the wealth of English cases recounted, the collection modified the style of narration, enhancing the focus on "small points" that would lead the reader to feel as though he or she were "carried into court," and expunging as much as possible of "sentiment."[31]

Craik's 1840 preface to the *English Causes Célèbres* likewise contrasted the French volumes' emphasis on a narrative about the lives of individuals with the more procedural orientation of his own collection. As Craik explained:

> [T]he present Collection of Trials at Law will be found to differ very considerably in its plan and character from the well-known French work called the *Causes Célèbres*. In general, no attempt will be made to work up the facts of a case into the form of a regular narrative; but the Trial itself, or all of it that is interesting, will be given, rather than any story or summary extracted from or founded upon it. If this be a less ambitious design than that of the original French work, and of various continuations and imitations of it in French and other languages, it is not without some other advantages besides its more easy execution. The story may not be so artificially disposed and developed as by the other method; but it may be given as fully, and probably will be given more faithfully, from the absence of all temptation to shape or adjust the

> incidents with the view of presenting them so as to produce the most harmonious or striking effect. They are here simply set before the reader in the order and manner in which they were brought out in court at the several trials.[32]

Rather than molding the material from cases into a more traditional narrative, the *English Causes Célèbres* relied on the form of the trial and the unfolding of incidents therein to provide the plot, allowing a legal instead of a literary approach to dictate the sequence of events.

The divergence between French and English styles corresponds to a difference in the balance of sources upon which the collections relied, a difference that is not simply pragmatic but also glossed with ideology. Both English collections represented themselves as drawing quite specifically on judicial documents and, in doing so, distinguished themselves from the French *Causes Célèbres*. The front matter of *Celebrated Trials* emphasizes the value in England of the openness and accessibility of judicial proceedings and the records of them. An epigraph attributed to one "Burke"—presumably Edmund—expresses wonder that "the English language contains no book like the *Causes Célèbres* of the French particularly as the openness of our proceedings renders the records more certain and accessible."[33] As the preface then insists, the openness of proceedings and the records thereof in England should render unjust convictions and subsequent executions less common, or at least more popularly reviled:

> Examples of punishment may deter the solitary criminal, but retributive Justice is rare in regard to those who commit murders in ermine, and under the sanction of legitimate authority. . . . In our days, one salutary check is the publicity of all judicial proceedings, from the charge before the magistrate to the sentence and execution; so that if prejudices are not artfully created, and successfully maintained, flagrant acts of injustice cannot now be committed without arousing the indignation of all contemporaries.[34]

The public's ability to attend judicial proceedings as well as the publication of the records of trials and judgments thus served the function of at once making justice more transparent and holding judges more accountable.

As Jonathan Grossman has elaborated in *The Art of Alibi: English Law Courts and the Novel*, by the end of the eighteenth century, "the right of the press to report ongoing and even pretrial public court proceedings was clearly articulated," and the result was a wealth of serialized newspaper and other reports on criminal proceedings.[35] Edmund Burke himself elsewhere asserted the desirability of public judicial proceedings; in his *Report on the Lords' Journals* in relation to the trial of Warren Hastings, Burke argued vociferously that the lords should pronounce their judgment and grounds for decision in open session. According to Burke, "[A]rgued judgments publicly delivered" serve better than any alternative method the aim of "enabling the learned of the bar and all intelligent laymen, to distinguish . . . changes made for the advancement of a more solid, equitable, and substantial justice . . . from . . . hazardous changes in any of the ancient opinions and decisions."[36] Burke therefore did not aspire to alert the politician or lawyer alone of changes in legal doctrine but to apprise the general public as well. Beneath his statements lies a notion that the transparency of judicial proceedings will operate as a check on miscarriages of justice or the distortion of legal doctrine.

The *English Causes Célèbres*, as Craik explained in his preface, was similarly oriented toward increasing the publicity of certain notable trial proceedings. Craik aimed to "present . . . , in a popular form, everything that can be made generally interesting in an extensive but little explored department of our literature, the records of proceedings of all kinds in Courts of Justice," and the collection relied heavily for its composition on these documents, making "free use . . . of any reports that [could] be obtained of curious or interesting trials."[37] At the same time, the edition supplemented these reports with "all the further details of an historical, biographical, anecdotical or other miscellaneous kind into which the subject may naturally expand."[38] Nor did the narrator of the cases refrain from making judgments about the merits of their outcomes.

The story of the murder trial of Count Königsmark in 1682 provides one example of how these narratives were composed. This report commences with a background story about the genealogy of the woman for whom the murder was supposedly committed, the Lady Elizabeth Percy, proceeds to an account of the victim, her husband, and continues through the murder and the subsequent arrest of various individuals, including Count Königsmark. With this introduction completed in under fifteen pages, the style of the treatment then shifts to that of court report, including dialogue among the judicial participants that is presented as though transcribed. This dialogue is sometimes interrupted by bracketed description, such as that of the biographies of the judges presiding at the trial and other scene-setting devices. Some material is explicitly summarized as well, rather than being included verbatim. When the jury acquits Count Königsmark but condemns his purported co-conspirators, editorial statements intrude to explain that various aspects of the trial procedures leading to the Count's acquittal had generally been judged bad law. Rather than simply stopping after the approximately forty-five pages of trial, the narrative concludes where it began, with the remaining history of the woman whose existence had set the chain of circumstances in motion.[39] As Craik's references in the preface to the "scene" suggest, the description of the trial of Count Königsmark presents and contextualizes a drama of the courtroom in a form intended not for viewing but for popular reading. The reader not only hears the attitude of the advocates and judge at the trial, as jurors or observers of the court proceeding would, but also receives a retrospective account of popular and critical opinion mediated through the vantage point of the editor. The narrative thus instructs the readers as to proper and improper modes of evaluating the progress and outcome of the original trial itself.

As a mode of increasing the transparency of the trial process, this type of documentation seems rather odd. Rather than presenting the evidence in an unmediated manner, furnishing all of the materials that the reader would need to reach his or her conclusions about the case, these collections provide a particular perspective—often one benefiting from the wisdom of hindsight—on the manner in which the case unfolded, its disposition, and its aftermath. Instead of putting the reader in the same position as a judge or member of the jury, these texts situate him or her in the place that the narrator thinks those decision-makers *should have* occupied. While enhancing access to judicial proceedings in the name of publicity and transparency, these works therefore simultaneously reveal a concern that court reports will not speak for themselves—or, at least, will not speak correctly for themselves—and that the reader must therefore be guided in the direction of understanding. Mark Seltzer has persuasively argued that "[t]he world of true crime is a self-observing world of observers";[40] it could be said similarly of these collections of celebrated trials that they encourage the reader to read his or her own practices of reading cases—whether reading the evidence as it unfolds in court or reading the report of this unfolding at a later point.

The factual basis and accuracy of the narratives included are, furthermore, far from established. The works rarely cite to their own sources; some cases derive from Howell's *State Trials*, but the *State Trials* is, as John Langbein has discussed, not a model of reliability itself.[41] Nor were the compositors reluctant to capitalize on the cases' proximity to fictional representations. Other kinds of trial reports in the period often assumed the generic form of sensation stories and were publicly received with the same fervor as fiction.[42] The prefaces to several of the collections of celebrated trials likewise observe the resemblance—but superiority—of their contents to fictional narratives. As Craik notes, "[Insofar] . . . as trials at law have had for their object the investigation of crime, they are a history of passion and adventure often as exciting as any fiction, with all the impressiveness and substantial value of truth."[43] Not only do these trials include the "chain of evidence" that can hold the attention of most readers, and which Craik suggests novels like those of William Godwin, Henry Fielding, or Daniel Defoe replicate, but they also are able to convincingly incorporate "an incident, or combination of incidents" that "may have actually occurred, and yet may be too strange and singular to be invented or supposed without violating the probabilities of fiction."[44] The title of the 1852 *Romance of the Forum, or, Narratives, Scenes, and Anecdotes from Courts of Justice*, contained in Collins's library and similar in many respects to the other celebrated trials collections, explicitly draws the analogy between the trial and the romance.[45] As Peter Burke, the lawyer who edited the work, explains, "[t]he reality displayed bears that affinity to romance which scenes produced by nature sometimes do to buildings that are the work of man."[46] Because these "narratives of justice" are "themselves so wild and wonderful," they are better presented unembellished than in a fictionalized version. These accounts of the relationship between legal and literary narratives suggest that it was less the veracity of the trial reports that the compositors valued than the ability to claim that they had depicted facts and had thereby surpassed fictional representations.[47]

Even the identity of some of the collections' editors suggests the tenuous line between fact and fiction. George Craik became a professor of English later in life.[48] George Borrow, who had articled with a solicitor, would likewise become a novelist subsequent to creating the *Celebrated Trials*, the task of compiling which he believed had, in part, taught him how to write.[49] Legal texts here spawned a mode of reading that would itself lead to literary writing.

The genre of the *Causes Célèbres* underwent yet one more conversion as it was transplanted into the American context in the form of the 1836 *Celebrated*

Trials of All Countries and Remarkable Cases of Criminal Jurisprudence selected by an anonymous "Member of the Philadelphia Bar."[50] This work adopted the same epigraph from Burke as *Celebrated Trials* would subsequently employ. Although the title of this edition suggests an international orientation, the collection largely comprehended English cases with French, German, and American ones sprinkled throughout. The preface envisions the audience as including lawyers, doctors, and the "general reader," and it both emphasizes the quality of its sources, with "recourse . . . had occasionally to manuscripts where printed documents could not be procured" and the preservation of what might otherwise be ephemeral records of trials.[51] As in the *Celebrated Trials*, the editor invokes the specter of unjust prosecutions, and he suggests that the collection furnishes examples of how to defend against them.[52]

In proclaiming its compilation by a member of the bar and its reliance on detailed sources, *Celebrated Trials of All Countries* conformed to a more general tendency of American trial pamphlets, which often announced the professional authority—despite anonymity—of those involved in producing the reports and emphasized the steps taken to render them accurate. The title pages and front matter of these pamphlets contained assurances of authenticity such as "Impartially taken by a Gentleman of the Profession," or "The following Report, although unsupported by a name, is given to the public with an assurance that it is impartial, correct, and minute—and what need a preface say more?" or "From the Short-Hand Notes of Marsh & Osbourne, Official Reporters of the Courts."[53] The same documents would, however, sometimes acknowledge their own possible errors; as the preface to the report of the 1871 trial of murderess Laura Fair, who had shot her married lover in front of his family, explained, "[b]elieving that this report of the proceedings on the trial will prove worthy the consideration not only of members of the Bar, to whom it will be invaluable, but, also, to the public generally; and hoping that a generous public will overlook and excuse the little inaccuracies to which we have already adverted, the volume is respectfully submitted by THE PUBLISHERS."[54] Rather than detracting from the overall impression of the text's authority, however, such disclaimers suggested that assiduous efforts had contributed to rendering the reports nearly perfect; any blemishes found on their pages emanated not from rampant fictionalizing tendencies but instead from inevitable obstacles to comprehensive transcription.

The very fact that the volumes of *Celebrated Trials* or *Causes Célèbres* comprised collections distinguished them, however, from the other trial pamphlets of the period, each of which generally focused on one particular case. Although both kinds of texts retained connections to fiction, the editorial stance embodied in the prefaces to the collections and in their compositional style was more conducive to reflecting on and intervening in the experience of the reader.

Circumstantial Evidence and Factual Precedents

The transplant of the French *Causes Célèbres* onto English and American soil occasioned another extremely important transformation—a shift from the treatment of a broad range of civil and other disputes to an exclusive focus on criminal prosecutions.[55] In England, this corresponded to a set of law reform efforts aimed at bringing to light the harms that might arise from relying on circumstantial evidence to convict and execute a defendant. Samuel March Phillips's 1815 treatise on *The Theory of Presumptive Proof; or, an Inquiry into the Nature of Circumstantial Evidence* announced itself as the first work in English to treat the nature of circumstantial evidence.[56] In this work, Phillips cast doubts upon the prevalent assumption of "the certainty of circumstantial evidence," objecting to it on three grounds: first, that it contradicted accepted jurisprudence, particularly that of the civil law; second, that experience demonstrated circumstantial evidence had led to the false conviction of a number of individuals; and, third, that only recently had English law insisted on the priority of "circumstances" over evaluation of the testimony of witnesses, the medium through which these circumstances could be ascertained.[57] The second reason—the risk of false conviction—provides much of the force of Phillips's argument, and motivates his selection of an exemplary case of a criminal prosecution based upon circumstantial evidence, that of Captain Donellan in 1781.[58] A range of cases summarized at the end of the treatise likewise primarily suggests that incautious deployment of circumstantial evidence leads to the death of innocent individuals.[59]

These appended case studies display a resemblance in tone and subject matter to some of the reports provided by the celebrated trials collections. The narrative given in the most detail in *Celebrated Trials of All Countries*, for example, is that of Captain Donellan, and a short final section on "Circumstantial

Evidence" includes five of the cases from Phillips's treatise almost verbatim.[60] Other collections of cases that bear no explicit relation to the *Causes Célèbres* appear slanted in a similar direction; an undated and anonymously edited *Cases of Circumstantial Evidence* not only comprehends some of the same materials as Phillips included, but also moralizes quite explicitly, both attacking false convictions and more generally lamenting the ills of capital punishment, which hinders the correction of mistakes occasioned by proof from circumstantial evidence. After one postconviction discovery that a supposed victim was not even dead, and by no means had been murdered, the narrative concludes that "this wonderful [but true] explanation was told to the judge and jury who tried the cause, and it is probable they never after convicted a man on *circumstantial* evidence."[61] The collection itself ends on a note not of caution but of abolition, stating:

> It is to be trusted, that, not alone from the chance of condemning a wrong party, but from general motives of humanity and a consideration of the utter uselessness of public executions in the way of example, capital punishments will ere long be numbered among the extinct barbarisms of a past age, and other and more rational means adopted for maintaining the integrity of the law and the peace of society.[62]

Hence, in at least some instances, the critique of circumstantial evidence underlies a reformist effort to abolish the death penalty itself.

The audience and readership of these case collections is not, however, self-conceived by the compilers to be legislators or those equipped to transform legal doctrine from above, but rather jurors and others who, although seemingly cogs within the wheels of the legal system, might be able collectively to change the direction of the entire leviathan's motion. The clearest evidence of this orientation is provided by the preface to *Celebrated Trials*, one of the works in Collins's own library. In addition to lauding the publicity of judicial proceedings as a check on the arbitrariness or misuse of judicial authority, the preface maintains that juries should serve to prevent the kinds of "legal murders" that "have in bad times disgraced our past annals."[63] The capacity of a jury to stem the flow of injustice derives from the variety of experiences that its members bring to bear upon the trial; to enhance this effect, "[t]he circle of judges ought therefore to be enlarged as much as possible, and the feelings of one caste, attempered by those of another, such as that of jurors drawn from the body of the people, in contrast with that circle in which live and move the permanent officers of tribunals."[64] Expanding the range of those entitled to exercise legal judgment thus minimizes the potential for particular prejudices to coalesce into an erroneous verdict.

At the same time, however, the preface does not suggest that jurors are entirely to be trusted to their own devices; instead, they should be educated about the responsibilities that their role entails. The preface therefore concludes with Sir Richard Phillips's Golden Rules for Jurymen and states that "the perusal of them will enable Jurors to understand their duties, and thereby perform them with intelligence and integrity."[65] Among these rules can be found one concerning the perils of relying too much on circumstantial evidence. As Rule 11 reads:

> Every juryman should be specially cautious of convicting persons on evidence merely presumptive and circumstantial; the conviction and legal punishment are positive, and so, as far as possible, ought to be the proofs: no reasoning, however ingenious, and no circumstances, however corresponding, being equivalent to one positive proof, either in behalf of, or against the accused. Doubt ought to produce a verdict of *not guilty*.[66]

This rule encapsulates the principal lesson suggested by many of the case reports involving false convictions—the notion that a chain of circumstances alone, without further support for a guilty verdict, should leave room for a reasonable doubt, and therefore for acquittal.

If the ideal reader of collections of cases like the *Celebrated Trials* is a jury member—or, in the context of the female reader not permitted to serve, a relative or friend of the jury member—then what, exactly, is the function of these works? One purpose is, as the prefaces' frequent references to the resemblance and superiority of these narratives to fiction makes clear, to entertain. Another aim is, however, to provide a kind of *precedent*—not a precedent in the modern sense of a case providing a rule for judges to follow, but instead *factual precedents* for consideration by jury members and for application to new trials. Certain of these precedents were, in a sense, canonized, by their inclusion in a variety of compilations, whereas others dropped out. And many of the precedents, although not all, involved elaborate demonstrations of induction—and erroneous induction—from individual pieces of circumstantial evidence. These precedents thereby furnished examples for jurors of how to weigh and consider the evidence adduced at trial or, in the alternative, prior mistakes to avoid. Those who would eventually become jurors would thus read surrogate decision-makers themselves reading and misreading circumstantial evidence.

The treatment of these kinds of cases as precedent emerges in two very different sources—the volume on circumstantial evidence in Jeremy Bentham's *Rationale of Judicial Evidence* and the argument to the jury in the Billings trial that Moak had sent to Collins. Bentham's treatise is addressed more to the legislator and the judge than to the juror, whom he refers to as a "sort of ephemeral judge."[67] Furthermore, because he deems few modifications to the law of circumstantial evidence necessary, and, in general, defends granting judges broad discretion to admit and consider all relevant circumstantial evidence, he explains that his work should be read as though it were "instructions . . . *from* the legislator"—or "the fountain of all authority"—"to the judge."[68] Circumstantial evidence, which is contrasted throughout with the direct evidence provided by a witness, constitutes a necessary part of any case in which "the body of proof . . . stands in need of any *inference* (though it be but a single inference, and that ever so close and necessary a one)."[69] Defining circumstantial evidence as that from which a judge or jury must make inferences to arrive at the fact to be proved places the evidentiary demonstration in the space between the witness and the decision-maker, as the latter can make circumstantial evidence even of what is offered simply as direct testimony. Bentham speaks to this point when he observes:

> The testimony of a witness operates as circumstantial evidence, not only in regard to all facts which, not having been actually perceived by him, are by him inferred from facts which he has perceived: his testimony (or at least the fact of his giving utterance to such testimony) may operate further in the character of circumstantial evidence, in regard to facts which have neither been perceived nor inferred by *him*, but which are inferred by the *judge*, from the fact of his having uttered the testimony. In this case, the evidentiary fact is not the testimony itself, but the delivery of it by the witness.[70]

Bentham thus deconstructs the opposition between direct and circumstantial evidence, displacing the priority of the former over the latter and indicating that neither provides direct access to truth and each merely supplies a different medium through which the judge can grasp at the "facts." Even "real evidence," which might seem to penetrate through the problems of interpretation, cannot be construed as invariably furnishing the facts, as it may itself prove susceptible to forgery.[71] The best "real evidence" to be discovered is, indeed, that which the jury sees upon the face or in the manner of testifying witnesses, which may allow them to discern whether or not these individuals are lying.[72] The circumstantial evidence that emerges from the manner in which direct evidence is given thereby also becomes real evidence itself.

Although presenting extremely valuable analyses of the relationship between the novel and the law of evidence in the Victorian period, both Alexander Welsh's *Strong Representations* and Jan-Melissa Schramm's *Testimony and Advocacy in Victorian Law, Literature, and Theology* tend to underestimate the extent to which Bentham, in particular, blurs the distinction between direct and circumstantial evidence and focuses instead on the relationship between evidence and its interpreter. Despite Welsh's acknowledgment that "[a]ll evidence . . . has to be read or interpreted as such," he concentrates on the narrative strategy of "strong representation"—or, in other words, the kinds of representations in "the later eighteenth and nineteenth centuries that openly distrust direct testimony, insist on submitting witnesses to the test of corroborating circumstances, and claim to know many things without anyone's having seen them at all."[73] Welsh further connects strong representations with prosecutors' and judges' attempts to create a persuasive explanation of the evidence in a case for the jury.[74] Schramm, by contrast, recuperates the role of testimony not only in the proof of fact in criminal cases but also in the rise of the third-person realist novel, connecting these historical developments with John Langbein's accounts of the role of the accused's testimony and the late arrival of defense counsel in the English criminal trial.[75] Neither of these treatments attends sufficiently to the relationship between the fact-finder and the evidence presented.

Because the probative force of evidence derives, for Bentham, less from whether it is direct, circumstantial, or real than from how it is probed and evaluated in the judge's or jury's construction of a narrative of what has occurred, he claims that an increase in the experience of exercising judgment rather than inflexible rules will improve the accuracy of verdicts. He therefore writes:

> In the history of law, be the country what it may,—the further we go back, the more numerous the instances we may expect to find of convictions and executions on insufficient evidence: but, for the opposite reason, the longer we go on in the track of civilization, the more rare we may expect to find the instances of such errors in judicature as have the weakness of the mental faculties for their cause. It is in the

> strength which, by the continually-increasing stock of information, may be given to the mental faculties of judges by apposite instructions drawn from correct and comprehensive views of the subject, that the true preservative against such errors is to be looked for: not in the restrictive operation of unbending rules of evidence.[76]

Given this posture, it would not be surprising for Bentham to endorse the deployment of celebrated trials collections to educate prospective jurors by providing factual precedents for the types of cases they might be asked in future to decide.

Although Bentham does not explicitly adopt such a position, he does cite the French *Causes Célèbres* throughout the text.[77] Bentham also extracts further examples from the anonymous *Treatise on Circumstantial Evidence*, focusing, in particular, on the case of Captain Donnellan, aspects of which he analyzes on numerous occasions.[78] In his allusions to this and other cases, Bentham several times observes that he is not concerned with the actual truth or falsity of the report, but rather with the principle that it exemplifies. Referring at one point to a "case which, whether real or fictitious, is famous in the history of French jurisprudence," he subsequently explains that "English law affords a story, which, whether meant for truth or jest, may alike serve for exemplification."[79] Both real and fictional narratives—including even a story from the *Arabian Nights*—can illuminate the problems presented by and proper mode of analyzing circumstantial evidence.[80]

Bentham's deployment of these exemplary cases demonstrates that the examples they provide are not univocal, and that these factual precedents, like legal precedents, could be mustered in service of conflicting or, at least, disparate, arguments. Treating the *Treatise on Circumstantial Evidence* and Donnellan's case renders it necessary for Bentham to deal with the claim that circumstantial evidence can lead to false convictions and the execution of the innocent. His response is that substantive law, not procedure, is to blame, and that the death penalty itself should be abolished directly instead of shifting procedure to minimize its impact. Discussing whether the desire of a defendant in a capital case for the production of character testimony in his favor should override the judge's discretionary judgment not to admit such evidence, Bentham opines that "the measure indicated" is "[n]ot the making the admission of this species compulsory, even in this case, but the forbearing to employ a mode of punishment, which in this as well as every other point of view is adverse to the interest of justice, favourable to them in none."[81] Treating the question of whether rules constraining the weight the decision-maker can give certain evidence should be established at least when the punishment will be irreversible, a set of cases for which the death penalty provides the paradigm, Bentham similarly writes: "But, of the consideration of this irreparability, what is the true result? The impropriety of this mode of punishment: not the propriety of those unbending rules."[82] Putting in place rules for the admission of evidence would thus be merely a poor substitute for fixing the law of punishment by eliminating the death penalty. Rather than endorsing the lesson other reformers drew from the cases in which false convictions led to execution—that circumstantial evidence should not be relied upon as the sole basis for such a conviction—Bentham instead extracted from them another lesson: that the death penalty itself should be eliminated.

The prosecutor Moak, who cited extensively to Bentham in the argument that he sent to Collins and adduced a number of authorities to convince the jurors that no difference existed in principle between direct and circumstantial evidence, and that they could legitimately follow a chain of evidence through to the verdict of guilty, also referred often to particular prior cases.[83] Focusing more on contemporary trial pamphlets than on the *Causes Célèbres* or their transplanted versions, Moak mustered these examples for a variety of ends, sometimes quoting from other judges' instructions to juries about how to weigh circumstantial evidence, sometimes supporting the propriety of his own production of evidence through the examples of prior cases, and, on one occasion, deploying the popularly reviled result of acquittal in a previous trial to urge the current jurors not to make the same mistake.[84] As Moak explained to his audience about the recent case of *People v. Cunningham*, "You recollect that that was a trial depending mainly upon circumstantial evidence. As to the *injustice* of the verdict, few who have ever considered the case, except the jury, have doubted. However, such things do sometimes strangely occur, and all we can say is, that they are incident to humanity. In that case few ever have doubted that a guilty woman escaped."[85] Moak here assumed a retrospective perspective on the verdict similar to that which the collections of celebrated trials had adopted—but his critique emphasized the under- rather than overvaluation of circumstantial evidence and, therefore, the acquittal of the guilty instead of the conviction of the innocent.

Maintaining that the jurors should rely on their own previous range of experience as a guide for judgment in the present case, Moak also explained the resemblance between reading and the deciphering of circumstantial evidence:

> For centuries, yes, for ages, if geology be true, the lightnings had played in the heavens and men were awed and shrank from their sight. Morse came with a capacity to read their laws, and he chained them, and taught them to carry our messages of affection, our messages of fortune and misfortune to friends thousands of miles away. When nature is correctly read she never deceives. . . . The only question for us to consider is, whether we have really read nature rightly or whether we are mistaken. The same Providence that, when we lay our heads upon the pillow at night, keeps the blood surging through our system to build up exhausted nature, with laws more certain than the laws of the Medes and Persians, has decreed that the man who commits a crime shall leave behind him some trail, shall throw around himself little circumstances which, if rightly read, point almost invariably to the guilty man.[86]

Whether employing their own experience or case reports as factual precedents for the situation at hand, jurors should, according to Moak, apply techniques of reading that they have honed in other areas to their evaluation of the case presented. For Moak, reading may entail difficulty but never impossibility; circumstantial evidence, like nature, operates according to a logic and law of its own that may readily be deciphered once the key is found. Here the doubts about the very possibility of providing a definitive "reading" of circumstantial evidence that had emerged in earlier treatises and collections of cases has been entirely effaced. In its stead stands a scientific vision of reading, through which a truth of nature can be ascertained.

Reading Trials in *The Law and the Lady*

In a number of novels, Collins explored legal documents and their newly expanded readership. Several of his works depict libraries containing legal volumes, which novice readers encounter for the first time. Whereas Collins himself, having been legally trained at Lincoln's Inn, could digest some of the more technical dimensions of works like Moak's "Argument,"[87] his novels represent a range of readers more or less capable of evaluating the legal texts they undertake. What emerges is an immanent critique of the belief that law will inevitably become more transparent with its increased accessibility to the ordinary reader, or that writing will itself render the representation of law more accurate. Instead, the very textuality of these legal documents may impede access to the posited "underlying" facts or law. Likewise, the process of translating the trial from event into text inevitably introduces error. At the same time, however, the critical reader, even if a novice, will ask the appropriate questions of the text and arrive herself at a less than credulous response to the document in question.

In the 1875 novel *The Law and the Lady*, the heroine Valeria Woodville is perplexed as to the nature of a secret that seems to be plaguing her husband, Mr. Eustace Woodville, aka (as she has already discovered) Eustace Macallan. Finding herself, on account of youth and attractiveness, with some sway over one of her husband's old friends, Major Fitz-David, Valeria persuades him to give her access to the possibility of discovering her husband's secret. Major Fitz-David does so by allowing Valeria free rein of his library for several hours. While Valeria first assumes that the clue must be provided by an object or letter contained within this room—focusing in particular on a peculiar vase—she suddenly realizes that "the clue might quite as probably present itself in the form of a book."[88] As Valeria subsequently recounts her process of searching:

> I looked along the lower rows of shelves; standing just near enough to them to read the titles on the backs of the volumes. I saw Voltaire in red morocco; Shakespeare in blue; Walter Scott in green; the History of England in brown; the Annual Register in yellow calf. There I paused, wearied and discouraged already by the long rows of volumes. How (I thought to myself) am I to examine all these books? And what am I to look for, even if I do examine them all?[89]

As she moves to higher shelves with the aid of a library ladder, Valeria discovers less uniform books, "some . . . bound in cloth; some . . . only protected by paper covers" as well as "empty spaces from which books had been removed and not replaced."[90] She eventually alights upon a cupboard with a large, "gorgeously-bound book," encased in blue velvet with "clasps of silver in beautiful arabesque patterns" and an accompanying silver lock.[91] Much to Valeria's disappointment and disgust, this volume contains not the secret for which she is searching but instead locks of hair documenting each of Major Fitz-David's female conquests. Almost giving up in despair at this point, Valeria is then interrupted by Major Fitz-David's current paramour, who storms into the room and launches a verbal assault. This jealous fit has fortuitous consequences.

When Valeria explains that she is simply in the library looking for a volume, rather than attempting to insinuate herself into the Major's good graces, the girl inquires, "Stop a bit! I wonder whether *that's* the book you have been looking after? Are you like me? Do you like reading Trials?" Valeria's response is to think, "Trials? Had I heard her aright? Yes: she had said, Trials."[92] The girl then recovers the volume from a space between the bookcase and the wall where it had fallen, and hands it to Valeria, accompanied with the statement, "I've read it twice over—I have. Mind you, *I* believe he did it, after all."[93] When Valeria looks at the title page, she is struck by horror and immediately faints. It reads: "A Complete Report of/ The trial of/ Eustace Macallan/ For the alleged poisoning/ of/ His Wife."[94] Although Macallan had not been convicted, he had not been acquitted either, but had suffered from the ignominy of what is called a "Scotch verdict," or the verdict of "not proven" rather than "not guilty." When Eustace discovers that his new wife has learned of his past and of his prior identity, he flees, too ashamed to face her again.

This chain of events leads Valeria to an increased resolution, and she determines to get to the bottom of the circumstances leading to Eustace's first wife's death and to demonstrate her husband's innocence. In service of this pursuit, she reads the entirety of the trial. Although an active and emotionally engaged reader from the beginning—as demonstrated by the fainting fit she had upon seeing the title page as well as an episode in which she admits to having torn out and trampled underfoot some displeasing pages of the report—Valeria is initially somewhat naive. She believes, for instance, the claims of the report to be especially accurate, claims that echo those of actual trial pamphlets, including ones to which Collins himself might have been exposed on his recent visit to America as well as after his return. As she recounts:

> Turning to the second page of the Trial, I found a Note, assuring the reader of the absolute correctness of the Report of the Proceedings. The compiler described himself as having enjoyed certain privileges. Thus, the presiding Judge had himself revised his charge to the Jury. And, again, the chief lawyers for the prosecution and the defence, following the Judge's example, had revised their speeches, for, and against, the prisoner. Lastly, particular care had been taken to secure a literally correct report of the evidence given by various witnesses. It was some relief to me to discover this Note, and to be satisfied at the outset that the Story of the Trial was, in every particular, fully and truly told.[95]

Rather than suspecting that the judge and lawyers might have taken the opportunity for revision to embellish rather than render accurate, Valeria gives credence to the account that the reporter provided.

It is revealed later in the novel that this faith was at least partially misplaced. As Valeria digs behind the text of the trial report into the nature of the witnesses' accounts and the background circumstances of the case, she discovers that the trial had been rendered logical and readable at some cost. One of the chief witnesses for the defense had been a friend of Eustace's, the aptly named Misserrimus Dexter, a man depicted as beautiful in his upper body yet lacking legs. Whereas his testimony had seemed quite convincing in the context of the report, Valeria soon discovers that he is plagued by episodes of insanity. Conversing with her mother-in-law, who has claimed that "in asking Dexter's advice . . . you appropriately consult a madman," Valeria responds, "You surprise me very much. . . . Mr Dexter's evidence, given at the Trial, seems as clear and reasonable as evidence can be."[96] Mrs. Macallan's more sophisticated understanding of the nature of trial reports emerges from her response. To Valeria's expression of surprise, her mother-in-law replies:

> Of course it is! The shorthand writers and reporters put his evidence into presentable language, before they printed it. If you had heard what he really said, as I did, you would have been either very much disgusted with him, or very much amused by him, according to your way of looking at things.[97]

The trial report thus forces the evidence into a coherent unity, at the expense of an accurate representation of the witnesses' testimony. The source for Collins's question to Moak about whether he might have felt anxious or nervous or was ever less than coherent—circumstances not evident from the text of his argument—thus begins to emerge.

During the course of the novel, Valeria's investigations teach her to be a critical reader of the trial report, refusing to accept the statements contained therein at face value. At the same time, however, the novel represents the naive reader as potentially endowed with characteristics that will enable her to discover "truth" more effectively than the professional. In particular, Valeria undertakes methods of inquiry that professionals are represented as disdaining.[98] A conversation with her uncle demonstrates the skeptical view on the inappropriateness of her endeavors. When she explains that she intends to clear Eustace of the imputations cast by the "not proven" verdict, he responds: "In plain English . . . you are conceited enough to think that you can succeed where the greatest lawyers in Scotland have failed. *They* couldn't prove this man's innocence, all working together. And *you* are going to prove it single-handed?"[99] The two principal techniques she intends to employ are reading the trial report itself to form a hypothesis about what actually happened to Eustace's first wife, and re-examining the witnesses. Upon telling her uncle that she plans to read the trial, he exclaims, affirming the connection between the legal and novelistic narrative and between English and French variants: "Nice reading for a young woman! You will be wanting a batch of nasty French novels next."[100] Valeria's goal in inspecting the trial is explicitly, however, one of reading against the grain; rather than accepting the legal truth established by the trial, she will employ it to "form some conclusion . . . as to the guilty person who really committed the crime."[101] After developing this account of what actually happened, Valeria will test her theory by seeking out witnesses who spoke in Eustace's favor and "ask[ing] all sorts of questions which grave lawyers might think it beneath their dignity to put."[102] This interrogation technique would have been endorsed by Bentham himself, who ridiculed English lawyers for not approving of or employing it more vigorously. In a section on "interrogation, as an instrument for supplying the deficiencies of Real Evidence," Bentham opined: "[T]he way to know is to inquire: a proposition that from the beginning of the world to the present day has never been a secret to any human being, unless it be to English lawyers."[103] It therefore appears precisely to be Valeria's nonprofessional role that allows her access to a truth that law has proved ineffectual in discovering.

The particularities of Valeria's identity affect her reading of the trial itself and allow her to approach the evidence from a vantage point that the original judge and jury would have lacked. Because of her allegiance to her husband, Valeria possesses a pre-existing belief in his innocence. As she insists to Eustace before even reading the trial report, "It is quite enough for me that I know you are innocent. When a man is innocent, there *must* be a way of proving it: the one thing needful is to find the way."[104] This belief does not simply prejudice Valeria in his favor, but it additionally leads her to evaluate the evidence provided by the trial report with the aim of achieving his acquittal in mind. It is, in large part, because of her continued faith in Eustace's innocence that Valeria sets in motion a set of events that culminate in the discovery and reconstruction of fragments of a letter in which the first Mrs. Macallan confesses to have, in fact, committed suicide upon discovering from her husband's diary—shown to her through the deviousness of Dexter—that he did not love her. The confidence that Valeria experiences allows her to serve as a much better advocate on Eustace's behalf than his original lawyers had been, and it permits her to pursue productive lines of investigation that had previously been neglected.

The editorial statements that Valeria makes during the reading of the trial report suggest both her ability to comprehend the attitude of the jurors and the slight remove from their perspective that she occupies. Her remarks also reaffirm that evaluation of the evidence calls for common sense more than professional qualifications. As she interjects at one point in the narrative, "Ignorant as I was of the law, I could see what impression the evidence (so far) was intended to produce on the minds of the Jury."[105] A little further on she verges on despair, explaining, "So far, I must own, the effect on me of reading the Report was to depress my spirits, and to lower my hopes. The whole weight of the evidence, at the close of the second day, was against my husband. Woman, as I was, and partisan as I was, I could plainly see that."[106] After most of the witnesses for the defense have been called, Valeria likewise observes that "[it] required no lawyer's eye to discern the fatal defect which was now revealed in the evidence for the defence. Every intelligent person present could see that the prisoner's chance of an honourable acquittal depended on tracing the poison to the possession of his wife—or at least on proving her expressed intention to obtain it."[107] Although not a professional reader, Valeria thus insists upon her ability to comprehend the evidence and refuses to situate herself in the same position as the jurors.

As her reference to herself as "woman" indicates, Valeria also views the difference between her gender and that of the jurors as significant. At the conclusion of the trial, the jurors deliberated for an hour before reaching the "not proven" verdict.[108] According to Valeria's aside, "A jury of women would not have taken a minute!," presumably to acquit.[109] Not only her personal interest in the case, but also her gender thereby affects Valeria's interpretation of the trial as recounted in the report.

Just as Collins opposed the novelist's perspective to the lawyer's in his letter to Moak, Valeria's vantage point as the "lady" is opposed to that of the "lawyers" and even the jurors in *The Law and the Lady*. Although eventually the lawyer

Mr. Playmore, one of Eustace's agents in the trial, assists in discovering and then reconstructing the letter that reveals Eustace's innocence, the lady provides a necessary supplement to the law in ascertaining the truth of the situation.[110] Like Collins himself in his reading of Moak's argument, Valeria investigates the characters behind the trial, exploring what lies beneath the persuasive facade of the trial report. Like Collins, too, she is attuned to the consequences of the verdict for the defendant, a man who happens here to be her husband. Valeria's emotion, her conviction, and her techniques of investigation are all represented as conducing to the eventual disclosure of what actually happened. Under this reading, the law needs the lady and cannot be complete without her contrasting vantage point.

Another reading, however, suggests the differential rather than opposing relationship between the law and the lady, and between the legal and novelistic narrative. According to this reading, the "truth" that Valeria and the novel itself establish remains no more definitive than that articulated in the trial report. The reader of the novel, too, must, on this reading, become, like Valeria, a critical reader of law and literature.[111]

On the one hand, *The Law and the Lady* contains and critiques the trial report—a trial report that resembles the Scottish one of the murder trial of Madeleine Smith, which had ended in a verdict of "not proven," that Collins had requested from his friend and solicitor, William Tindell, in preparation for writing the novel.[112] On the other hand, *The Law and the Lady*'s own form recalls that of the *Celebrated Trials* collections and other works evaluating and criticizing the uses of circumstantial evidence. Like these legal documents, the novel adopts a retrospective standpoint, analyzing the presentation of evidence and the jurors' judgment from hindsight. Similarly, the novel attempts to establish the innocence of a defendant upon whom the imputation of guilt was falsely cast. Rather than arriving at the tragic recognition of innocence after the execution of the supposed perpetrator, however, the novel instead substitutes the lesser verdict of "not proven" to avert the ultimate irreversibility of death. A certain indelible stain upon Eustace's reputation does, however, remain at the conclusion, because, on Valeria's urging, Eustace refrains from opening and publicizing the letter from his first wife confessing her suicide, and, therefore, fails to clear himself.

The underlying narrative itself bears a significant relation not only to the trial of Madeleine Smith, but also to the case of Captain Donellan, which appeared widely throughout the celebrated trials collections, and had also been the subject of two contemporaneous shorthand reports.[113] Captain Donellan was accused and convicted of killing his brother-in-law through administering arsenic in the form of a supposed dose of medicine. Eustace Macallan was similarly tried for giving his wife arsenic through her composing draught and later a cup of tea. In each case, the victim was in bed suffering from a minor ailment at the time. The evidence suggesting the culpability of the poisoners was, in both instances, entirely circumstantial in nature.

In *The Law and the Lady*, Valeria is represented as emulating a court of appeal, which would serve to review the original verdict and acquit her husband. She therefore assents when her mother-in-law inquires: "Your notion of turning yourself into a Court of Appeal for a new Trial of Eustace, and forcing the world to pronounce a just verdict on him. Do you really mean to try it?"[114] Works like *The Theory of Presumptive Proof* adopted a similar perspective on the Donellan case, demonstrating how the verdict of the jury in that instance had resulted in a miscarriage of justice. Collins's novel thus resembles a particular type of legal writing prevalent at the time.

Nor does Collins attempt to establish for his own work a veneer of accuracy smoother than that of legal documents. Although the reader learns of Eustace's innocence at the end of the novel, and is asked by Valeria to "think kindly of Eustace, for my sake,"[115] his wife's responsibility for her own death is established by a text that, even when fully reconstructed, bears the marks of incompleteness. After various inquiries, the fragments of the letter are discovered in the dust heap at Eustace's ancestral residence, Gleninch. Although the lawyer, Mr. Playmore, and Valeria's uncle's former clerk, Benjamin, engage in a valiant and nominally successful effort to reconstruct it, the letter in final form remains accompanied by several footnoted disclaimers, explaining that "we have been obliged to supply lost words" although "the utmost pains have been taken to supply the deficiency in exact accordance with what appeared to be the meaning of the writer, as indicated in the existing pieces of the manuscript."[116] The materiality of the written text remains an impediment to transparency not only in the trial report contained within the novel but even in the context of the truth that Valeria believes to have been established at the conclusion of the narrative.

The collections of celebrated trials suggest the possibility of honing the experience of the lay reader upon particular factual precedents, and, in doing so, encourage the creation of a new kind of juror. Collins similarly depicts Valeria's progress from naive to critical reader in *The Law and the Lady*; Valeria provides the model of a reader who would ask, as Collins did of Moak, how the protagonists experienced the trial, and how it ended. Collins simultaneously indicates, however, that the critical reader must recognize the impact of the form in which law appears upon her experience of it and must read while acknowledging the secrets that the text retains. In the wake of each reading, a remainder persists, one that may create an incentive for ever more texts of explanation and simplification, but will never be entirely exhausted.

Notes

I am extremely grateful to the participants in the "Secrets of Law" seminar at Amherst for their responses to this paper and am indebted as well to the comments of Ayelet Ben-Yishai, Amalia Kessler, Doug Kysar, Simon Stern, and Jim Whitman. I would like to thank the former director of the Cornell Law Library, Professor Claire Germain, former collections manager Brian Eden, and research librarian Thomas Mills, as well as former research librarian Julie Jones, for their invaluable assistance with materials from the law library's Trials Collection as well as other sources.

1. Stephanos Bibas, "Transparency and Participation in Criminal Procedure," *New York University Law Review* 81 (2006): 911, 917.

2. Dan Esty, "Good Governance at the Supranational Scale: Globalizing Administrative Law," *Yale Law Journal* 115 (2006): 1490, 1530.

3. Thomas N. Hale and Anne-Marie Slaughter, "Transparency: Possibilities and Limitations," *Fletcher Forum on World Affairs* 30 (2006): 153.

4. Ibid.; Mark Fenster, "The Opacity of Transparency," *Iowa Law Review* 91 (2006): 885.

5. See Patrick Birkinshaw, "Freedom of Information and Openness: Fundamental Human Rights?" *Administrative Law Review* 58 (2006): 177, 189–90. ("Access to information is a component of transparency, but the latter also entails conducting affairs in the open or subject to public scrutiny. It means keeping observable records of official decisions and activities [for subsequent access]. Transparency includes the provision of reasoned explanations for decisions, the giving of adequate reasons when power affecting the public weal or individuals is exercised in a negative or positive fashion. It also means

making processes of governance and lawmaking as accessible and as comprehensible as possible—to simplify them so that they are more easily understood by the public. Complexity, disorder, and secrecy are all features that transparency seeks to combat.")

6. The manuscript of this letter, which has not been previously published, is contained in *Closing Argument of Nathaniel C. Moak* (Albany, NY: Weed, Parsons and Co., 1879), available in the Trials Collection of the Cornell Law Library.

7. Ibid.

8. As one of Collins's biographers described the novelist's route in America, "After spending a few days with Fechter at the beginning of October on his small Pennsylvania farm, he opened his tour with Readings in a number of towns in New York State, including Troy, Syracuse, Albany and Rochester." Kenneth Robinson, *Wilkie Collins: A Biography* (London: Bodley Head, 1951): 267. Collins himself wrote from Albany on October 8, 1873, that he had "'read' here, last night, for the first time. The story so riveted the audience that not a soul stirred—and even when there was an alarm of fire in the neighbourhood, and the alarm-bell ringing outside!" Letter from Wilkie Collins to Dion Boucicault, October 8, 1873, in William Baker, Andrew Gasson, Graham Law, and Paul Lewis, eds., *The Public Face of Wilkie Collins: The Collected Letters*, vol. 2 (London: Pickering and Chatto, 2005): 420.

9. Collins's letters from this time period indicate that he had just completed the novel *Heart and Science*. Letter from Wilkie Collins to Frances Power Cobbe, April 24, 1883, in Baker et al., *The Public Face of Wilkie Collins*, vol. 3: 402.

10. Collins appears to have traveled for about a week with Edward Pigott in the yacht *Phyllis*. Letter from Wilkie Collins to A. P. Watt, July 20, 1883, in ibid., vol. 3: 422–23; letter from Wilkie Collins to A. P. Watt, July 27, 1883, in ibid., vol. 3: 423; letter from Wilkie Collins to Edward Pigott, August 1, 1883, in ibid., vol. 2: 461.

11. The transcription from the manuscript is mine. Indecipherable or ambiguous words are bracketed.

12. One of Collins's characters expressed a strangely similar sentiment with regard to his own fate after reading French trials and conceiving the idea of emulating them. As the individual who calls himself "the Cur" inquires of his own circumstances, "How will it end?" Wilkie Collins, *The Guilty River*, in *Miss or Mrs?, The Haunted Hotel, The Guilty River*, Norman Page and Toru Sasaki, eds. (Oxford: Oxford University Press, 1999): 272.

13. Stephen Roger Fischer discusses the dynamics of nineteenth-century travel reading in *A History of Reading* (Chicago: Reaktion Books, 2004): 291–92.

14. Several of Collins's novels, including, in particular, *Armadale* and *The Moonstone*, were widely acclaimed in America. See Norman Page, ed., *Wilkie Collins: The Critical Heritage* (London: Routledge, 1974: 17–19).

15. *Closing Argument of Nathaniel C. Moak*: 33.

16. Wilkie Collins, *Armadale* (London: Penguin Classics, 1995): xvi.

17. During his 1873–74 reading tour in America, Collins alighted upon at least one, if not more, trial reports, tracing his novella *John Jago's Ghost* back to a narrative about a man's false conviction for murdering someone who remained alive. As Collins explained in his note to *John Jago's Ghost*:

> The first idea of this little story was suggested to the author by a printed account of a trial which took place, early in the present century, in the United States. The recently published narrative of the case is entitled "The Trial, Confessions and Conviction of Jesse and Stephen Boorn for the murder of Russell Colvin, and the return of the man supposed to have been murdered. By Hon. Leonard Sergeant, Ex-Lieutenant-Governor of Vermont. (Manchester, Vermont, *Journal Book and Job Office*, 1873)." It may not be amiss to add, for the benefit of incredulous readers, that all the "improbable events" in the story are matters of fact, taken from the printed narrative. Anything which "looks like truth" is, in nine cases out of ten, the invention of the author.

Wilkie Collins, *John Jago's Ghost*, in *Who Killed Zebedee?* (London: Hesperus Press, 2002): 103. A recent book juxtaposes Collins's tale with a narrative of the original wrongful convictions. Rob Warden, *Wilkie Collins's* The Dead Alive: *The Novel, the Case, and Wrongful Conviction* (Evanston, IL: Northwestern University Press, 2005).

18. William Baker, *Wilkie Collins's Library: A Reconstruction* (Westport, CT: Greenwood Press, 2002): 133.

19. William Baker has provided the valuable service of reconstructing the contents of Wilkie Collins's dispersed library. Collins's collection included a number of compilations of trial reports from disparate countries. The list comprehended: George Henry Borrow's *Celebrated Trials and Remarkable Cases of Criminal Jurisprudence from the Earliest Records to the Year 1825* (6 vols., 1825); Peter Burke's *The Romance of the Forum, or, Narratives, Scenes, and Anecdotes from Courts of Justice* (2 vols., 1852–53); John Hill Burton's *Narratives from Criminal Trials in Scotland* (2 vols., 1852); *Causes Célèbres* (2 vols.); William Jackson's *The New and Complete Newgate Calendar: or, Malefactor's Universal Register* (3 vols., 1800–3); Maurice Mejan's *Recueil des Causes Célèbres, et des Arrêts qui les Ont Décidées* (26 vols., 1808); Francois Richer's *Causes Célèbres et Intéressantes, avec les Jugements qui les Ont Décidées* (18 vols., 1772–81). William Baker, *Wilkie Collins's Library*: 81, 83, 87, 121, 133, 143.

Finally, although Baker's reconstruction of Collins's library does not list Blackstone's *Commentaries*, it does include Henry John Stephen's *New Commentaries on the Laws of England Partly Founded on Blackstone*. Baker, *Wilkie Collins's Library*: 152.

20. Sue Lonoff, *Wilkie Collins and His Victorian Readers: A Study in the Rhetoric of Authorship* (New York: AMS Press, 1982): 121.

21. D. A. Miller, "From *roman policier* to *roman-police*: Wilkie Collins's *The Moonstone*," *NOVEL: A Forum on Fiction* 13, no. 2 (Winter 1980): 167–70.

22. Another important episode of legal reading occurs in *Armadale*, when Allan Armadale and his beloved, Neelie, peruse Blackstone's *Commentaries on the Laws of England* to determine whether any obstacles stand in the way of their marrying. *Armadale*: 454–58. Although there is not enough space to analyze this passage here, it vividly dramatizes the mistakes of the uncritical reader, which include reducing legal doctrine to negatives and positives in a utilitarian fashion and envisioning the law on the books as automatically entailing its own execution.

23. One example of a relatively late American collection containing stories of this kind is Horace Fuller's *Impostors and Adventurers* (Boston: Soule and Bugbee, 1882). As *The Literary Gazette* described an earlier volume, "The *Causes Célèbres* (a collection of French trials) are a mine of interesting histories, which novelists or dramatists may dig for centuries without exhausting. The following anecdote is a member of that family: in a romance it would be despised as frivolous. So true it is, that while in works of fiction we demand probability, the actual life around us is daily teeming with apparent impossibilities." "Miscellany," *Literary Gazette and American Athenaeum* (January 13, 1827): 3, 19.

24. Sarah Maza, *Private Lives and Public Affairs: The Causes Célèbres of Prerevolutionary France* (Berkeley: University of California Press, 1993): 24–25. Historical attention has been less focused on these particular collections than on the *mémoires judiciares*, trial briefs written by barristers for consumption by the courts of prerevolutionary France but also published in volumes of several thousands at a time for perusal by the general public. Ibid.: 34–39. As Maza emphasizes, these *mémoires judiciares* self-consciously partook of the literary, playing upon the motifs of contemporary drama and fiction: "The new genre of trial briefs . . . drew on the subject matter of the *drame*. It also adopted some of the *drame*'s style and technique, its use of hyperbole, exclamation, faltering speech, and the awkward emphasis on identity and state of mind that served as signposts to a theater audience." Ibid.: 63.

25. Ibid.: 25.

26. Baker, *Wilkie Collins's Library*: 133, 143.

27. Collins, *John Jago's Ghost*: 38.

28. Collins, *The Guilty River*: 270.

29. George Henry Borrow, ed., *Celebrated Trials and Remarkable Cases of Criminal Jurisprudence form the Earliest Records to the Year 1825* (London: Knight and Lacey, 1825): title page, iii.

30. Ibid.: iii–iv.

31. Ibid.: iv.

32. George L. Craik, ed., *English Causes Célèbres or Reports of Remarkable Trials* (London: Charles Knight and Co., 1840): vi.

33. Ibid. The first reference to this quotation that I have discovered occurs in *The*

New-York Literary Gazette from 1825. "Miscellany," *New York Literary Gazette, and Phi Beta Kappa Repository* 1, no. 3 (September 24, 1825): 48.

34. Craik, *English Causes Célèbres*: vii.

35. Jonathan H. Grossman, *The Art of Alibi: English Law Courts and the Novel* (Baltimore, MD: Johns Hopkins University Press, 2002): 32.

36. "Report on the Lords' Journals," in Edmund Burke, *The Works and Correspondence*, vol. 8, at 39 (London: Francis and John Rivington, 1852): 64.

37. Craik, *English Causes Célèbres*: v–vi.

38. Ibid.

39. Ibid.: 1–85.

40. Mark Seltzer, *True Crime: Observations on Violence and Modernity* (London: Routledge, 2007): 3.

41. John H. Langbein, "The Criminal Trial before the Lawyers," *University of Chicago Law Review* 45, no. 2 (1978): 263.

42. Daniel Cohen, "Trial Reports and the Rise of Sentimental Fiction," *Legal Studies Forum* 17, no. 2 (1993): 119–32; Caleb Crain, "In Search of Lost Crime," *Legal Affairs* (July/August 2002): 29. Seltzer argues along similar lines about true crime, that it "operates in that counterfactual region between truth and falsity: the region of social and collective belief, the situation of modern credibility." Seltzer, *True Crime*: 38–39.

43. Craik, *English Causes Célèbres*: v.

44. Ibid.: v–vi.

45. Peter Burke, ed., *The Romance of the Forum, or, Narratives, Scenes, and Anecdotes from Courts of Justice* (London: Colburn and Co., 1852).

46. Ibid.: v.

47. Both Jan-Melissa Schramm's and Alexander Welsh's work on law and the Victorian novel touch upon the competition between legal and literary forms implied here. Jan-Melissa Schramm, *Testimony and Advocacy in Victorian Law, Literature, and Theology* (Cambridge: Cambridge University Press, 2000): 23; Alexander Welsh, *Strong Representations: Narrative and Circumstantial Evidence in England* (Baltimore, MD: Johns Hopkins University Press, 1992): 7–18, 42.

48. Stanley J. Kunitz, ed., *British Authors of the Nineteenth Century* (New York: H. W. Wilson Co., 1936): 158.

49. Michael Collie, *George Borrow: Eccentric* (Cambridge: Cambridge University Press, 1982).

50. *Celebrated Trials of All Countries and Remarkable Cases of Criminal Jurisprudence* (Philadelphia: L. A. Godey, 1836).

51. Ibid.: 3.

52. Ibid.: 4.

53. *Report of the Trial of Henry Bedlow, for Committing a Rape on Lanah Sawyer*

(New York, 1793); *Report of the Trial of Richard D. Croucher, on an Indictment for a Rape on Margaret Miller* (New York: George Forman, 1800); *Official Report of the Trial of Laura D. Fair, for the Murder of Alex. P. Crittenden* (San Francisco: San Francisco Cooperative Printing Co., 1871).

54. *Official Report of the Trial of Laura D. Fair*: 4.

55. Maza, *Private Lives and Public Affairs*: 25–26.

56. Samuel March Phillips, *The Theory of Presumptive Proof; or, an Inquiry into the Nature of Circumstantial Evidence* (London: W. Clarke and Sons, 1815): preface.

57. Ibid.: 23–29.

58. Some sources employ the spelling "Donnellan" and others use "Donellan."

59. Ibid.: 65–107.

60. *Celebrated Trials of All Countries*: 111–79; 587–94.

61. *Cases of Circumstantial Evidence* [S.l.], [18–]. *The Making of Modern Law*. Gale, Cengage Learning. February 17, 2012: 16.

62. Ibid.: 32.

63. *Celebrated Trials of All Countries*: viii.

64. Ibid.

65. Ibid.: ix.

66. Ibid.: x.

67. Jeremy Bentham, *Rationale of Judicial Evidence Specially Applied to English Practice. From the Manuscripts of Jeremy Bentham, Esq.*, vol. 3, bk. 5 (London: Hunt and Clarke, 1827): 116.

68. Ibid.: 2, 245.

69. Ibid.: 5.

70. Ibid.: 8.

71. Ibid.: 249–50.

72. Ibid.: 249.

73. Welsh, *Strong Representations*: 7–8.

74. Ibid.: 15, 25.

75. Schramm, *Testimony and Advocacy*: 20–23.

76. Bentham, *Rationale of Judicial Evidence*, vol. 3, bk. 5: 227–28.

77. Ibid.: 60, 63, 174.

78. For references to the *Treatise on Circumstantial Evidence*, see ibid.: 74, 253–57; for references to the case of Captain Donellan, see ibid.: 36, 52, 65–66, 72, 188, 232.

79. Ibid.: 49, 168.

80. Ibid.: 36.

81. Ibid.: 199.

82. Ibid.: 228–29.

83. *Closing Argument of Nathaniel C. Moak*: 5–6, 22–23, 25.

84. Ibid.: 14–19, 20, 52.

85. Ibid.: 18.

86. Ibid.: 22–23.

87. Collins, who began studying at Lincoln's Inn in 1846, became a barrister in 1851. Robinson, *Wilkie Collins*: 41, 51.

88. Wilkie Collins, *The Law and the Lady* (London: Penguin Classics, 1999): 78.

89. Ibid.

90. Ibid.

91. Ibid.: 81–82.

92. Ibid.: 87.

93. Ibid.: 88.

94. Ibid.

95. Ibid.: 119.

96. Ibid.: 186.

97. Ibid.: 187.

98. As Robert Ashley observed, Valeria in this respect inaugurated a motif that would "become [a] stock device . . . of the detective story," that of "the attempt of the amateur . . . to succed where professionals . . . had failed." Robert P. Ashley, "Wilkie Collins and the Detective Story," *Nineteenth-Century Fiction* 6, no. 1 (June 1951): 54.

99. Collins, *The Law and the Lady*: 112.

100. Ibid.

101. Ibid.

102. Ibid.: 112–13.

103. Bentham, *Rationale of Judicial Evidence*, vol. 3, bk. 5: 45.

104. Collins, *The Law and the Lady*: 109.

105. Ibid.: 133.

106. Ibid.: 144.

107. Ibid.: 161–62.

108. Ibid.: 170.

109. Ibid.

110. Ibid.: 120.

111. Two recent articles on *The Law and the Lady* reach divergent conclusions about the extent to which the novel reaffirms a disciplinary structure, as D. A. Miller argued *The Moonstone* did, or instead demonstrates the indeterminacy of language. According to Rosanna Cavallaro, the conclusion of *The Law and the Lady* "reconstitut[es] norms against attempted subversion." Rosanna Cavallaro, "Solution to Dissolution: Detective Fiction from Wilkie Collins to Gabriel García Márquez," *Texas Journal of Women and the Law* 15, no. 1 (Fall 2005): 4. By contrast, for Janice Allen, in *The Law and the Lady*, as elsewhere, "Collins . . . consistently acknowledges the instability of language, denying

the primacy of the signified and reinscribing the textuality repressed by classical detective fiction." Janice M. Allen, "A Lock without a Key: Language and Detection in Collins's *The Law and the Lady*," *Clues* (Fall 2006): 46. My argument accords more with Allen's than Cavallaro's conclusions.

112. Letter from Wilkie Collins to William F. Tindell, June 14, 1874, in Baker et al., *The Public Face of Wilkie Collins*, vol. 3: 36–37. *A Complete Report of the Trial of Miss Madeline Smith for the Alleged Poisoning of Pierre Emile L'Angelier*, rev. and corr. John Morison, Esq. (Edinburgh: William P. Nimmo, 1857).

113. Welsh, *Strong Representations*: 27.

114. Collins, *The Law and the Lady*: 185.

115. Ibid.: 383.

116. Ibid.: 362.

Historiographic Secrets of the Labour Contract—The Law and Literature of Lewis Jones 'Cwmardy' and 'We Live'

MELANIE L. WILLIAMS

Introduction

Those living beyond the shores of the British Isles may be forgiven for a failure to understand why Wales—the country still in the process of devolution of government from Westminster, London, which lies to the west of central England—has been described as 'England's Oldest Colony.'[1] A country of great beauty, conquest by outright invasion and industrial exploitation has been influential in the politicisation of a people steeped in poetic and religious oratory, fiercely protective of an ancient language and culture, yet still today suffering the effects of rural and postindustrial poverty. Such hardship gives rise to vehement truth-seeking and, in common with many countries around the globe at the time, Wales at the beginning of the last century became steeped in debate concerning the nature of power, labour, and law. Such debate was fuelled particularly by the events of just over one hundred years ago leading to what are known as the 'Tonypandy Riots.'[2] In 1909, management at the Ely Pit in Penygraig, owned by the Naval Colliery Company, wanted to open up a new seam. But they claimed that during a test period miners were working deliberately slowly so they could demand a higher price per ton of coal. This would not have benefited the miners, since they were paid by weight of product, not by hours—they argued that the work was slowed by a tranche of rock running throughout the seam. The dispute led to a 'lock-out' of the miners by the owners, followed by strike which was met with the use of 'blacklegs.' Even more contentious was the use of the police both to assist with continuing essential work in the mine but also as a concerted force to meet the striking miners; a terrible culmination occurred when police responded to a relatively small group of troublemakers by charging at the strikers en masse with batons, resulting in widespread injury. This use of police 'against the people' is still recalled as a betrayal of relations between citizen, capital, and government. Yet such perspectives were quickly buried and the strikers portrayed as troublemakers and traitors to the economy, by 1911 forced to accept a mediated wage short of the sum they had fought for. Subsequent socialist activists worked to keep alive the flame of political engagement, though at times the appetite for activism flagged as the relevance of the 'story' seemed to abate. Lewis Jones, a youth in those times, applied his narrative skills to the task of reinvigorating the trade union and political life of the working people as privations continued. Though his text remained unfinished—he died at the close of a day in 1939 at the age of forty-two, having addressed more than thirty meetings that day to generate support for the republican struggle in the Spanish Civil War—it bears vibrant witness to the nature of the struggle.

With his novel set, *Cwmardy* and *We Live*,[3] a tale of the struggles and privations of the mining community in the industrial south of Wales in the early decades of the twentieth century, Jones, former miner and socialist activist, put aside the usual tools of political activism—of oratory and pamphlet propaganda—and instead turned to fiction as a means of educating and mobilising the political energy of the workforce. In doing so, Jones represented the extent to which the law was pivotal to the social organisation delivering injustice to working people. As this chapter will show, examination of this 'revolutionary' use of literature highlights the extent to which history and the legal record both gloss and subsume contestable accounts; the elisions and absences from the record speak eloquently of the extent to which selective doctrine contribute to that injustice. The resultant message resonates with debates on the relationship between society, politics, and the rule of law itself. Revealing the means by which hegemonic discourses subordinate the unwelcome voice, the fiction provides an intersection between law, literature, and history, an intersection which highlights just how such voices, their reasonable claims and rightful place in the doctrines of law, are kept from knowledge or view—the very definition of the word 'secret.'

Introduction: Law, Literature, and Historiography

With interdisciplinary study has come increasing recognition that concerns as to the contestability of accounts and truths may reveal the influence of narrative, as well as institutional, power. Not only is there recognition that assertions of truth are most easily made by those with the power to harness authoritative media[4]—and in this may be included the law as well as the press; increasingly scholarly attention has also turned to the role played by the power of narrative in such assertions. In the interdisciplinary body of scholarship that has come to be known as 'law and literature' in particular it is argued that, as a human activity steeped in the dilemmas of the moment, the world of literature may often provide insights otherwise lost to the formal record.[5] In addition it may be argued that narrative processes are so intrinsic to every account as to provide reason to query the status formerly accorded to 'factual' as opposed to 'fictional' sources, given that all will carry contestable elements.[6]

Although lawyers refer to a linear legal 'history' as the touchstone of authoritative knowledge concerning the foundations and development of the law, it is increasingly apparent that historiography—history with a consciousness of multiple influences, of interpretative practice, contestable truths, and narrative strands—is an enriching additional approach to understanding past and present questions. A historiography of law undertaken from a vantage point sufficiently distant to provide a truly dispassionate account of the role and impact of the law in the daily lives of its citizens has yet to be written. Not only the separation of politics from law, but also the streamlining of doctrinal authority and the separation of allegedly independent cognate strands into legal specialisms, have all contributed to the artefacts of law.

As mentioned heretofore, the present chapter, questioning the relationship between historiography and the law—that relating to the labour contract in particular—was prompted by the potent work of fiction *Cwmardy* and *We Live* by Lewis Jones. The power of the work comes in part from its urgent yet simple depiction of the politicisation of a community, a community based upon the real industrial communities of South Wales. In terms of its power to contest the 'truths' of more authoritative canons, the text is perhaps less radical than some in that it bears some relation to factual events and personalities, being in part a dramatisation of a real community and its history. Doubtless the sequence and magnitude of events as represented to some extent serve political as well as dramatic imperatives in the text; the fictional status must be admitted. Nevertheless the central issues of exploitative practices, compliant jurisprudence, and a vulnerable labour force reflect genuine aspects of the historical and legal moment, a moment itself poorly and partially represented by the conventional historical gloss. In particular the dramatisation highlights a polarisation, where a divisive and questionable fabric of public and private law interaction alienates a citizenry of drive and integrity.

South Wales in particular bears witness to the remarkable social and industrial history of the country. A tradition of oratory and fierce debate combined with a precocious and exacting industrial revolution has produced some fiery challenges in politics and law. Wales, the site of the Rebecca Riots of 1843, as well as being a pivotal player in the Chartist movement of 1848, has produced numerous prominent political figures, including David Lloyd George and Aneurin Bevan. Stimulated by harsh social conditions and resultant socialist sympathies, informed by Nonconformist notions of integrity, political activism has played a natural and pivotal role in Welsh cultural as well as political life, and the reputation of the working people of Wales in this regard is widely known. In the early part of the twentieth century, links stretched from Wales to Russian trade unionism and the International Communist movement. From America, Paul Robeson, singer, actor, and civil rights activist, visited South Wales many times between 1929 and 1939. In 1938, Robeson sang to the seven thousand people who attended the Welsh International Brigades Memorial in Mountain Ash to commemorate the thirty-three Welshmen who had died in Spain. He told the audience, 'I am here because I know that these fellows fought not only for me but for the whole world. I feel it is my duty to be here.'[7] In Wales in particular, the struggle was impassioned and informed because of the working-class commitment to faith, to community, and to education.[8] This commitment was enduring because of the intimate link between the issues and the very terms of existence—that is, the preservation of a bare living wage in return for labour conditions of danger and uncertainty.

It would appear that the work of Lewis Jones came into being precisely because of a conviction that the offices of oratory, politics, or law were not sufficiently responsive to meet the challenge of human need. Though guided by a fellow activist toward his narrative turn, Jones was clearly receptive to the development. Against a background of constant suffering in the working community—a community hopeful of empowerment and equity through the ballot box—Jones had witnessed the failure of this promise of equity: a failure of meaningful representation in local and national politics, the dilution and exhaustion of union activism, the criminalisation of key representatives (including Jones himself), biased reporting by the media, and prejudicial treatment by the law. This chapter therefore examines the convergence of historiographic, legal, and cultural processes represented in the recourse to narrative. It does not set out to provide an exhaustive critique of industrial relations law or of the origin and use of force by state agents per se, but rather looks at the core ideas giving rise to such difficulties—of the nexus between labour, contract, and coercion on the one hand, and political, legal, and historical narrative on the other.

Lewis Jones has received very little recognition in literary terms—his workaday characters and settings do not attempt a profoundly literary approach, nor is the text imbricated with overtly philosophical or metatheoretical perspectives. Though one can readily identify the work as 'political' literature, it does not sit easily within the genre, being neither political satire nor intrigue. The text receives minimal notice—barely a paragraph—in texts dedicated to British political fiction. Harvie[9] briefly observes that

> 'Revolutionary' literature . . . diminished the sense of historical change in class and economic relationships, and the religious-radical tradition of millennial protest. Perhaps we see this best in the 'working-class novel.' Lewis Jones's *Cwmardy* (1937) and its sequel *We Live* (1939) take a Welsh mining valley from the 1900s to the Spanish Civil War. Jones's own Mardy, in Rhondda, was one of the 'Little Moscow' fortresses of the Communist Party, but Jones presents Cwmardy as *typical:* communism and autodidact materialism take a back seat to *Gemeinschaft* . . .

whilst Raymond Williams notes that

> *Cwmardy*, the plot of which spans a whole lifetime, reveals a new class consciousness manifest in the cohesion of a mining town, which transforms the very nature of the struggle. In a brief early review, W. H. Williams pointed out that the evolution of class consciousness—something 'lacking in D. H. Lawrence'—added a new note to the novel. What Williams detected in *Cwmardy* was obviously the power of a new sensibility reaching forward into the future. The novel shows the inadequacy of mine management and opens up the possibility of control by the miners themselves.[10]

Neither comment reflects the power of Jones's message—the kind of elegiac truth that filters through regarding the utter failure of politics and law. For both these commentators, whilst the *themes* sit pleasingly with certain political motivations, there is little to say about the stylistic qualities of the text—Jones is not consciously a modernist, a satirist, a lyricist. Arguably, this is absolutely deliberate, rather than merely a reflection of literary limitations—such stylistic interjections might well have interfered with the receptivity of the audience, a straitened community audience, to the message. Jones does, however, draw upon certain elements of modernist writing to empower the message of revolutionary politics, most notably in the realism with which he represents the brutal physical manifestations of prevailing cultural and political cruelties—the violent and needless industrial deaths, the brute reality of death itself, unmitigated (even for a young girl, Jane and her newborn child) by the religious nostrums which hitherto had solaced the workers:

> The men worked in the most intolerable conditions. Excessive heat and the foetid atmosphere melted their flesh and left them like empty sacks at the end of their short shifts. The bodies they discovered each day were simply ghastly lumps of greasy putrefaction. Very few could be identified. In a short time it became known to the people of the valley that the explosion had left no survivors. (Jones, *Cwmardy*, 81)
>
> This was to be the last occasion before they screwed the coffin down ready for the funeral next day . . .
>
> Len looked down and a look of horror filled his eyes. Jane's beautiful face was gone. In its place was a dirty yellow mask with snarling lips that curled back from shiny white teeth. A blackened penny grinned at him mockingly from each of her eyes. The roses had died and were now withered blotches on the white lace of her shroud. Dark blobs filled the places where her cheeks had been. The tiny shrunken form at her side was covered. A fusty smell rose from the coffin and reminded Len of the odour in his bed the night after Jane had died. (112)

Action, rather than a fatalistic piety, will allow the people to overcome the injustices in life and in unnecessary deaths—this realism is key in giving force to the political message—'the new sensibility reaching into the future' (as Raymond Williams expresses it, above). Such realism is also central to the carefully conveyed, micromanaged account of the network of corruptions and failings in the political system, from local council to state government, giving *reason* to the political message—that the people must take a stand. More prominent, literary, political writers, such as George Orwell, arguably fail on this front—the satirical fable of *Animal Farm* proving too allegorical, the deadly pessimism of *Nineteen Eighty-Four* too destructive. Jones is singular in combining the dramatisation as educative tool (conveying the vital links between the concepts of labour, power, politics, and collective action, with the fabric of systems, of councils, federations, unions, laws, states, on a different register to the admittedly magnetic writings of Marx and Engels) with the signal to future political transformation. Indeed, elsewhere Raymond Williams lambasts the writings of Orwell—in Williams's view, Orwell suffers from 'the paradox of the exile,' and Orwell's alienation, his inauthentic membership of the working community, contributes to the failure of his political message.[11] In contrast, one might believe that Jones would have fulfilled the aesthetic and political aspirations of Trotsky, whose expectations of a new 'revolutionary and socialist art' in Russia were largely disappointed. In *Literature and Revolution,* Trotsky decries the fact that postrevolutionary writers are failing the reasonable expectation of a literature of revolution. Returning instead to a misplaced romanticism, of the 'old' country and of the peasant, postrevolutionary Russian writers decry the very existence of 'proletarian' poetry and of industrial landscapes and workers, and thereby fail to deliver the long-awaited transformative message while the organisation of labour in a system of capital accumulation implicates forms of exploitation beyond the presumptively normative free labour contract and the only real freedom workers possess under capitalism or any system of domination is their power of resistance.

> Of 'industrial rhythms,' of proletarian poetry, of the very principle of it, Kliuev speaks with the natural contempt that comes to the lips of every 'strong' peasant when he glances at the propagandist of socialism, the houseless city worker . . . . When one speaks of revolutionary art, two kinds of artistic phenomena are meant: the works whose themes reflect the Revolution, and the works that are not connected with the Revolution in theme, but are thoroughly imbued with it.[12]

Although Jones more closely fulfils this kind of artistic hope, creating seamless links between the values and identities of people and the broad ideological context, his revision of history—what might be called his historiographic position, and adherence to a simple, workaday prose, are practical, rather than aesthetic or ideological moves. Thus he demonstrates an interesting, 'pre-genre' example of what has come to be known, in the modern terminology, as 'historiographic metafiction.' Such texts have an association with 'postmodernist' literary and artistic development, in their playful engagement with history and with the notion of truth. Jones could not (and perhaps would not wish to) be counted as a legitimate member of this movement. His purpose is far from playful, and indeed his practical engagement with the 'facts' of history, though to some extent politically aware, aesthetically it would appear, is quite unconscious. Yet the deliberate moves of historiographic metafiction—especially given a frequently political motivation—resonate quite closely with the less conscious coordinations of Jones. In her definition of 'historiographic metafiction,' Hutcheon (*Poetics of Postmodernism*, 5), for example, places emphasis upon the self-awareness of history and fiction as human constructs. Though the work of Jones cannot be described as 'self-reflexive,' his awareness of history and fiction as human forms of construct, each capable of ideological manipulation, is clear. His awareness of history as an artefact is surely informed by brutal personal experience as well as by his political education, whilst his use of fiction as tool as well as canvas suggests a freedom from the seductive powers of art.[13]

The patent injustice suffered by his beloved community was the driving force for Lewis Jones in his journey from oratory to fiction. Already engaged by political ideas as a result of the hardships of their working environment, the working communities of South Wales had experienced limited success in pressing their claims for fairer wages and conditions. Much of Jones's text dramatises a struggle that is pivotal in Welsh industrial history, the story of Tonypandy in 1910–1911. As Smith recounts, this was a time when

> Rhondda labour leaders who variously combined a fervour for 'syndicalism' (workers' control to be achieved through the direct action of democratically organised unions) with the politics of the ballot box . . . then add the assembled forces of imported police and over twelve thousand colliers and their families out on strike until starved back after almost a year's embattled struggle. (Smith, *Wales*, 102–3)

Smith adds, 'No wonder John Morgan set out to write a libretto for his opera *Mabon* based on Tonypandy,' and quotes the stimulus for Morgan, for whom

> [t]he scale of that drama in 1910–11 . . . was epic. . . . Nowhere else in Europe was there such a startling revelation of the new political order of the century. Therefore to convey this scale the opera will need as large a chorus as is feasible. It cannot be a chamber work.

The origins of the dispute lay with increasingly harsh working conditions. As the mines were worked more intensively, extracting profitable coal became more dangerous and technically challenging. With the men obliged to extract a proportion of useless stone along with the coal, management forced the men to bear the impact of the losses, leading to an industrial dispute deriving from the men's plea that, already on minimal wages, they would be at the lowest subsistence point if management did not make some allowance for the unproductive element of the work. With an unrelenting management and already ravaged by a series of appalling industrial accidents, the men went on strike. The management attempted to circumvent the strikers by drafting in blackleg labour and colliery officials to keep the mines in working order, and this led to unrest and the drafting in of police. Confrontations, exacerbated by a relatively small group of agitators attacking property, led to criminal charges being made against certain strikers and allowed the strikers to be characterised, not as the victims of a harsh and unjust industrial regime, but as an unruly mob, acting against the interests of the entire country. Though some advances were made on behalf of the workers in the ensuing years, the scale of those advances was small and the political efficacy of collective activity undercut by broader political intrigues.[14] For some, such as Lewis Jones, the democratic process had proved itself to be of doubtful utility even when political representation was within sight. Global politics acquired an intimate relevance as fascism stalked with the Spanish Civil War, and revolutionary politicisation of the workforce seemed the only way forward. Orthodox methods of political education and mobilisation—through lectures and pamphleteering—were proving somewhat slow. The turn to fiction was a concerted educative tool in the attempt to mobilise the revolutionary political message.

In his tale of the travails of a mining community and the crises and tragedies pursuant upon the industry, Jones represents certain encounters with the law and notions of justice. These provide a plausible and plangent account of the encounters with the law in the 'real' as lived by the workers of the time and justify some examination, illuminating the use of narrative in this regard. Though many issues of legal note arise in the text, three engagements with direct mechanisms of law are directly recorded: an inquest, a deployment of police—as well as army forces—and a criminal prosecution. These events reflect some simple but fundamental criticisms of law. It is however the second, the deployment of force—that of police force in particular—which is most clearly indicated by Jones as a source of concern. With the potential to be easily 'naturalised' as an everyday part of domestic order, this issue forms the key focus of the present essay.

The Deployment of Force against Strikers

The deployment of the police and army as a containment measure in the management of an industrial strike provides a potentially instructive and significant illustration of the engagement between the people and the law. Such encounters are easily represented in the media and in history as a necessary move in the face of imminent chaos. At the height of the Tonypandy troubles, both police and troops were mobilised, and this was indeed characterised in the press as a necessary response to violent disorder, though the local account recalls an entirely different interpretation, of decent and desperate people needlessly dishonoured and brutalised by such intervention, an intervention apparently supported by the government in distant London. In *Cwmardy*, Jones represents all this, the strife, the attempt to exert state force through the police and the army, the indignant people and the resultant media version of events. Nevertheless, as far as the deployment of force is concerned, Jones directs most narrative suspicion and incredulity at the question of the legality of police deployment in particular, perhaps recognising that, whilst army forces may be easily and somewhat impenetrably submitted as a crucial resource for states *in extremis*—the use of the police is a different matter. Already a routine part of the domestic 'furniture,' their use can all too readily be normalised as a neutral instrument of domestic order whilst serving the interests of the powerful.

In narrating the development of industrial dispute, the reader gains insight through the eyes of the main protagonist, Len, son of experienced miner Big Jim. Len moves from fledgling miner, keen to learn the finer points of the craft, to politically aware representative of his peers as, time and again, he witnesses injustices wrought upon his fellow workmen. The inducement to strike is provided when the colliery company declares that it will no longer pay for the 'small coal' mined by the men, but only 'large coal.'[15] The men calculate that on average small coal accounts for around 40 percent of each tram filled. Already working to capacity on bare subsistence wages, and constrained by the technical difficulty of extracting 'large coal,' the edict portends ruin for the men. As Dai Cannon, miner and preacher expresses it:

> Mr Chairman and fellow workmen, at last the octopus is closing his tentacles about the living bodies of our women and children. Like a gloating vulture, the hireling of the company is waiting to fill our valley with the sighs and sobs of starving people .

> ... [If] we are to starve let it be in the sun with God's pure air around us. If we are to die let it be fighting like the slaves of old Rome. I stand, like Moses, for my people. (Jones, *Cwmardy*, 193)

Beside this resonance with images of slavery, the text provides a panoramic view of events, relating the stance adopted by the mine owner, Lord Cwmardy, and his manager at the Big House, who agree that the miners will 'assuredly strike' but that with no organisation, no money, and no leaders, they will not be able to strike for long. To ensure the continued lack of leadership, the management consider whether Ezra Jones, an influential old mining leader, can be 'bought off,' but in concluding that he is 'incorruptible,' they are anyway assured in the range of their influence in every other realm. It is thus made clear not only that the miners have no real choice but to strike and that this is the only effective method of exerting influence open to them, but also that the contest of wills is to be utterly uneven from the start, as democratic mechanisms are entirely manipulated by those in power. The trusting integrity trained into the ordinary worker by elementary religious and state education, mortally endangered as he is by his conditions of work,[16] is pitted against the crude commercialism of the captains of industry.

The strike action deepens with confrontations between mine officials (designated 'blacklegs' and 'scabs' by the miners) and striking miners. In continuing to work, the mine officials seriously undermine the effectiveness of the strike, a strike which the men are only able to maintain at the price of great privation to themselves and their families. Attempting to exert further control over the situation, the mining company call in the police. The utilisation of a police presence in such a context has deep political as well as legal implications, as the text makes clear. One may come to appreciate the complex jurisprudential nature of such implications and their submersion in the actual world of law.

In Lewis Jones's text, the use of the police force against them bewilders the workers:[17] As the omniscient narrative comments (ibid., 221): 'What they failed to understand was why, when the advantage was with them,[18] the police should be placed at the disposal of the owners.' The police presence proves menacing as, with little provocation, batons rain down 'with smashing regularity' on the heads of the miners whilst 'posses of uniformed men' parade through back lanes and 'burst their way' into houses at will. The offence is compounded by inaccurate and propagandist newspaper accounts portraying the striking men as hooligans and looters subjecting the police to wild attack and forcing the police to draw batons in self-defence.[19] The politically acute Ezra and Len understand that a report in the newspaper will be perceived as 'truth' and that such 'evidence' will be significant for the law:

> What you see in black and white is truth and you must always believe it . . . . Right has always been, and always will be, determined by might. There can never be one law that is at once good for the tiger and the lamb. Neither can there be one law that binds together the interests of workmen and owners. (Ibid., 231)

In an attempt to overcome the impasse, the striking men promise that the officials and 'safety men' will be guaranteed free movement provided the police are withdrawn, but a manager claims that this would be 'impossible,' that the matter was 'entirely out of [their] hands,' and that 'the police are under the control of the authorities and have nothing at all to do with the company.' That this is a debatable assertion is however again acknowledged by the text. The status of the call upon the services of the police is recognised as pivotal to the confrontation between capital and worker. Claiming that the police are under the 'control of the authorities' implies the political neutrality of the management in their deployment, whilst signalling that such intervention on behalf of representatives of the state is entirely necessary to a policy of containment. In discussions with Union activists, Len and others divine that the status of the police deployment is a truly significant issue.

The Legal Record

The particularly harsh period of global struggle in the early part of the twentieth century was characterised by the Great Depression, which affected individual fates and fortunes on both sides of the Atlantic. Industrial Wales had in fact provided a sensitive barometer of erratic world markets for decades, forming a crucible for the politicisation of the workforce from the mid-nineteenth century. In the coal industry, the volatile impact of the market was passed on to the miner through the mechanism of the sliding scale, so that the rise and fall in prices was reflected in the weekly wage.[20] On the political landscape, struggles were occurring with momentous implications for the law, yet if one looks to the legal record of the period, hints of this vast world are halting.[21]

Being educated into the law, one tends to accept its major structural organisation as integral, but viewing the law through the prism of fiction promotes fresh consideration of such structures. For the ordinary citizen it may seem strange and perhaps even a kind of cultural failing that such struggles are scarcely represented on the legal record, or indeed reflected upon in legal theory. In dramatising the life of this industrial community Jones depicts the relationship between private and public life in order to explicate the systematic failures of public process. Considering the three events identified in the text, the formal hearing of an inquest by its nature would be unlikely to gain a place in the legal record. Given its identity as a tribunal of fact, the mechanism for enquiry into issues of justice is minimised and where the representational power of any party is at all compromised, so too is any such mechanism. The deployment of police (as well as troops) in the context of industrial action, though of deep potential significance to the polity, may be characterised readily as a response to impending civic disorder, a practical and essential containment measure, dealing only with a threat of violence and of little lasting significance to the legal record. Similarly, as the text by Jones implies, the displacement of individuals like Len (politicised citizens capable of exposition and articulation of faults in the status quo) into the marginalising system of criminal process, consigns their reasonable, legitimate concern to ignominy and obscurity, 'naturalising' them as criminals. Though all three juristic events are significant as part of an organic critique of the law, the basis of police deployment in particular is most contentious. Inquest findings may be partial as a result of the influence and prejudices of local individuals, as may the 'criminalisation' of political activists. But the use of forces, and the question of who finances them, is an even broader juridical issue, going to the heart of the state and law. Any attempt to navigate the processes of history via the processes of law will prove problematic. Though the early twentieth century saw some legislation and some caselaw in relation to industrial issues, this was piecemeal, given the scale of the issues, with the caselaw often normalising the prevailing hegemonic view. Of course the key purpose of the legal record is to identify significant practical legal rules and the purpose of legal history to formulate a coherent account of the development of principle. But the fact that the record both disregards events and crystallises them into a principle utterly in denial of the wider context, fuels the mutual alienation of subject and law and is in itself a cultural and hermeneutic phenomenon of note. As already indicated, Jones's fiction dramatises the struggle in Tonypandy in 1910 when striking miners were suppressed both by a police and then army presence. The army presence was the most gross insult—and threat—to the working community, revealing the taking up of a clear position by the state in relation to these particular citizens. The use of police as well as troops signalled this same message. As Smith recounts:

> Churchill was reluctant to accede to the somewhat intemperate demands of the local magistracy and judiciary who had been sending out distress signals as early as 2 November 1910. They were anxious for a military presence to overawe the miners on strike in both the Cynon and Rhondda Valleys (in separate disputes) . . . . [T]he troops, as well as over 1000 police, were, in essence, an army of occupation . . . . [T]he troops ensured that all mass demonstrations against blackleg labour would be controlled and thereby rendered ineffective . . . . [T]heir presence prevented the mass picketing which the leaders of the strikers had seen as their only real hope of an early victory . . . . [T]he defeat suffered by the men of the Cambrian Combine was, in the eyes of the local community, attached directly to the state intervention authorised by Churchill. (Smith, *Wales,* 104)

Note that it was said that a probable key purpose of the deployment was to *control* and *render ineffective* the use of industrial action. Crucial to the issue of the deployment of forces and the status of that deployment is the question of whether there was any real threat of mass violence. Certainly the local population and social commentators believed that the small outbreak of violence which did occur was in *response* to ill-treatment and violence, and was anyway perpetrated by an unrepresentative group.[22] Yet, though so central to the annals of Welsh industrial history, subtle differences in accounts of the events only serve to highlight the strongly interpretative element present in general—as well as legal—history. In addition the struggle bears scant recognition in general British historical accounts of the period, even those with a social and political remit.[23]

The Case of Glasbrook Brothers

In relation to this particular period, the variable recorded histories and the prompts of narrative fiction outlined above drive scrutiny of formal precedent in relation to the use of police. It is not until a strike of 1924 in a neighbouring coalfield that the common law principle underlying the deployment of police in such circumstances is discussed, in much diluted form, with the case of *Glasbrook Brothers v. Glamorgan County Council* (1925).[24] As already mentioned, even taking into account the legislative developments during the early decades of the twentieth century, the 'legal record' provides little hint of the vast human story unfolding throughout, and this case is an oblique encounter for the working person, given the fact that the workers at the heart of the dispute giving rise to the case were not participating litigants. Thinking from the point of view of the working citizen, searching for some clue, some pathway through the annals of legal precedent, a clue which might acknowledge the facts of their recent history, the case of *Glasbrook Bros.* presents an odd visible landmark in the voyage to law, and arguably illuminates Jones's turn to instructive fiction, recourse to law and politics proving nugatory. Indeed it may be that Jones, writing in the late 1930s, recounts the events of Tonypandy (in fact occurring in 1910–11) and compresses them alongside an emphasis upon the legality of police deployment (and a query concerning the fiscal support for such deployment), with a consciousness of the stance of this case, occurring as it did in the1920s. To compress the message of the unfolding decades was to elucidate the ideological challenge of the times.

To lawyers, the significance of the case lies in its doctrinal importance in the law of contract. The point at issue is whether fees are payable where the police authorities provide a policing service over and above that required by their own assessment of the extent of duty in the need to preserve order. For a contract lawyer, the case is a question of commerce—of whether, if at all, contractual 'consideration' had been provided for the claim to fee and the relationship of that concept to the exercise of duty.[25] For this reason, the case of *Glasbrook Bros.* is found in textbooks on the law of contract, rather than those on the law of employment or indeed—where the relationship between politics and law is most actively debated—in jurisprudence.

Insofar as law may be treated as a factual record of significant legal mechanisms and significant legal events, we might expect to be able to gain a fairly enriching insight into an event or period of legal consequence from the legal record. Even taking account of the constraints of the historical moment, the claims of law—to forensic precision, detachment, objectivity, formal consistency, substantive flexibility, and so on—might nevertheless reveal some sense of the immanent issues. Thinking about these issues in relation to the specific case of Glasbrook begs questions on many points of legal convention, from the relationship between political and legal philosophy to the notions of social, civic, and labour contract—the very structure and concept of contract law itself. Yet, throughout the law of contract, the case is glossed as a simple precedent regarding the boundary of contractual and noncontractual duty.

The case arose as a result of a national miners' strike, in circumstances bearing a significant relation to those concerning Lewis Jones. At a group of collieries near Swansea, the manager at Glasbrook Bros. mines responded to unrest and resistance[26] to the call to return to work by applying for police protection for the colliery and insisting that

> [it] could only be efficiently protected by billeting a police force on the premises. The police superintendent was prepared to provide what in his opinion was adequate protection by means of a mobile force, but refused to billet police officers at the colliery except on the terms of the manager agreeing to pay for the force so provided at a specified rate.[27]

The county council employing the police force subsequently brought an action against Glasbrook Bros. for payment of the fee, which had been resisted for want of consideration. The *ratio decidendi* in the House of Lords was that 'there was nothing illegal in the agreement, nor was it void for want of consideration.'[28] In standard textbooks on the law of contract, the case is reported as a straightforward precedent on the doctrine of consideration. Viscount Cave, delivering the judgement, outlined a firm account of legal principle:

> My Lords, the practice by which police authorities make a charge for 'special services,' that is to say, for services rendered outside the scope of their obligations, has been established for upwards of sixty years and is constantly followed by every police authority in the country with the approval of the Secretary of State; and it is difficult to understand on what grounds it should now be treated as illegal.[29]

To explain how an opposing model of the principle might be fashioned, Viscount Cave quoted Lord Atkin,[30] who had stated:

> Either they were performing this public duty in giving this protection asked for, in which case I think they cannot charge, or, which no-one suggests, they were at the request of one individual doing something which it was not their duty to do, in which case it seems to me both public policy and s 10 of the county Police Act 1839, make the contract illegal and void.[31]

Viscount Cave deploys this argument in order to refute it, positing a failure, on the part of Atkin LJ, to recognise a distinction between a 'duty' and a 'power':

> With great respect to the learned Lord Justice I am disposed to think that this reasoning rests on an ambiguous use of the word 'duty'. There may be services rendered by the police which, although not within the scope of their absolute obligations to the public, may yet fall within their powers, and in such cases public policy does not forbid their performance. I do not understand the reference in the above passage to s 10 of the Act of 1839.[32]

It is unlikely, however, that the great Lord Justice Atkin was really guilty of such an oversight. On one reading, Atkin is merely applying a particular technical approach to the issue in the law of contract—if duty extends to these circumstances, there is no basis for contract, if no duty extends but money is paid, the contract is illegal and void. But characterising it in this particular way may also betray the political position of the judge. For arguably a strict duty/no duty account of the principle envisions a world in which circumstances either clearly and unequivocally call for the necessity of police intervention—as a matter of duty, in their role as mediators of state and public peace, or they do not, and contract here is 'illegal' and 'void on grounds of public policy' because of the shadow of a contract for mercenary services. Conversely, once Viscount Cave posits a world in which police may render

> services . . . which, although not within the scope of their absolute obligations to the public, may yet fall within their powers and in such cases public policy does not forbid their performance[,][33]

he is evading the issue foreshadowing such a model—the prejudicial use of police services as a coercive force.[34] Where once the role of the police moves from that of public protection to industrial 'strong arm,' an 'ambiguity' indeed arises around the notion of 'duty.'

For the discussion here is one of an elemental struggle for power. The capital power of the industrialist (in his manipulation of contractual terms) cannot be challenged by the poor labourer alone; it can only be challenged by the collective entity of the workforce. And confirming that a garrison of police can effectively be hired to challenge such a workforce—confirming that such a contract can sound in law—is a deeply political finding and not simply an interesting doctrinal point on consideration. There is perhaps the slightest intimation of this point in the rhetoric employed by Viscount Cave, in his statement that 'public policy *does not forbid*' the performance of such contracts.[35] This surely betrays at least a subliminal awareness of the political sensitivity of the issue—signalling that, whilst there may be no formalised *veto*, there is surely a concern.

The dissenting judgment of Lord Carson was not an assertion of concern over such civic principles. Quite the contrary: Lord Carson was concerned to uphold the right of individuals ('individuals' here relating to the property-owning classes only) to take steps to protect life and property,[36] and on the facts concluded that the supply of police was necessary to the preservation of the pit. He did not dispute the proposition that the doctrine of consideration could be brought into play in such a case; rather he contended that it had not come into play on the facts of this particular case, judging police involvement on the large scale requested by the manager necessary to induce the safety men to continue pumping the mines.

The second dissenting judge, Lord Blanesburgh, similarly believed that the police presence was necessitated by duty. His examination of the evidence focussed upon the fact that the lower courts had failed to challenge the police superintendent's assertion that sufficient police protection could have been afforded without a police garrison, but merely a police presence. According to Lord Blanesburgh, though such an opinion was no doubt formed in good faith, it was a mistaken opinion, flying in the face of evidence that the safety men would not have continued work without a full garrison. At issue here was not so much a suggestion that violence was truly objectively imminent (for the superintendent believed the situation to be perfectly containable with a minimal police presence). Rather it was that, since the safety men felt sufficiently intimidated to doubt whether they should continue work, there was sufficient subjective *apprehension* to interfere with the continued labour of the safety men. This formed the basis of Lord Blanesburgh's dissent. Yet in effect this is not a focus upon a threat of violence or a direct threat to property. It is rather about the extent to which police involvement is justifiable in the maintenance of industrial property, coloured as it is by a perceived threat. For on one view we may say the primary function of the safety men was to carry out essential work to prevent flooding of the mine in order to preserve its functional capability. On another view, they functioned as blacklegs,[37] deeply undermining the efficacy of strike action. On yet another view, the withdrawal of labour—the cessation of coal production, justifiably could be treated as a separate issue from the maintenance of property. On whatever reading, the opposition of property to labour is much more politically charged than is indicated by a merely technical debate about the doctrine of consideration. For the men involved, the 'placing of police at the disposal of the owners' (as Jones expresses it in *Cwmardy*) identifies the police as something other than community servants, their role and their master the fundamental gauge of the link between public law, private law, and the very concept of the rule of law itself, in a state where, apparently, 'right' may be determined by 'might.'

Historiography and the Labour Contract

If one accepts a key element of Jones's account—that principled people are denied justice, are criminalised and brutalised—and thereby politicised—one is stimulated to consider the legal framework underlying such a process. The novel brings force to some fundamental issues—to the absolute linkage between labour and survival, power and coercion; the need for authentic access to the political and legal mechanisms for change. The lived, subjective experience of the privations leading to the dramatisation by Jones and a case like *Glasbrook Bros.* is one of unremitting hardship. The legal principles and legal record bear scant witness to these facts, and we may therefore consider the very structure of those principles, of the historiography of law and the labour contract.

Somewhat surprisingly, texts tracing the history and origins of the law of contract pay scant attention to the doubtful foundation of the labour contract.[38] With classical contract law providing a largely normalising role for the case, one might expect *Glasbrook Bros.* to appear again and more discursively in the texts of labour law perhaps with more consciousness of its political significance. It is after all—quite apart from being an intriguing sight of the nature of the labour contract of the police themselves—a case touching upon the engagement between a containment force and the very function of industrial action as a means of negotiating the labour contract. Yet though a central precedent in the law of contract, learned by all British undergraduates in law, the case is absent from the texts on labour law. Though Kahn-Freund (a seminal writer on the political and coercive context of labour relations), in *Labour and the*

Law, 3rd rev. ed. (London: Stevens and Sons, 1983), 24, readily recognises, for example, that

> [it] is necessary for the law to see relations of subordination in terms of co-ordination, that is, an act of submission in the mask of a 'contract,' because this is the fiction through which it exorcises the incubus *of 'compulsory labour[,]'*

there is no mention of *Glasbrook Bros.* in any part of the book.[39] Especially surprising is the failure of textbooks on labour law to trace the long-standing role of the law in the history of labour itself.[40]

Though the issues as indicated by the case therefore appear to have been elided both in the courtroom and in the text, the 'incubus' of 'compulsory labour' is, as Kahn-Freund indicates, ever present. For the labour contract to have any genuine connection to the notion of contract effective collective bargaining and where necessary, action, is crucial in that it provides some cogent meaning to the idea of a meeting of minds by a levelling of powers. Ultimately,[41] the collective agreement, when it is reached, may simply be an agreement to accept defeat, to return to work in virtual acceptance of the miserable terms imposed by the mine owners. It is a collective 'bargain' in name only.

It may be argued that the case has little to do with labour law. Even the labour of policemen[42] is oddly circumvented as a commodity of oblique significance to the question of consideration. Yet the case is of profound significance to the issue of labour. For not only is the issue of the deployment of police labour deeply political and therefore significant to the ethics and integrity of the rule of law. The deployment of such labour is of even greater significance when it relates to the withholding, and ultimate coercion, of labour by others. Thus the narrative 'truth-space' claimed by the legal record and the status accorded to this doctrinal significance effectively subsumes the narrative possibilities to be found in the broader historical record. And it is perhaps at this juncture that narrative—such as that produced by Jones—must be deployed in order to reinstate the profound truth of lived experience.

Legal and Political Theory and the Labour Contract

In reading of the struggle to win a 'living' wage and achieve a degree of autonomy in the regulation of their working lives, the travails of the miners in *Cwmardy*—especially where the coercive forces of the state are brought to bear—are a vivid reminder of how very thin is the mask of contract upon a face of 'compulsory labour.' Given this context, the analysis of such forces provided by Marxist theory must have seemed compelling and wholly logical. As is well known, Marx addressed the issue of the relationship between labour, the living wage, and coercion many times. As he stated in his early lectures:

> Wages are only a special name for the price of labour, for the price of this peculiar commodity which has no other repository than flesh and blood.[43]

For the workers of South Wales, the literal truth of such analysis no doubt presaged hope that wider understanding of their predicament was at hand. Yet even today, though the philosophical impact of the Marxist position has been explored by many writers, this relationship, between the notions of labour, coercion, and payment, remains resistant to full exposition. One scholar willing to embark upon an engagement with the implications of the spectre of coercion is Cohen, and it may be helpful at this point to track some aspects of Cohen's discussion,[44] in order to derive some broad insights into the discourse discoverable in relation to labour and coercion. Reminding us that, according to Marx,

> a member of a social class belongs to it by virtue of his position within social relations of production. In keeping with this formula, Marx defined the proletarian as the producer who has (literally or in effect) nothing to sell but his own labor power[,]

Cohen suggests a clear inference, that for Marx, the worker 'is *forced* to sell his labor power (on pain of starvation).' Cohen sets out to explore the putative 'truth' of the claim that workers are 'forced' to sell their labour power, in the process examining possible 'leftist' and 'rightist' responses to the claim.[45] A central plank of Cohen's discussion proposes that a worker is

> forced to sell his labor power in the presently required sense if and only if the constraint is a result of *standard* exercises of the powers constituting relations of production . . . . The relevant constraint must reflect use of *economic* power, and not, moreover, just any use of it, but a *standard* exercise of it. I do not yet know how to define 'standard,' but it is not hard to sort out cases in an intuitive way. If, for example, a capitalist forces people to work for him by hiring gunmen to get them to do so, the resulting constraint is due to a non-standard exercise of economic power . . . . [A] philanthropic capitalist might be willing to transfer large shares in the ownership of his enterprise to workers . . . . [T]hat would not be a standard use of capitalist power.

Already this juxtaposition of a constraint deriving from economic power alongside the notion of a *standard* exercise of such power is less straightforward than it might appear. When illustrated by the extreme examples of what would *not* comprise a standard exercise of such power—the use of hired gunmen on the one hand and a philanthropic gift on the other—the examples only serve to demonstrate the utterly pivotal importance of the status accorded to the deployment of a state force. Cohen is attuned to the possibility of state involvement in coercive phenomena,[46] yet, though one might expect this discussion to lead naturally into some recognition of the possible relevance of coercive 'state officials,' no such discussion ensues. Instead, Cohen is diverted into a detailed analysis of the notion of coercion, its content explored by comparing the alleged predicament of the coerced worker with the imagined predicament of persons locked into a room with limited opportunity for escape.[47]

Arguably, such an analogy only serves to emphasise the degree to which abstracted examples of a dilemma diverge from their real counterparts, where the freedom to 'stay' or 'escape' is very much affected by the actual presence of coercive forces. And though workers may elect to 'escape' or 'walk away' from the constraint that is their labour, the social, economic, and geographical conditions make such choice near impossible for most.[48] A myriad of other reasons are likely to inhibit them from doing so, not least concern for holding fast to existing personal bonds, as the intimate community of Cwmardy implies.[49] As one might surmise and as *Cwmardy* demonstrates, however, such 'collective loyalty' does not tend to be the force driving attempts at liberation; rather, such cohesive relationships are in part a *result* of the dearth of choices available individually and collectively. They are not the fruits of 'choice' in our usual understanding of the term; rather, they are the fruits of absolute reason in the absence of 'true' choice. Cohen's model posits a somewhat 'automated' scheme, where escape by one inmate activates a sensor which locks the remaining inmates inside. However, nowhere does Cohen recognise the direct relevance of the analogy to the use of coercive forces: the problem of lack of choice is not in fact a merely mechanical or numerical one. And the irony here is that 'collective bargaining' *is* dependent, for its effectiveness, on individuals *staying* within the unit.[50] Yet Cohen elides the clear relationship of the analogy to collective action and collective bargaining, again becoming sidetracked into a discussion of the possibility of 'co-operatives' as a means to freedom, whilst failing to see the clear significance of the phenomenon of unions as a means of collective power. Though he concludes, rather weakly, that

> it might be, though false, nearly true that the overwhelming majority of the proletariat are forced to sell their labor power . . . because there are virtually no exits available at any given time[,] (Cohen, 'The Structure of Proletarian Unfreedom,' 442)

Cohen does not recognise the relevance of the use of compulsive forces to this 'virtual' lack of exits. Nor does he address a key issue linking labour with compulsion—that of whether the 'deal' available offers meaningful payment for the work.[51] For 'subsistence' wages limit freedom of action in a practical sense—affecting the degree of energy available to approach the exit. The fact that this essay by Cohen provides an extensive exploration of the philosophical links between the labour contract and coercion, yet fails to provide recognition of the dilemma in a form more potent than that it might be 'nearly true' that workers are forced to sell their labour power, goes some way to explaining the resistance of the concept, its vulnerability to dilution and reconstitution through abstraction.

Thus philosophy as well as law may fail to give recognition to the depth of the dilemma, and history in its turn—as well as philosophy—contributes to the construction of these 'realities' in law. Modern historiographic accounts of the journey from feudalism to capitalism, in particular in relation to the labour contract, are a recognisable strand in the background to the process of narrative elision and uncertainty, adding to the complex, layered visions of labour discoverable in politics, law, fiction, and the media. Holton for example identifies a whole range of theories.[52] Differing interpretations of this crucial historical pathway—the transition from feudal to capital—are often grounded upon differing criterial perspectives and evidential origins; such uncertainties assist in the successful promotion of certain ideological assertions, not least the myth of equality underlying the idea of the labour market and contract.[53] Writers such as Banaji[54] set out to argue that such assumptions fail to give recognition to the primacy of the analysis put forward by Marx whereby the notion of 'free labour' was contested.

Banaji's discussion focuses very much upon the issue of consensuality and voluntariness—or lack of it—in the labour contract.[55] Dramatically noticeable, however, both in the review of the differing theories concerning the history and origins of the labour contract put forward by Banaji and in his own synthesising assessment, is the failure to recognise that payment around the bare subsistence level makes the distinction between the wage contract and virtual labour slavery disappear to the vanishing point. The submersion of notions such as sharecropping and labour tenancy into the concept of the wage contract is after all not so very controversial—'wages' may take different forms.[56]

Given little or no mention in the theorisation of texts devoted to labour law, it transpires that the issue is also given minimal treatment in texts concerned with Public Law, yet the payment and deployment of a state force in the midst of industrial action lies on the very nexus—the boundary, howsoever imagined, *between* public and private law, pivotal to the relationship between state and citizen and thereby to the very identity of these branches of law—of what law *is*. That this is in turn determined by economic relations was a fact divined by Engels as well as Marx:[57]

> If the state and public law are determined by economic relations, so, too, of course is private law, which indeed in essence only sanctions the existing economic relations between individuals which are normal in the given circumstances. The form in which this happens can, however, vary considerably. It is possible, as happened in England, in harmony with the whole national development, to retain in the main the forms of the old feudal laws while giving them a bourgeois content; in fact, directly reading a bourgeois meaning into the feudal name.[58]

As the doubtful boundaries between contract and labour, private and public law unravel so seriously, one may sympathise with a sense that, for the wage labourer, subject to state force supporting capital interests, the very notion of the 'rule of law' becomes suspect. The meaning ascribed to the term 'rule of law' is itself contentious, and is more apparent as an assertion of state hegemony than as a test of legitimacy. As this excursion through the scholarship associated with the histories of labour and law has revealed, it is no doubt with a historical purview that we may best come to understand the defensible limits of the term;[59] yet it is least likely to be asserted on behalf of the wronged worker, even by those sympathetic to their cause. Even the Marxist historian E. P. Thompson, surveying his understanding of the concept of the rule of law via events in British history, assured himself of a meaningful security in the idea, yet for parameters he asserts:[60]

> Did a few foresters get a rough handling from partisan laws? What is that beside the norms of the Third Reich? Did the villagers of Winkfield lose access to the peat within Sinley Rails? What is that beside the liquidation of the *kulaks*?

Certainly, a 'few foresters' getting a 'rough handling' and a few villagers losing access to their local peat-cutting facilities *do* seem trivial grievances in comparison with the norms of the Third Reich and the kulaks. Such examples are surprising from this socialist historian of the English working class when one considers the much closer analogy presented by the perspective of the beleaguered industrial community illustrated by Lewis Jones.[61] Perhaps a more global view of history is necessary. As Simmonds explains,[62] Pashukanis theorizes the entire trajectory, from feudalism to public law sanction:

> '[W]ithin feudalism, rights were thought of as naturally and inherently unequal'.... Within the framework of bourgeois legal thought, rights are no longer thought of as in principle unequal. The actual inequality of concrete rights must be explained at the level of principle by reference to willed transactions entered into by the legal subject.... In so far as the state acts as guarantor of private relationships of exchange, it can appear as a public authority pursuing the impersonal interest in the maintenance of order. But when it acts beyond its role as guarantor of the market, the state is launched in a realm of pure expediency. This area of state activity does not really admit of legal interpretation. Legal theories that seek to cover all the state's activities, therefore, must necessarily distort reality.

The dramatised account of police deployment provided by Jones, set alongside the juridical discussion presented in Glasbrook Bros., points up the absolutely fine line indicated here. Indeed, the example, fictional and real, leads one to acknowledge that the state role as 'guarantor of the market' is itself inevitably politically and legally contestable, quite apart from any action 'beyond' such a role. In short, the Marxist position is logically unavoidable. Simmonds is led to ask, in a clear challenge to modern glossatorial accounts of public law:

> [Is] there anything very 'legal' about public law theory or public law reasoning? Or are the forms of reasoning involved here basically the purposive and expediency—oriented forms of thought characteristic of the administrator or the bureaucrat? ... [If] the conceptual structure of the legal order is a product of the exchange relations of the market ... we could read Pashukanis as pointing to the fact that, when the bourgeois state extends its role beyond that of general guarantor of the market, and

> uses rules in a markedly instrumental manner, it moves beyond the sphere which provides its basis of legitimacy. In enforcing rules that give clarity and stability to the legal relations of the market, the state can appear as the impersonal embodiment of the rule of law. But when it employs the law to implement *ad hoc* goals and purposes, the state can no longer plausibly cover itself with the trappings of legal right and obligation. It is revealed as lacking any claim to legitimacy.

No doubt this discussion touches upon a myriad of uses of public law and of the reach of public law vis-à-vis private law. But, seen in this light, the issue of who *pays* for the deployment of a police force—the local council, as handmaiden of the state, or private industry, in circumstances of economically and politically sensitive dispute—is at the very heart of the theorisation of public and private law, with a significance far beyond the purely technical question of consideration in the law of contract, instead touching the very question of the rule of law itself. And arguably, beyond the narrative space, it is only with Marxist and neo-Marxist critiques of law that such insights become clear.[63]

Payment near or at bare subsistence level deprives the worker, not only of *just* payment, but also of sufficient payment to bestow any real freedom of action or of identity. What is clear from the historical facts and the dramatisation provided by *Cwmardy* and *We Live* is that the use of coercive forces in situations of just dispute and labour—a dangerous labour—yielding significant profit for others, is effectively an extraction of labour on sufferance. It is salutary to find that the textual references to slavery are more than merely rhetorical, that there is an ancient and direct link between these modern workers, mining, and the very notion of slavery. In classical Roman law, the physical labour of mining had a symbolic as well as practical savagery—as well as a direct definitional link to slavery itself: enslavement by *Jus Civile* included *Servi poenae*—those condemned to death, or to enforced *labour in the mines*,[64] or to a contest with wild beasts in the arena, were considered enslaved.[65] Garnsey notes the association in the collective ancient mind between underground *work* and *shame*—

> The early history of forced labour as a criminal sanction in Rome is badly documented. *Metallum* and *Opus* were both recognised penalties under Tiberius and Gaius. Both emperors are said to have imposed them on men of rank, and this was clearly considered outrageous. *Metallum* and *opus metalli* were 'plebeian' penalties, in the view of Marcianus' contemporary Callistratus.[66]

With their deaths trivialised, expert testimony ridiculed, and just dispute criminalised, such images of slavery seem pertinent to those more recent figures failed by society and by law. The historiography of the labour contract is a cultural and philosophical as well as political and legal question, its relation to the individual and to state forces complex and subtle. Though political theory—most notably in the writings of Marx and Engels—chronicles these failings, the 'dramatised' chronicle reasserts the urgency and the rationality of the desire for change.

Conclusion—'There Can Never Be One Law'

In this chapter, the initial stimulus provided by the fiction of Lewis Jones prompted examination of the component ideas constituting the very fact of labour, of the forces impinging upon that fact and the rhetorics surrounding it. At very least it would appear that law, history, and philosophy have all proved somewhat inadequate to the task of providing a direct and wholly earnest response to the material relationship between coercive practices and the human commodity that is labour. In particular, the rationales of law, from discrete doctrinal gloss to the broad and contestable conceptual boundary between public and private domains, all contribute to concealing these truths as liminal—as a kind of 'secret' subtext to the visible world of law. Against this background, it becomes clear why the Marxist analysis of the conundrum provided a most compelling account of the 'truth' for the workers of the time. Yet by the 1930s even Marxist theory had been overtaken by historical events and, given this context, fiction provided an accessible vehicle for understanding and reviewing the vigour of the outstanding political challenge. Nevertheless, as the above analysis has indicated, the theoretical vision provided by Marx still remains a potent force in moving forward with a critique of the boundaries of law.

Some reading this discussion may have been perplexed by the avoidance of clearly prominent issues—of the law concerning the management of public order, of the law concerning the 'right to strike.' The discussion could have been characterised as one concerning the nexus between public order and civil liberties, of the boundary between state controls and individual—and collective—freedoms.[67] Certainly, the issue of public order was pivotal to debates of the time. The people of Tonypandy and of Wales, were utterly shocked by the ready deployment of police and of troops, and of the ready use of violence, in the name of the British government—despite the fact that there was never any 'reading of the Riot Act.'[68] But to keep faith with the central jurisprudential enquiry thrown up by the events and by the text, the discussion has focussed upon the intimate relationship between the opportunity for effective engagement with the terms of the labour contract through industrial action and the use and financing of coercive forces—'[W]hat they failed to understand was why, when the advantage was with them, the police should be placed at the disposal of the owners.'

As has been suggested, this question was answered, some years later, by judges in a seemingly less significant dispute; that adjudicated in *Glasbrook Bros. v. Glamorgan County Council.* Taking advantage of dramatic license, Lewis Jones choreographs elements of the Tonypandy *debacle* with other significant events—altering some aspects of chronological precision in order to render more potent the unfolding of educative political narrative. Writing from the vantage point of the 1930s—looking back over the preceding decades—his text pulses with the injustice of the apparent juristic support for capital with coercion. In a direct expression of their experience of a failure of law, the workers of Cwmardy believe that 'right' is determined by 'might,' that there 'can never be one law that is good for the tiger and the lamb,' and that this corrupted norm forms the foundation of the support of the state for capital and against citizens. The failure of their struggle to win meaningful influence through the democratic process alongside the partiality of state mechanisms, convince them of the failure of law. Singular in the creation of a historiographic, political fiction capable of educating a community to action, the work of Lewis Jones highlights some key issues for political and legal theory. No doubt for many legal commentators, the juxtaposition and 'politicisation' of the case of *Glasbrook Bros.*—after all, a case distant from the Tonypandy dispute and simply adjudicating the parameters of payment in a particular case—is an unnecessary excursion to place alongside this novel. Yet viewed through the eyes of this community, searching throughout to understand the roots of their impotence, the normalisation of the use of force by state actors in domestic industrial conflict is an issue central to the immanent impotence of the workforce, to an understanding of the relationship between public and private law and, ultimately, to the credibility of the rule of law itself.

From the failure of justice in the public inquest, to the public/private deployment of police, to the criminalisation of workers of integrity, Jones demonstrates the organic strictures of purportedly independent legal nomenclatures. His attempts to represent the interests of the workers thwarted, the main protagonist, Len, is sentenced to hard labour. His 'real' counterparts, Will John, Henry Hopla, and John Hopla, were similarly arraigned and wronged by the law. John Hopla 'died a broken man' in his early twenties, shortly after his release.[69] With this context, the perspective of Pashukanis[70] is not merely an analysis of some eccentric and dystopic capitalist legal system, but instead demonstrates the interdependence of these nomenclatures in the creation of capitalism, particularly in relation to the link between criminal law and labour law:

> In the Middle Ages, every person who tried to follow a trade without being a member of a guild was thought to be a law-breaker. The capitalist bourgeoisie, scarcely had it emerged, declared that the workers' attempts to join forces in associations were criminal .... [F]rom the purely sociological standpoint, the bourgeoisie maintains its class rule and suppresses the exploited classes by means of its system of criminal law. In this respect, its courts and its private, 'voluntary' organisations of strike-breakers are pursuing one and the same end.

Though there was formal legislative support for trade unions and voluntary associations by the early twentieth century, the rapid path from collective action to criminalisation depicted by Jones provides corroboration that capital power still ruled—though the *form* of law vouchsafed democratic structures, practice could still diverge. And, as we have seen, more recent critical insights may become blunted in the explication of theory as well as by doctrine.[71] Global political change too may intervene—in the late 1930s, the 'pure' ideological wars at home and in Spain became submerged by the overpowering and new threats posed by World War II. No doubt as a result of the fact that the larger political failures of communism were apparent by the time of writing the novel, in 1937, Lewis Jones indicates to his readers that communism as Marxism is not the way forward,[72] but the text is clear regarding the utter failure of democratic process and of law. Jones did not live to complete the narrative directive in relation to this, but the ghost-written *finale* remains obdurate on the significant failure of integrity in law:

> They are fighting to keep a principle which they and their fathers won through suffering many years ago . . . . [T]he company has been clever and used the poverty of our own people to turn some of them into scabs . . . . [T]hey have kept our men down the pit through fear of starvation on top . . . . [Y]es . . . they made us sell our freedom for a job.
>
> During the strike, some of us wondered why the police should be sent in against us. But since then, we have learned the Government doesn't keep them just for chasing criminals. No. They keep them to maintain law and order and everything that we do that is in our own interest and against that of the company is illegal and disorderly. They use the police to smash us with their batons; then summons us for a riot which they themselves have made. And after this, before we know where we are, they use magistrates and judges to twist the law and turn us into criminals, then send us to jail.[73]

Jones's dramatisation demonstrates that fiction may assist in retrieving a more complete and representative account of cultural and legal failings than can be achieved by history and theory alone. It can certainly lead one to view cognate specialisms in law, as well as individual doctrine, with a fresh eye. This retrieval may extend to a more profound engagement with the public-private divide and to the very notion of law itself. Fictions may be needed, not merely as an educative tool, but also to counter the 'truth' of history and of law with the truths of historiography and critique. A truly conscientious legal theory should take account of the possibility of present, as well as historical instances of such elisions. Modern industrial disputes may continue to pose such difficulties,[74] but so too will larger disputes of ideological note, where individuals and groups of political integrity are denied their own narrative, demonised and crystallised within the formal structures and logics of law. In South Wales in the early twentieth century, and in the dramatisation by Jones, the state's willingness to turn force against a significant body of citizenry had signalled a failure not simply in political process but also, we may come to believe, of law.

Notes

1. Niall Griffiths, 'Wales: England's Oldest Colony,' *New Statesman*, April 23, 2007, at http://www.newstatesman.com/politics/2007/04/welsh-language-wales-england.

2. See David Williamson, '100th Anniversary of the Tonypandy Riots,' *Wales on Sunday*, June 27, 2010.

3. Lewis Jones, *Cwmardy* and *We Live* (Cardigan: Parthian Books, Library of Wales, 2006; first published 1937). Actually a 'pair' of novels, now published together as one narrative, the first section, *Cwmardy*, relates the 'story' of the mining community, their relationships and struggles, while *We Live*, a continuation of this story, concentrates more fully upon consolidating a vision of political activism, culminating in support for the freedoms threatened in the Spanish Civil War.

4. A long-standing realisation, as satirised by George Orwell and his Ministry of Truth in the novel *Nineteen Eighty-Four*, but more recently the concept of the alternative and notionally predominant 'truth' has been admitted into jurisprudential process, for example in the Truth and Reconciliation hearings of South Africa.

5. Several texts may be cited in this regard,, but see, for example, works on law and literature by Maria Aristodemou, James Boyd White, Adam Gearey, Brook Thomas, Ian Ward, and Melanie L.Williams.

6. The authors cited at note 5, above, all deal with this issue in various ways, but in broader philosophical terms; so too does Stanley Fish, *Doing What Comes Naturally* (Oxford: Clarendon Press, 1989), for example.

7. See page dedicated to Paul Robeson on the Coalfield Web Materials site at www.agor.org.uk.

8. The working communities of Wales each contributed their tiny savings to the establishment of the University of Wales in the later nineteenth century; the Miner's Library in Swansea holds a remarkable collection of philosophical and political literature, again bought with the contributions of the miners themselves.

9. Christopher Harvie, *The Centre of Things—Political Fiction in Britain from Disraeli to the Present* (London: Unwin Hyman, 1991), 182.

10. Raymond Williams, 'The Language of the Working-class Novel of the 1930's,' in *The Socialist Novel in Britain*, ed. H. Gustav Klaus (London: Harvester, 1982) 133–34.

11. For further discussion of Raymond Williams on Orwell, see Paul Thomas, 'Mixed Feelings: Raymond Williams and George Orwell,' *Theory and Society* 14, no. 4 (1985): 419.

12. Leon Trotsky, *Literature and Revolution*, ed. Wm. Keach (Chicago: Haymarket Books, 2005; first published 1924): 66.

13. The discussion in Hutcheon points up links between postmodernism, historiographic metafiction, and the twentieth-century political mind, links intimated in early form by Trotsky, at least in relation to the location of art. Hutcheon: 'It is no longer big news that the master narratives of bourgeois liberalism are under attack . . . . [W]hatever narratives or systems that once allowed us to think we could unproblematically and universally define public agreement have now been questioned by the acknowledgement

of differences—in theory and in artistic practice.' Linda Hutcheon, *A Poetics of Postmodernism: History, Theory, Fiction* (London: Routledge, 1988), 6–7.

14. In the Trades Disputes Act (1906) trade unions were provided with notional immunity from liability for damages arising from strike actions. The statute was a belated political response to a series of controversial and adverse court decisions affecting the capacity of trade unions to strike, culminating in the *Taff Vale* judgement of 1901, which had rendered union funds, as funds of legal corporations, subject to economic liability for losses incurred by others as a result of union action. The royal Commission on Safety resulted in the Mines regulation Act of 1911, still a cornerstone of protective legislation for underground workers; nevertheless, health and safety legislation did little to prevent the continuing occurrence of major disasters. The Minimum Wage Act of 1912 remained on the statute books until 1947, but its ameliorating intent was diluted in the final form. At the beginning of the twentieth century, the minimum age of entry into the coal industry was raised to thirteen years. In 1906, the mineworkers union participated for the first time in a Royal Commission on safety in the mines. Incessant campaigning alongside industrial action brought about the 1908 Eight Hours Act for mineworkers underground. As already indicated, in spite of the increasing health and safety legislation, however, the death toll in the industry remained high.

15. Jones, *Cwmardy,* 188. The situation is analogous to that driving the Tonypandy debacle.

16. The worst explosion in British mining history occurred on October 14, 1913, when 439 miners were killed at Senghenydd in South Wales.

17. In Tonypandy itself, some acknowledgement of correct process would have been signalled by a reading of the Riot Act at some stage prior to the deployment of aggressive force, but according to the record, this did not occur.

18. 'Them' being a reference to the owners.

19. According to first-hand accounts, an unrepresentative group *was* involved in perpetrating some damage; nevertheless it seems that troop and police action in Tonypandy was wholly disproportionate, with striking miners 'charged' with fixed bayonets. In the clash with police on November 8, 1910, one man, a bachelor collier, Samuel Rays, died as a result of head wounds. The inquest jury, after being advised that 'if they found that his injuries were caused by a policeman's truncheon' they would also have to decide if 'the police were justified in the action they had taken in using force to repel force for the purpose of preventing disorder,' decided that it was not 'sufficiently clear' how the injuries 'caused by some blunt instrument' had been received.—see Dai Smith, *Wales: A Question for History* (Bridgend: Seren, 1999) 99.

20. Throughout the 19th and early 20th century, wages in the mining industry were linked to market prices of coal in a 'sliding scale,' a volatile and unpredictable measure.

21. For example, the story behind the 'minimum wage' is epic. From 1911, Mining Federation delegates voted for strike action unless the principle of a minimum wage

was conceded by the coal owners. By a massive majority of four to one, the membership voted to take strike action at the end of February 1912. This was the first time a coal dispute affected the nation as a whole. By March 1, more than a million miners were out on strike. From other sections of workers all around Britain there was substantial support for action taken to secure a fixed minimum wage. The dispute lasted six weeks; it was called off by the Federation when the then Liberal government promised to introduce protective legislation on pay. Yet once the government secured the miners' return to work, it was decided that there would be no actual minimum wage figure in its bill. Another ballot saw mineworkers voting by nearly 54 percent to continue the strike, but as this fell short of the necessary two-thirds majority, a return to work was agreed and a compromise Minimum Wage Act appeared in 1912. Without the entrenchment of additional employment securities, however, the minimum wage itself proved a poor source of stability.

22. See Smith, *Wales*, 116. This point is made by Jones's narrative version.

23. A brief survey of histories has borne this out. For example, the social historian Trevelyan provides a timeline which refers to events in Wales and includes the fact that miners struck for a minimum wage in 1912, but the Tonypandy events are not recorded; see G. M. Trevelyan, *A Shortened History of England* (London: Penguin Books, 1986).

24. *Glasbrook Brothers v. Glamorgan CC* (1925) A.C. 270. The key ratio of the case stated: 'Although the police authority are bound to provide sufficient protection to life and property without payment, if in particular circumstances, at the request of an individual, they provide a special form of protection outside the scope of their public duty they may demand payment for it.'

25. Questions concerning the doctrine of consideration are much beloved by contract lawyers and indeed the doctrine has a deeply convoluted narrative history of its own involving a complex excursus upon the relationship between payment, deed, and bond.

26. That is, a refusal to return to work in compliance with a national agreement to end strike action, picketing with some unrest, including pulling a safety man off his bicycle, and a declared resolve to 'get all the safety men out.'

27. From the summary of facts, paragraph one, *Glasbrook Bros. v. Glamorgan County Council* [1925] A.C. 270; 1924 WL 19840 (HL).

28. The court at lst inst and the Court of Appeal had reached the same conclusion as the House of Lords.

29. *Glasbrook Bros.*, 1924 WL 19840, 5.

30. In the Court of Appeal.

31. The Police Act 1839, s. 10 stated: 'And be it enacted, that all Chiefs and other Constables appointed under this Act shall be restrained from employing themselves in any office or Employment for Hire or Gain other than in the Execution of their Duties under this Act' ('The Police Act: An Act for the Establishment of County and District

constables by Authority of Justice of the Peace'; CAP XCIII, Pickering's Statutes Vol. LXIX 2 & 3 Vict 1839 (511).

32. *Glasbrook Bros.*, WL 19840, 5.

33. Ibid.

34. Although the police force, as the Metropolitan Police Force (the 'Peelers') was established in 1829 in part as a response to the movement of large populations into urban, industrial communities, with the attendant risk of disorder, it was with the stated principle that their function was the protection of the public against 'criminal' types.

35. Italics added.

36. *Glasbrook Bros.*, WL 19840, 12. 'I should like to supplement these statements by one further observation—namely, that it is not in the power of the executive through the Secretary of State or otherwise to limit the rights of the subject in obtaining such protection for life and property and that any attempt to do so would be absolutely unconstitutional and illegal.'

37. Jones, *Cwmardy,* 216, suggests that the 'officials' brought in to 'keep the pits in working order' are more numerous than needed for the purpose.

38. Consider, for example, P. S. Atiyah, *An Introduction to the Law of Contract* (Oxford: Clarendon Press, 1995); James Gordley, *The Philosophical Origins of Modern Contract Doctrine* (Oxford: Clarendon Press, 1991); and Hugh Collins, *The Law of Contract* (London: Butterworths, 1993).

It is in the feminist critique of the models of labour contract, domestic contract, and social contract provided by Carole Pateman, *The Sexual Contract* (Oxford: Polity Press, 1988) that the link between classical rhetorics and doctrines of freedom and coercive practice is explored.

39. Nor is it mentioned in *Labour Law in Britain,* ed. Roy Lewis (Oxford: Blackwell, 1986), nor even the comprehensive Simon Deakin and Gillian Morris, *Labour Law,* 2nd edition (London: Butterworth, 1998).

40. In mediaeval Europe, serfdom of course imposed a peonage between the land, the labourer, and his lord as a matter of birth rather than bargain. According to M. Keen, *English Society in the Later Middle Ages 1348–1500* (London: Penguin Books, 1990), one of the side effects of the plague in the 1300s was for landlords to assert with renewed vigour their rights to dues and services from tenants, as the value of such fees and work was heightened by the collapse of rental income from freemen cut down by plague. This formed a contributing factor in the Peasant's Revolt of 1381. As Keen explains:

> There was also a rudimentary ideological level to the revolt. It is perhaps most marked in the demands of the rebels for 'freedom', for the abolition of serfdom and equality of status before the law .... Langland says that revolutionary friars were preaching a kind of primitive communism. A significant feature in the provocation of the peasants was the utilisation of legal principle in their oppression, with the enactment of the Ordinance of Labourers in 1349 followed by the Statute of Labourers

> in 1351. A development of great significance in the history of the labour contract, this statutory move crystallised the link between labour and politics. . . . The object of the act was clear and straightforward, to hold up the economic weather by protecting the interests of lords and employers. (Ibid., 42–43)

This formed a key issue in the manifesto of the Peasant's Revolt, where Wat Tyler demanded that '[no] one should work for any man but at his own will, and on terms of regular covenant.' According to Keen the demand was just as revolutionary and pertinent as it suggests, aiming '[a] clear and direct blow at the clause in the Statute of Labourers that gave a lord a preferential hold over his men's labour and demanded the freedom to negotiate on wages it inhibited.' Clearly demonstrating a belief in the idea of security of contract—covenant—and in the intrinsic liberty indicated by the expression of 'will,' the demand reflects a very modern and idealistic conception of contract, perhaps already tapping into the myth that would declare the defeat of status by contract centuries later.

41. As was the case with Glasbrook Bros.

42. Note that Deakin and Morris, however, explain the modern position of the police qua 'employees' or 'workers':

> Police officers are excluded from most of the protective statutory provisions available to 'employees' or 'workers.' 'The balance of judicial opinion is that police officers do not have contracts of employment, although the terms in which the statutory exclusion is framed leaves open the possibility that they do. In constitutional terms, police constables are regarded as 'independent officers' capable of exercising legal powers derived from the nature of their office; for this reason, it was held that for the purpose of vicarious liability in tort they were not the employees of the relevant police authority (*Fisher v. Oldham Corpn* [1930] 3KB 364).' (*Labour Law*, 186)

These ambiguities, with an utterly selective deployment and displacement of concepts deriving from contract, tort, and administrative law, only serve to demonstrate the politically nuanced nature of this arm of state control. It must be noted in addition that members of the profession can pursue discrimination rights, are entitled to written particulars of their terms and conditions, have minimum notice and redundancy rights, and are within the scope of the Working Time Regulations insofar as is practicable. In recent years (see http://news.bbc.co.uk/1/hi/uk/7409679.stm) they have been active in pursuing the question of the right to strike, though Richard Edwards ('Police Offered Right to Strike,' *The Telegraph*, October 1, 2010, http://www.telegraph.co.uk/news/uknews/law-and-order/8038086/Police-offered-right-to-strike.html) reports that this may be subject to the termination of lucrative overtime payments.

43. Quoted in *Karl Marx, Selected Writings*, ed. David McLellan, 2nd edition (Oxford: Oxford University Press, 2000), 275.

44. G. A. Cohen, 'The Structure of Proletarian Unfreedom,' in *Contemporary Politi-*

cal Philosophy, ed. Robert Goodin and Philip Pettit, Blackwell Philosophy Anthologies (Oxford and Malden, MA: Blackwell, 1997), 429–45.

45. Cohen's hypothesising of such responses, and his own counterarguments in relation to such hypotheses, though intriguing, do not demand attention in this particular discussion.

46. Ibid., 431.

47. Ibid. 'For capitalism requires a substantial hired labor force .... [D]oes [this] refute the claim that most proletarians are not forced to sell their labor power? I think not. An analogy will indicate why. Ten people are placed in a room the only exit from which is a huge and heavy locked door .... [W]hoever [uses the key first may unlock the door and leave the room, but photoelectric devices will only allow one person to exit. At least nine people will remain in the room]. Now suppose that not one of the people is inclined to try to obtain the key and leave the room. Perhaps the room is no bad place, and they do not want to leave it. Or perhaps it is pretty bad, but they are too lazy to undertake the effort needed to escape.'

48. Although emigration to escape poverty was a clear phenomenon of the period, the mining communities of South Wales were themselves already the product of migration—from the poverty and poor employment opportunities of rural Wales. The industrial areas were typified by tiny terraces of houses containing large struggling families. For most, movement of the family on any scale must have seemed an impracticable dream.

49. Ibid., 433, touches upon this possibility at a late stage in his analysis:

> [H]uman motivation shows that sometimes people care about the fate of others, and they sometimes have that concern when they share a common oppression .... [A] fourth possible explanation of the absence of attempt to leave now suggests itself. It is that no one will be satisfied with a personal escape which is not part of a general liberation .... [We] can conclude ... that although most proletarians are free to escape the proletariat, and, indeed, even if every one is, the proletariat is collectively unfree, an imprisoned class.

50. And indeed, the 'real' and dramatised men 'stay down' in the mine as a response to the usual 'lock-out' imposed by industrialists.

51. As well as whether there is a meaningful correlation between labour expended by worker and capital realised, and accepting that the capitalist must provide outlay costs and, in taking capital risks, has claim upon certain proportion of capital.

52. Robert J. Holton, 'Marxist Theories of Social Change and the Transition from Feudalism to Capitalism,' *Theory and Society* 10, no. 6 (1981): 833–67, concentrates an entire study upon the divergence of views amongst academics in the debate over the transition from feudalism to capitalism in Europe. Holton reviews the difficulties inherent in Marx's own changing accounts of the transition:

> [D]ivergences ... stem in part from the incomplete and rather unsystematic comments that Marx made on this specific historical problem. These range from the bald propositions of *The Communist Manifesto*, through the suggestive sketches in *The German Ideology* and *Pre-Capitalist Economic Formations*, to the sustained discussion of 'primitive accumulation,' and 'merchant capital' in *Capital*. Such comments, though highly suggestive, are nonetheless far from definitive theories free from ambivalence. (Ibid., 836)

Holton then explores the theoretical positions of the major contributors to the debate, quoting Sweezy-Wallerstein pursuing an 'exchange relations' perspective, where the dynamic for feudal decline and capitalist development is the influence of international trade and forms, a process 'external' to feudalism, alongside mercantile development; Dobb, Hilton, and Brenner pursuing perspectives expressing Marx's teleological view of man as capable of growing and overcoming alienating social relations, wherein feudalism declines because of its inherent inefficiency, coupled with the weakening effects of class struggle between lords and serfs and the overwhelming effect of agrarian transformation, and Anderson's view, where a Renaissance vision of man—as essentially civilised and self-motivated—is reclaimed as part of a process of capital success wherein 'the classical past awoke again within the feudal present to assist the arrival of a capitalist future' (ibid., 856).

53. See ibid., 862: '[S]ome authors approach ... feudalism in terms of generic economic criteria ... while others see it far more in terms of particular genetic characteristics defined in terms of the interpenetration of economic, legal, and political criteria, unique to feudalism .... [A] second dilemma concerns the relationship between teleological aspects of theoretical reasoning and the problem of scientific verification.'

54. Jairus Banaji, 'The Fictions of Free Labour: Contract, Coercion, and So-Called Unfree Labour,' *Historical Materialism* 11, no. 3 (2003): 69–95. Definitional difficulties abound: '[T]he upshot of their stark dualities is that Brass and Ramachandran both subscribe to a liberal-individualist notion of wage-labour as essentially free labour, labour based on the "consent" of the individual worker and the free bargain that embodies that "consent"' (ibid., 74).

55. His survey takes account of studies of bonded labour in India, of debt peonage in Mexico, of the 'feudal remnant in the governance of American labour in the nineteenth century.' Referring to Orren's discussion of master and servant law, of 'the position of nineteenth-century English wage-earners who faced criminal sanctions for breach of contract,' Banaji concludes that, 'while the organisation of labour in a system of capital accumulation implicates forms of exploitation beyond the presumptively normative free labour contract [, ...] the only real freedom workers possess under capitalism or any system of domination is their power of resistance.'

56. Note, for example, the intimate tie between industrial urban tenancies and the

immediate industry itself; also, of tied markets, such as 'tommy shops,' where workers were forced to buy weekly necessities, at inflated prices, from shops owned by their masters.

57. Taken from *Marx and Engels on Law,* ed. M. Cain and A. Hunt (London, New York: Academic Press, 1979); original reference: 'Engels, Ludwig Feuerbach and the End of Classical German Philosophy,' *MESW* [3], III, 370–72 [taken from *Marx and Engels Selected Works, Vols. I and II* (Moscow: Progress, 1969)].

58. Cain and Hunt, *Marx and Engels on Law,* 123 (from Marx, *Capital* I, 505): 'The wage-form thus extinguishes every trace of the division of the working-day into necessary labour and surplus-labour, into paid and unpaid labour. All labour appears as paid labour. . . . This phenomenal form, which makes the actual relation invisible, and, indeed, shows the direct opposite of that relation, forms the basis of all the juridical notions of both labourer and capitalist, of all the mystifications of the capitalistic mode of production, of all its illusions as to liberty, of all the apologetic shifts of the vulgar economists.'

Ibid., 156 (from Engels, 'Origin of the Family, Private Property and the State,' *MESW* [3], III, 326–30): 'The state is, therefore, by no means a power forced on society from without; just as little is it "the reality of the ethical idea," "the image and reality of reason," as Hegel maintains . . . . The people's army of the Athenian democracy was an aristocratic public power against the slaves, whom it kept in check; however, a gendarmerie also became necessary to keep the citizens in check, as we related above. This public power exists in every state; it consists not merely of armed men but also of material adjuncts, prisons and institutions of coercion of all kinds, of which gentile [clan] society knew nothing. It may be very insignificant, almost infinitesimal, in societies where class antagonisms are still undeveloped and in out-of-the-way places as was the case at certain times and in certain regions in the USA. It [the public power] grows stronger, however, in proportion as class antagonisms within the state become more acute.'

Ibid., 164 (from Engels, 'Letter to Van Patten,' 18.4.1883, MESC 340–41 [selected correspondence]: 'Marx and I, ever since 1845, have held the view that *one* of the final results of the future proletarian revolution will be the gradual dissolution and ultimate disappearance of that political organisation called *the state;* an organisation the main object of which has ever been to secure, by armed force, the economical subjection of the working majority to the wealthy minority.'

59. See, for example, W. Burnett Harvey, 'The Rule of Law in Historical Perspective,' *Michigan Law Review* 59, no. 4 (1961): 487–500; and Richard H. Fallon, '"The Rule of Law" as a Concept in Constitutional Discourse,' *Columbia Law Review* 97, no. 1 (1997): 1–56.

60. See Daniel H. Cole, '"An Unqualified Human Good": E. P. Thompson and the Rule of Law,' *Journal of Law and Society* 28, no. 2 (2001): 177–203; for this quotation (from

E. P. Thompson, *Whigs and Hunters: The Origins of the Black Act* [London: Allen Lane, 1975]), see Cole, 'An Unqualified Human Good,' at p. 183. See also Robert Fine, 'The Rule of Law and Muggletonian Marxism: The Perplexities of Edward Thompson,' *Journal of Law and Society* 21, no. 2 (1994): 193–213.

61. Nor was Lewis Jones exaggerating the gravity of the position—depending on your point of view, *some* threat to the idea of the rule of law was present throughout the early period of the twentieth century, with contingency plans for industrial unrest to be met with a formalised domestic military presence discussed at length—see Keith Jeffery, 'The British Army and Internal Security 1919–1939,' *Historical Journal* 24, no. 2 (1981): 377–97.

62. Nigel Simmonds, 'Pashukanis and Liberal Jurisprudence,' *Journal of Law and Society* 12, no. 2 (1985): 135–51, at 145.

63. Contrast, for example, Dawn Oliver, *Common Values and the Public-Private Divide* (Cambridge: Cambridge University Press, 1999), whose useful text, like those texts on labour law, places emphasis upon the relationship between the public-private divide and the *individual* employment contract.

64. Italics added.

65. L. B. Curzon, *Roman Law* (London: M&E Handbooks, 1981), 61.

66. P. Garnsey, *Social Status and Legal Privilege in the Roman Empire* (Oxford: Oxford University Press, 1970), 61.

67. In recent times, the law of England and Wales has become more orientated toward this approach, with the discourse of 'human rights' catering to individual freedoms and responsibilities, aligned with (some may say, counterbalanced by) more restrictive 'public order' legislation. The issue of collective action in industrial dispute in particular has been affected by the subtleties of cultural, political, and legal change—the perspective in labour law texts already described is partly accounted for by the emphasis upon individual employment rights, with a diminution in collective bargaining powers. With such protections for individuals (ranged alongside redundancy, unemployment, and welfare provisions), union membership and collective bargaining, it may be argued, no longer reflect the 'life and death' conflicts of yesteryear. Nevertheless, the miner's strike of the 1980s provides some powerful discussion points. With jobs and communities under threat, industrial action remained a key tool. When it came to the problems in the Nottingham coalfield the Metropolitan Police were called in to strengthen the local police presence, and their brutal tactics proved controversial. The failure to hold a full ballot of members robbed the miner's union (the NUM) of its legitimacy, and this was exploited to the full by Conservative politics. It is now widely recognised that had a ballot been held, the vote would have been strong and the strike would have been formally supported. Thus, however attenuated, such rights need careful protection. My thanks to Helen Milgate for comment on this matter.

68. It is intriguing to consider to what extent this response from London was affected by prejudices of class; even more intriguing to consider the extent to which it was affected by race—for decades the Welsh as a people had been oppressed by draconian language laws and remained the butt of a kind of 'neighbour state racism' in many subtle ways. The policies were also no doubt a reflection of more extensive political anxieties—see Jeffery, 'The British Army and Internal Security.'

69. Smith, *Wales*, 135.

70. Evgeny Pashukanis, *Law and Marxism: A General Theory* (London: Pluto Press, 1989), 173.

71. Hugh Collins, *Marxism and Law* (Oxford: Oxford University Press, 1982), for example, recognises the particular partiality discoverable in the history of the law of contract yet chooses the formalistic example of individual employment law in the case of *Sagar v. Ridehalgh and Son, Limited* [1931] 1 Ch. 310, to make his point, a surprising though perhaps strategic choice for a book entitled *Marxism and Law*: Collins (ibid., 59) acknowledges that 'the tangled web of legal doctrines can conceal anachronistic survivals as well as permitting subtle metamorphoses of the existing legal doctrines.' For a survey of the contribution of American scholarship to the notion of labour law and in particular to the notion of collective bargaining, see Joanne Conaghan, 'Critical Labour Law: The American Contribution,' *Journal of Law and Society* 14, no. 3 (1987): 334–35.

72. Marx is described in Jones, *Cwmardy*, 320, as not only 'heavy and dry' but also 'out of date.'

73. Jones, *We Live*, 817–18.

74. As did the miners' strike of 1984–85, where Prime Minister Margaret Thatcher analysed the dispute in terms of external and internal 'war' with the 'rule of law':

> We had to fight the enemy without in the Falklands. We always have to be aware of the enemy within, which is much more difficult to fight and more dangerous to liberty. . . . I must tell you that what we have got is an attempt to substitute the rule of the mob for the rule of law, and it must not succeed. (John Campbell, *Margaret Thatcher, the Iron Lady* (London: Jonathan Cape, 2003), 374)

Duly Noted or Off the Record? Sovereignty and the Secrecy of the Law in Cinema

RICHARD BURT

Preliminaries: The Divisibility of the Secret

> The law prohibits interfering with and deferring the "ference" [*férance*], the reference, the rapport, the relation . . . . That is the law of the law, the process of a law of whose subject we can never say, "there it is," it is here or there. It is neither natural nor institutional, one can never reach it, and it never reaches the depths of original and proper taking-place. . . . It is always cryptic; this is a secret which as caste . . . pretends to possess by delegation. The secret is nothing—and this is the secret that has to be kept well, nothing either present or presentable, but this nothing must be well kept.
>
> —Jacques Derrida, "Before the Law"[1]

> In more political terms, the Nixon tapes may offer a (conspiratorial) equivalent to the 'photographic realism' . . . suggesting . . . not merely a unity of place and action, but also strongly representational aesthetic . . . in which, as in so much historiography and historical fiction, what the reader/spectator longs for is to be present at the scene: to see, to hear, to find out the secret truth.
>
> —Frederic Jameson, *The Geopolitical Aesthetic*[2]

> What psychoanalysis and deconstructionist philosophy "inscribe" into the model of the trace, is when observed in light of changing filing technologies, the distinction between two mutually constitutive forms of writing: an erasable writing on wax tablets and transcription into a durable inscription. The latter can attain validation and truth functions because it is preceded by a canceled *ur*-writing that has been rendered illegible. The doubling of writing into draft and clean copy puts an end to the time of the magistrates with its emphasis on pure transmission without duplicates. Based on the technique of *acta facere*, writing inscribes

> itself into the force of law. With the taking of minutes, the law designs its own truth of reality. What Paul de Man, from a linguistic point of view, termed a "fact of language" cold from a media-theoretical point of view applied to the act of taking notes: it is a performative, fact producing act. From the media-technological point of view, the synonymous use of "acts" and "*taking note* of the *fact*," as performed by Derrida in "Acts," his reading of Paul de Man, is perfectly admissible.
>
> —Cornelia Vismann, *Files: Law and Media Technology*[3]

In this essay, I call into question a series of related, uncritically examined and positivist and historicist assumptions about the law, secrets, sovereignty, and media. These assumptions may be quickly enumerated here: (1) secrets are indivisible, hidden but waiting to be revealed; (2) whatever media the law allows admitted in court as evidence are transparent, not opaque, and hence the evidence is evidently legible; (3) live testimony is primary, its records secondary because communications technologies are regarded as instrumental and external to human beings; (4) transparent and complete legal records can be easily preserved and stored in documents, files, and archives which have a fully functionally topographical space allowing for retrieval; (5) these records, some of which may include documents obtained by subpoena or secret documents only the judge reviews in chambers, can be reconstructed by historians, journalists, attorneys, and ordinary citizens, all of whom may thus reveal the empirical truth and make it possible for historians to render the past in narrative, positivist form; (6) the judge, or sovereign, is indivisible; and (7) fiction and testimony are opposites; fiction amounts to perjury, fully conscious testimony being "the truth, the whole truth, and nothing but the truth."[4]

Synthesizing these points, we may generalize that the law is understood by positivist and historicists to be indivisible. Legal evidence resists division when it is admitted. According to Cornelia Vismann, the document is the indivisible unit of the legal archive: "[D]ocuments are stored individually, partly because of their external appearance (parchment, format, hanging seal), while files are always a blasted, bundled, or bunched collection" (2008, 75). Law limits the divisibility of media proceeding on a case-by-case basis: indivisible written and other media transcriptions are filed and stored in the metaphorically indivisible unit of the case number. Only if conceptualized as indivisible units of indivisible media can documents be classified as top secret or declassified. The assumed indivisibility of the law enables an idealization of the unified totality of its documents and of its archive. "According to the ideal of the archive," Vismann writes, "the law is the sum of all files on record. They are the capital of the law" (ibid., 58).

Close readings of two "conspiratorial films," *All the President's Men* (dir. Alan Pakula, 1976), *JFK* (dir. Oliver Stone, 1992), and of two films directed by Fritz Lang, *Fury* (1936) and *The Testament of Dr. Mabuse* (1933), will show that they deconstruct the presumably indivisible secrets of the law, better understood as the in/divisible secrecy of the law: the law, that is, ceaselessly redivides the very units it divides up into material documents, the document being the indivisible unit, enclosed by a file, a case, and so on.[5] Once we see how these films deconstruct the presumed indivisibility of the secret, sovereignty, the law, and media, we will be able to understand how the secrecy of the law deconstructs the presumed indivisibility of political sovereignty as well. Whether sovereignty takes the governmental form of a democracy or an authoritarian regime, is it is always a government in writing, dependent on the word itself become law.[6]

Further Preliminaries

> Only in retrospect will we be able to understand if the symbolically suffused collapse of the capitalistic citadels in lower Manhattan implies a break of that type or if this catastrophe merely confirms, in an inhuman and dramatic way, a long-known vulnerability of our complex civilization. . . . [O]nly "effective history" can adjudicate its magnitude in retrospect.
>
> —Jürgen Habermas, *Philosophy in a Time of Terror*[7]

> "History. We don't know. We'll all be dead."
>
> —George W. Bush[8]

In order to grasp why the secrecy of the law requires an oblique psychoanalytically inflected deconstructive analysis from the perspective of cinema, we must first put deconstructive pressure on the positivist and historicist assumptions of the rule of law and secrecy in general. The transmission of information through recording media, especially in its current digital form, may be at odds with media transparency, which is nothing more than a mirage called up by the computer screen interface. As Andrew McNamara and Peter Krapp write, "[T]he medium is too often assumed to be a transparent phenomenon that simply transmits meaning from one place to another without delaying or transforming the intended meaning. In political discourse, transparency is an important issue because it goes together with accountability as a central tenet of liberal democracy and the rule of law. Is it merely perverse, then to stress 'opacity' as an equally fundamental feature in examining the role of media?"[9]

In her book *Files: Law and Media Technology*, Vismann points out even more pressing problems with the law's administration of the recorded truth, however transparent, through file storage. "The law," she writes, "operates not *in mundo* but in the medium of literality; it believes only what is written—more precisely, what it itself has written down. This is the highly effective mechanism of public belief (*publica fides*) in minutes. With the compilation of a file, a truth attains a common status; it becomes generally valid" (2008, 56). Files became necessary in European law, she shows, because records were multiple, not single, and hence were open to manipulation:

> Whatever was preserved in files for subsequent reuse had to remain legible and therefore to be neither crossed out nor written on erasable slates or scraps of parchment. But once erased was itself erased, the hierarchy of textual stages, according to which a single original presides over and legitimizes copies, breaks down. . . . The preserved drafts could be retroactively altered. Parchment erasures or pencil-written drafts allow for countless undetected corrections that leave scarcely visible marks . . . . Whenever drafts are collected, files come about. (Ibid., 92)

Vismann adds the crucial observation that "the erratic side of the law—the administrative operations, the transmission medium itself—remains a blind spot for legal history" (75), pointing out that "it is not until the beginning of the twentieth century that files turned into an object of historiography" (75).

In addition to depending on an undeconstructed account of media (transparency is transparently opposed to opacity, as it were) and the (organized or disorganized) administration of law through files, positivists and historicists depend on an undeconstructed, idealized account of the archive. In *Archive Fever: A Freudian Impression* (1995), Derrida maintains that there is always a remainder, an ash of the archive that cannot be archived.[10] Along similar lines, Peter Krapp says that the "question of the archive is not reducible to memory. . . . There is a need for a memory of the archive, as well as for the separation of the archive from cultural circulation. . . . [F]or media theory, memory is not associated with presence but with absence, and forgetting not with loss, erasure or omission but with the hidden."[11]

Along similar lines, Vismann conceptualizes the archive as an object of desire: "Files are the mirror stage of any administration," she writes. "Subsequently they become the object of desire for a positivist historiography that uses files to deduce their administrative as well as their political background" (2008, 92). The archive as object of desire produces an irresolvable problem of narrative closure both for the historian and for the citizen. In her discussion of the release, shortly after the reunification of Germany in 1989, of the Stasi (the East German secret police) files to former citizens of the now nonexistent GDR, Vismann writes that "the right of access to one's records, Stasi files . . . can be used for purposes of self-enlightenment in much the same way as keeping and reading a diary." A German government clerk read the file before releasing it to the person who requested the file and decided which parts could or could not be released. The clerical reading and releasing of files produced uncertainties in their reception, Vismann writes, fueling "the suspicion that the legible file is nothing but an inferior secondary text lacking the truly important pages. It does not contain the *whole* life. . . . [O]ne's own story turns out to be illegible, something that can only be found in the *complete* file." The file became, in the viewer of the person reading her or his file, an envelope that "attract[ed] all kinds of phantasms" (156). Instead of producing complete, whole stories, then, the files produce neither biographies nor autobiographies, just some of the materials for them. The imaginary of the archive produces what I call "secrecy effects": the release, or revelation of the unredacted files comes with spectral back ups, faux-similes of records that have either been destroyed or are still secretly being kept off the record. These paranoiac effects are endless and uncorrectable mis/recognitions of what is secret and what is not. Germans who got their Stasi files lived out their living deaths as a kind of declassification of state secrets by making it impossible for citizens to determine whether they had all the necessary papers to write their own autobiographies.

Finally, positivists and historicists assume that both fiction and testimony and life and death are conceptually mutually exclusive sets of terms: fiction is either outside the law, or, if found in the legal archives, waiting to be reconstructed as a true story, as history, by historians; similarly, only the living can testify, and testimony is to be given in person by the witness in court. Derrida deconstructs these seemingly obvious distinctions in careful close reading of Maurice Blanchot's possibly autobiographical short story "The Instant of My Death," in which the narrator narrowly escapes execution in Nazi-occupied France.[12] Derrida maintains the law must proceed on the assumption that testimony is given by a fully present living person. "For to testify," Derrida writes, "the witness must be present at the stand himself, without technical interposition. In the law, the testimonial tends, without being able to succeed in this altogether, to exclude all technical agency. One cannot send a cassette to testify in one's place. One must be present, raise one's hand, speak in the first person and in the present, and one must do this to testify to a present, to an indivisible moment, that is at a certain point to a moment assembled at the tip of an instantaneousness which must resist division. If that to which I testify is divisible, at that moment it is no longer reliable, it no longer has the value of truth, reliability, or verifiability that it claims absolutely" (2000, 32–33). The law maintains its indivisibility, delivers a stable referent ("the record") and the unmediated, absolute truth, by absolutizing differences between ontologically separate media, moments, and spaces. Only then may the gathering of evidence proceed in an orderly fashion that moves linearly from eyewitness testimony, to inscription, to transcription, and so on, and, when assembled, given a sequential narrative structure.

In practice, however, the law self-deconstructs positivist and historicist assumptions about it, actually delivering the referent as both spectral effects and truth effects, sometimes making it impossible to distinguish between them. Consider again Vismann's example of the released Stasi files. Former East Germans wondered if they had received their complete dossiers, Vismann observes, because the bureaucratic workings of the law that enabled the release their files could never be made visible; conversely, referent effects that have absolute truth-value are produced in the law by their concealment, not by the materiality of an original document. Whether or not they have been lost or destroyed is of next to no account. Secrecy is internal, not external to the operations of the law and hence is not reducible to individual secrets kept from it. Conspiracy theories about particular secrets are not by-products of the law but effects produced by secrecy of the law.

The Unreadability of Secrecy

> I rather believe the idea came to me one day in the Bibliotheque Nationale when I was reading an internment register drawn up at the very beginning of the eighteenth century.
>
> —Michel Foucault, "Lives of Infamous Men,"[13] (76)

> Unless being able to read makes the law less accessible still. Reading a text might indeed reveal that it is untouchable, literally intangible, *precisely because it is readable*, and for the same reason unreadable to the extent to which the presence within it of a clear and graspable sense remains hidden as its origin. Unreadability thus no longer opposes itself to readability. Perhaps man is the man from the country as long as he cannot read; or, if knowing how to read, he is still bound up in unreadability within that very thing which appears to yield itself to be read. He wants to see or touch the law, he wants to approach and "enter" it, but perhaps he does not know that the law is not to be seen or touched but deciphered. This is perhaps the first sign of the law's inaccessibility or of the delay it imposes on the man from the country. The gate is not shut, it is "open as usual" (says the text), but the law remains inaccessible.
>
> —Jacques Derrida, "Before the Law," 197

> I withdraw into the secret of irony . . . . But here is yet one more turn, and it is political: is it not also democracy that gives the right to irony in the public space? Yes, for democracy opens the public space, the publicity of the public space, by granting the right to a change of tone (*Wechsel der Toene*), to irony as well as fiction, the simulacrum, the secret, literature, and so on. And, thus, to a certain nonpublic within the public, to a *res publica*, whether the difference between the public and the nonpublic remains an indecidable limit.
>
> —Jacques Derrida, *Rogues: Two Essays on Reason*, 91–92

What follows from my notion of the secrecy of the law? Perhaps most important, the law is rendered resistant to reading. As Vismann says in a somewhat literary turn of phrase, the law produces truth only through writing that "writes itself" (2005, 56–57).

A secret that is not completely legible or capable of being fully disclosed in a complete story renders any distinction between readable and unreadable secrets difficult to read, as it were. The secrecy of the law must be un/read indirectly through allegory, whether in Wilhelm Jensen's novel's *Gradiva* and Sigmund Freud's essay on it, with a "fictional" autobiographical passage; philosophy crosses over into literature, as Derrida very subtly makes evident in his pseudo-autobiographical conclusion to *Archive Fever*, or in other media such as narrative cinema. The law is not immediately accessible, and it is not immediately readable. Another name for allegory is "un/reading."

The unreadability of the law, its rerouting of access through allegory, bears directly on the presumed indivisibility of sovereignty. In *Rogues: Two Essays on Reason*, Derrida undertook a deconstruction of the indivisibly of sovereignty in political theory from Plato to Carl Schmitt, exploring the aporias of justice, force, and law. And in his essay "Force of Law," a close reading of Walter Benjamin's "Critique of Violence" and *The Politics of Friendship*, Derrida acknowledges the power of Benjamin's and, in different ways, Schmitt's withering critiques of existing modern democracies. Derrida nevertheless held out for a "democracy to come" (*Specters of Marx* 1994; *Rogues* 2005, 78–94). According to Derrida, "[T]he 'to-come' not only points to a promise but suggests that democracy will never exist, in the sense of a present existence: not because it is deferred but because it is aporetic in its structure. . . . As for the 'democracy to come,' it actually announces nothing" (2005, 86, 90). Yet it is not clear to me that Derrida can save even an "*im-possible*" (ibid., 84) democracy from modern democracy by offering it in the form a promissory note that can never be cashed. And even if one allows that Derrida does save democracy through "the secret of irony" (ibid., 85)—by permanently deferring its arrival because it can n/ever arrive—one has to ask if Derrida is not playing out his own version of Kafka's man of the country standing before the law until the door is shut, placing himself before democracy to come and hoping the door will never be shut.[14] Is Derrida waiting for something like Habermas's "effective history" (2003) that will some day (who knows when) render judgment retrospectively? Is exchanging the failure of existing modern democracies in return for a "democracy (not) to come" anything more than a way of severing democracy from the question of the "force of law," from the violence on which all modern democracies have been founded, even if that deferral is in some ways more than one could hope for?[15] I am not prepared to decide these questions here (or anywhere else, no doubt). I will, however, ask preliminary questions about the way allegory deconstructs the law's putative legibility, accessibility, and indivisibility through a nonlinear, nonsequential serialization of events that interrupt, disturb, or haunt a chronological narrative capability of retracing and reconstructing cause and effect events to their origins. Allegories of the law's unreadability, as we will see when we turn to the conspiracy thriller and then to Fritz Lang's *Fury* and *The Testament of Dr. Mabuse*, follow both from the law's divisibility and from the divisibility of its media supports.

Yet More Preliminaries: BeFor/c/e/of/ the/Law

> Before even speaking of force, would justice be reducible to law [*droit*]? What about the law [*Quoi de droit*]? . . . [J]ust who has the right to give or take some right, to give him- or herself some right [*droit*] or the law [*droit*], to attribute to or to make the law in a sovereign fashion? Or the right to suspend law in a sovereign way?
>
> —Jacques Derrida, "Preface: Veni," in *Rogues: Two Essays on Reason*, xi

What is the force of law when one is always before it, when one has to "read" it allegorically? What happens to justice if the law has not only to be backed up by force (the bailiff and police, for example) but by the violence that inheres in any legal decision? (In the law, an ultimately sovereign, extralegal ruling on what the law means or whether it is in fact law.) If, as Carl Schmitt famously said, "[S]overeign is he who makes the decision" (2006, 5), what happens to legal sovereignty when a decision to declare a state of emergency and suspend the law in order to uphold it is already suspended by the law's allegorical inaccessibility?[16] To respond to these questions, we must understand that the law—and justice—arrive not only mediated but through storage media akin to palimpsests. Records—hand-written, audiovisual in both analog and digital media—function in law not because they have a referent but because they constantly loop back to a referent that is not "there," much the way editors of literary texts without manuscripts function by positing an original version or versions. We might call this p/recursive looping "reading interrupted." Vismann usefully historicizes a break between reading and archiving in nineteenth-century German chancellery, pointing out the precise moment when the last archivist read the material being archived.[17] The law's un/readability cannot fully be reduced, however, to any one moment of linear, chronological time; rather, the law becomes "readable" only by appearing to solve what is essentially a narratological problem: a recursive looping back to a phantom/real referent gets linearized and sequenced so that narrative closure, at least in legal terms, can occur. The law becomes allegorical, concealing and unconcealing the *evid*ence of evidence, as it were, as it operates in inaccessible secrecy.

How the serial recursiveness of law's secrecy necessarily fails to produce a linear narrative and narrative closure is often the subject of literature and film. Even before we get to Kafka's man from the country, we are already in the realm of allegory in the courtroom. The secrecy of the law may be un/concealed only through the law's allegorization of its paradoxical dependence on divisible closed narrative events; these events may be sequenced but are themselves made divisible by the narrative's recursive and proleptic structure and its deconstruction of written and audiovisual media as always reliable means of inscription, transcription, and transmission. To understand the secrecy of the law and its implications for sovereignty and justice, we will have to un/read the law's inaccessibility not only as articulated by Kafka in "Before the Law" (2008) but also the law's relation to violence as articulated by Walter Benjamin in his essay "Critique of Violence" (1996) the terrifying implications of which have been acutely articulated by Derrida in his close reading of it in "Force of Law" (2002).[18] My limited aim, which must remain enigmatic here, is to synthesize Derrida's essays on Kafka and Walter Benjamin, making "before the law" and the "force of law" a literary and philosophical question of reading "be-force" of law.[19]

Even Further Preliminaries: The Dis/Appearing Evidence of Notes, On and Off the Record

If the allegory or unreadability of the law produces an irreducible secrecy through a recursive looping back to an extradiscursive referent, a discourse turned into a thing that is stored in another thing, we may perhaps best unfold and fold up that secrecy if we examine closely one of the most fundamental recording media that arrives at "the truth," namely, handwritten notes, which are sometimes also the most effectively concealed and hardest to read, (Derrida, "Force of Law," 2002, 215–57). Arguably the most divisible of all documents and not part of any binary opposition, notes have a certain tendency to go missing, and not just in the law.[20] Hans-Jörg Rheinberger observes that "an increasing amount of literature in the history of science, especially from historians of science and technology concerned with micro-historical reconstructions, has been devoted to laboratory notebooks and other forms of laboratory and research inscription" ("Scrips and Scribbles," 2003, 624).[21] In what Rheinberger calls the "scrips and scribbles" of the laboratory, "scientific knowledge is made to emerge and can be grasped in its emergence" (ibid.).[22] What counts as scientific knowledge is gained, Rheinberger maintains, through a "double loss" (ibid.) of inscribed and transcribed notes mistakenly regarded as inert, transparent, and extrinsic to the research process.[23]

Notes have a somewhat similarly extrinsic status in the law. Jurors are not allowed to see transcripts of the trial, but the compensatory practice of note taking by jurors during trials is not uniform in the United States.[24] Some judges and states allow jurors to take notes; some provide jurors with notebooks to do so; and some judges and states forbid jurors to take notes. The law also regulates the passing of notes between jurors during a trial. More states and judges have allowed jurors to take notes (but not to pass them) because they seem to help jurors remember and understand evidence during jury deliberations. Even if the jurors' notes are accurate, they are not entirely transparent and their allowance hardly logical. If jurors need help remembering, logically they should get a copy of the transcript, since it is after all the official court record and taken by a court appointed stenographer. As it stands, notes occupy an odd place both inside and outside the law, used as evidence when questioning witnesses who took them and hence part of the record, on the one hand, and an extrarecord supplement based on the trial transcript and never published after the trial by jurors when they are permitted to take them, on the other. Notes record only part of the record and, because they are divisible, therefore always remain partially off the record, the unarchivable ash of the archive: transcripts do not delineate, for example an "Ah ha" moment of discovery, and other such reactions.

Un/Clear Channel

> Jameson died 9/11.
>
> —*The Manchurian Candidate* (dir. Jonathan Demme, 2004)

> In its broadest sense, technology *resists* being simply returned to the simpler level of pure objectivity, whatever its aspects of systematic and dynamic dimensions that appear to the senses on any given day—such

> that the designation "object" seems no longer to suffice for thinking it. . . . [It] is well known there is in technology a heterogeneous force that might be called techno-logical, a strange power (perhaps foreign) though completely human, even superhuman, increasingly difficult to control, whose dynamism puts into question opposition to a different mode of subjectivity than the opposition of the subject to its object. This feeling of foreignness generates fear.
>
> —Bernhard Stiegler, *Technics and Time 3*[25]

I turn to cinema in order to clarify how allegory delivers the law through media, media understood, however, not as prosthetic devices and technologies that are used instrumentally by humans.[26] Notes, along with other media such as telephones, televisions, typewriters, writing pads, computers, video, film, among others, operate as referents in the conspiratorial film by their deconstruction a seemingly obvious and questionable distinction between humans and technology: in Avital Ronell's terms, Being is already hard-wired; the essence of technology is not an add-on or extrahuman.[27] Notes are not merely a theme in films about the law and secrets: their resistance to re/reading and their relative invisibility ground the commonplace understanding of secrets as hidden information stored and retrieved only under certain conditions by certain people. The medium of film makes that resistance and relative invisibility furtively visible.

I turn first to the divisibility of newspaper reporters' notes in *All the President's Men* by way of Frederic Jameson, who calls it a postmodern "conspiratorial film." According to Jameson, media allegories in conspiratorial films operate through analogy as a cognitive mapping of global flows of capital, to provide at least some access to the always already unrepresentable "social totality." According to Jameson the always already empirically unrepresentable social totality may also be (totally) cognitively mapped through analogy. Jameson maintains that postmodern conspiratorial films deconstruct a crucial narrative distinction that enabled the clarity of the earlier detective story: "The detective story presupposed an absolute distinction between the story of the crime and the story of its resolution; here the distance between the two has been reduced to an absolute minimum by the positing of a 'crime' as informational and media-centered as its own solution."[28] If the minimal distance between the two stories based on information and media produces problems of evidence when storing it, the conspiratorial film dialectically recuperates this opacity by constructing a linear history of media as the history of its obsolescence. In *Three Days of the Condor*, Jameson writes, "[No] matter how systematically reorganized and postmodernized, telephone technology is still marked as relatively old-fashioned or archaic within the new post-industrial landscape."[29]

Concluding his chapter with *All the President's Men*, Jameson almost arrives at a paradoxical formulation of the way media become secret as they reveal state secrets: "[It] seems crucial that the Library of Congress' slips are still on paper; that the checks and Segretti's credit card receipts are not yet stored away in the computer; that the typewriter . . . should thereby be allowed to celebrate an anachronistic if not indeed posthumous triumph . . . . [S]uch archaic technology impacts on the possibilities of representation to the very degree that the newer communicational machinery—the data bank, for instance—evades conventional representation altogether. . . . [We] can most adequately represent the contemporary by way of what is already past, slightly out of style, or in the process of historical obsolescence. . . . [T]he representability of this narrative material is somehow deeply related to what is already archaic about it, to *what is already secretly no longer actual*, what is outmoded and already old-fashioned, whether or not the participants or indeed the viewers are aware of it."[30]

Jameson cannot quite arrive at a paradoxical formulation of secrecy, however, for two reasons: first, his dialectical cognitive mapping of the social totality is structuralist, media being indivisible; and second, his notion of allegory is mimetic: one invisible unit that resembles another may therefore be substituted for it. Jameson embeds a structure dividing visible from invisible media within another structure dividing representation from the unrepresentable: the social totality of late capitalism can still be represented and historicized in cinema by its concrete representations of media. By allegorizing media as indivisible units, Jameson can linearize them and thereby advance his understanding the postmodern space of geopolitics: out-of-date, transparent media such as photography are replaced by new, opaque media in the form of storage devices.

"We Have the Notes"

> When I was very young—and until quite recently—I used to project a film in my mind of someone who, by midnight, plants bombs on the railway: blowing up the enemy structure, planting the delayed-action device

> and then watching the explosion or at least hearing it at a distance. I see very well that this image, which translates a deep phantasmatic compulsion, could be illustrated by deconstructive operations, which consist in planting discreetly, with a delayed-action mechanism, devices that all of a sudden put a transit out of commission, making the enemy's movements more hazardous. But the friend, too, will have to live and think differently, know where he's going, tread lightly.
>
> —Jacques Derrida, *A Taste for the Secret*[31]

> The wall designed to surround the symbolic order of the law once the codification is complete turns everything outside into rubbish and file trash.
>
> —Cornelia Vismann, *Files*[32]

One could put critical pressure on Jameson's account of the postmodern conspiratorial film by showing that its modern antecedents in journalist and police procedurals such as *The Picture Snatcher* (dir. Lloyd Bacon, 1933), *From Headquarters* (dir. William Dieterle, 1933), and *Call Northside 777* (dir. Henry Hathaway, 1948) were already questioning the transparency of what was then "new" media. Instead, I want to put critical pressure directly both on what I take to be Jameson's mimetic account of allegory and his fundamentally structuralist account of a postmodern period of the conspiratorial film: only by presuming that information is stored in discrete media units by discrete media storage devices can Jameson allegorize the relative legibility of a given medium to its vanishing and replacement by "newer communicational technology machinery" that evade "conventional representation altogether."[33] The indivisibility of media allows Jameson to temporalize them both into micro moments in which some media become "anachronistic," and even "posthumous," on the one hand, and into macro periods, modern and postmodern, on the other. Through a deft dialectical maneuver, Jameson freeze frames this temporalized flow of successive, invisible media, as it were, by rendering that flow spatially. Jameson can then save the concept of social totality by making it representable in cinema even while conceding that the social totality can never be empirically represented. Allegory always lags behind what it tries to map through analogy.

To show how the postmodern conspiratorial film calls into question Jameson's mimetic account of allegory and the ahistorical, structural oppositions on which Jameson's account of media allegory depends, I turn now to an analysis of reporters' notes in *All the President's Men.* Taking Carl Bernstein's (Dustin Hoffmann) and Bob Woodward's (Robert Redford) investigative reporting as its narrative center, Pakula's film tells the story of Watergate: President Richard M. Nixon's plot to make George McGovern the Democratic Party's presidential nominee in 1976. Pakula begins his film with the break-in at the Democratic Headquarters at Watergate, Nixon's attempt to cover up his criminal dirty tricks, and Nixon's resignation.

Notes appear prominently at a number of points just after the police capture the criminals, or "plumbers," breaking into the Democratic Party offices in the Watergate hotel. Woodward is first shot taking notes at the arraignment of the plumbers, then at his office desk, and then in several extreme close-ups of handwritten notes to show how he first follows up that lead. When Woodward and Bernstein go to Bradlee's office, they always carry their notes. "Deep Throat," an F.B.I. source Woodward knows, leaves a typed letter for Woodward that says, "I'll leave a note on page twenty four of the *New York Times*" if he wants to speak to Woodward. Woodward says, "It's down on the record," after taking notes on a phone conversation. Bradlee asks Woodward and Bernstein if they've "got good notes," and Bernstein says, "Verbatim." And near the end of the film, after checking with an F.B.I. source, Bernstein says triumphantly, "We have it in the notes." The reporters' notes become more important when they become divisible into writing that is discarded and writing that is kept. When Bernstein returns to Woodward's apartment after staying up all night to interview a source, he takes out all kinds of pieces of paper from various pockets on which he has taken notes. But Woodward, seated at his desk about to type, gathers these pieces of paper together, bunches them up, and then leaves them to the side on his desk. He asks Bernstein if he has something he can take the story down with, and Bernstein says yes, giving him a book with notes in it, joking that he is a "walking litter basket" as he takes still more notes out of his shirt and pants pockets. Yet we never see either of the reporters throwing the bunched up fragments of notes into a wastebasket, nor do we see either reporter keeping them in a file. And even the notes Bernstein gives Woodward don't matter because Bernstein starts summarizing the story aloud and Woodward takes down Bernstein's dictation based on memory alone.

The reporters' notes paradoxically become more powerful as they gradually disappear from view. Parallel medium close-up shots of Woodward and Bernstein at their desks interviewing sources on the phone first show them taking notes, with the notes being visible; in a later scene with Woodward talking on the phone to Kenneth Dahlberg, however, Woodward's notes are not shown. We can tell Woodward is taking notes, but we only see the eraser tip of his pencil. The next shot is a tighter close-up, and we can infer from his eye direction and his facial expression when he is writing; we can see Woodward insert paper into his typewriter but not the machine and not the typing (we hear it). In a later, parallel shot of Bernstein when he is talking to Mitchell on the phone, we see only the eraser end of his pencil. Similarly, early shots of Woodward and Bernstein reporting to Bradlee in his office always show them holding their notes. Later in the film, when the story has gotten stronger, Woodward and Bernstein are shot in Bradlee's office without any notes at all. Bradley does not ask to see their notes, saying that he can't do the reporting for his reporters and so has to trust them.

By the end of the film, the journalists no longer need their notes to authenticate their story. None of the three *Washington Post* reporters on the same telephone line holding three different earphones in the same shot write anything down during or after the conversation. The fact that the three reporters heard the same person speaking effectively does away with any need for notes. In the final, racking-focus, long shot of the film, the camera zooms in slowly, showing—in focus—Nixon on a TV set in the left foreground being inaugurated for a second term—and slowly racking the focus to Woodward and Bernstein, alone at their office desks, while cross-cutting at regular intervals full frame shots of the events happening on the TV screen. When the camera stops zooming in, all we see and hear are the reporters typing, the cannons at the inauguration firing on TV. The shot dissolves into a series of extreme close-ups of very loud teletyped stories about the convictions that preceded and ended with Nixon's resignation, the date of which loops back to the very first extreme close-up shot of the film, when that date is slowly typed in letter by letter and number by number, on typing paper so hypervisible that its grain becomes evident.

Notes function both as the extralegal and legal "record" insofar as they get remaindered in *All the President's Men*. The film's narrative unity and clarity, its linearization of the story's epilogue into verdicts and sentencing in the final shot, are achieved by redividing the record in ways that paradoxically, if not ironically, disintegrate, or, in the film's diction, shred that record to the paradoxical point where it becomes a referential nonreferent (like a "nondenial denial"). We may grasp now the importance of the divisibility of the singular overhead shot of the Library of Congress that Jameson celebrates as a mirror image of the long shots of the White House. Never showing the inside of the White House and showing Nixon on TV or members of his staff at their apartments or relaying their voices through a telephone is not merely a clever narrative strategy but a condition of the film. The divisibility of notes secures the indivisibility of the executive's sovereignty. By ending with a teletyped report of Nixon's resignation rather than with footage of its TV broadcast, *All the President's Men* saves the presidency from a particularly bad president, dividing the office from the office-holder, the sovereign from sovereignty, and thereby recuperates the democracy that almost wasn't.

Jameson closes his chapter "Totality as Conspiracy" by attending to "the very famous and seemingly gratuitous shot of the Library of Congress, which literally rises from the very small (the reading-room call slips) to the social totality itself."[34] Jameson's account of this show is worth citing in full:

> This mounting image, underscored by the audible mergence, for the first time in the film, of the solemn music that so remarkably confirms the investigation's and the film's telos, in which the map of conspiracy itself, with its streets now radiating out through Washington from this ultimate center, unexpectedly confirms the possibility of cognitive mapping as a whole and stands as its substitute and yet its allegory all at once. The mounting camera shot, which diminished the fevered researches of the two investigators as it rises to disclose the frozen cosmology of the reading room's circular balconies, confirms the momentary coincidence between knowledge as such and the architectural order of the astronomical totality itself, and yields a brief glimpse of the providential, as what organizes history but is unrepresentable within in it.[35]

Jameson's account is technically incorrect, however: the overhead shot of the library is not a single take but three different shots, each of which dissolves into the other taken from a higher point from the same angle.[36] The shot is divided into three shots. More crucially, the library is a dead end for Woodward and Bernstein. They go there in order to "get something on paper," but come out, directly after the overhead shots, frustrated and empty-handed. The library's divisibility immediately produces conspiracy effects: Woodward and Bernstein offer several explanations as to how the slips may have gone missing but can't decide if they missed it or if it was removed. Unlike the overhead library shot, there is no similar shot of Bernstein's notes, and the only one that comes close is a long shot of Woodward and Bernstein sitting in a hotel room with Segretti's receipts laid out on the floor that follows a montage of close-ups of the receipts as they are stacked on top of each other.

The *Washington Post* reporters whom Bradlee comes to call "WoodStein" assemble their story not only by linearizing successive moments but by looping back to a source after rehearsing whatever information they have in the form of "the story" whenever they reach a dead end.[37] At one point, editor Ben Bradlee (Jason Robards) yells, "Where is the goddamn story?" The answer depends less on the number of confirmations the reporters have then it does on a medium that escapes Jameson's notice—namely, notes taken by the *Washington Post* journalists. The gradual divisibility and final erasure of their notes during the course of the film paradoxically serves to guarantee the notes' referential status: having "it down on record" depends on the recording itself going off the record, becoming waste, not to be filed.

Jameson's allegorical account of *All the President's Men* reproduces the film's narrative structure: just as the notes serve most strongly as an indivisible referent for "the record" when they are not represented, so the impossibility of empirically representing the "social totality" serves as an indivisible referent for Jameson's division of history into modern and postmodern histories of increasing media penetration of global flows of capital. In addition to circling back to Michel Foucault's paranoiac account of biopower as the always increasing intensification of discipline of docile bodies through surveillance and what we would now call the biometrics of dataveillance, Jameson necessarily reinscribes a revamped reflection model of historicism. Cognitive mapping of social space proceeds by way of analogy and speculation. Cinema is a crucial resource for Jameson, even though he does not say so, because it frames other media and can reflect itself. Jameson's notions of allegory and cinema are both indivisible: film may narrate history allegorically because one term may be substituted for another, politics for economics, or vice versa, just as a newer medium displaces an older one. The unrepresentable, like a secret, is assumed to indivisible.

To achieve total allegorical clarity, Jameson must exorcize both paranoia from cognitive mapping and an historical spirit, or *Geist*, from conspiracy: as in *The All the President's Men*, paranoia is always on the side of the investigator determined to discover the secret truth even only by way of analogy; just as we are never given access to the paranoia inside the White House that drove the desire to know what the Democrats were doing, Jameson does not grant access to us to the social totality, just the conspiracy in which it takes form. The White House, not the Library of Congress, figures the unrepresentable as a storage container, a black box, a total archive (the missing minutes from Nixon's tapes are never mentioned in the film) that can never be called up even if it can eventually be called to account. The way state secrets do not allow for reflection may be grasped if we move comparatively to consider how they were formulated in Prussia. Vismann observes that "the wording of all administrative instructions was classified as a 'state secret' . . . to ensure that the traffic between cabinet and chancery remained secret" (2008, 108). Subaltern scribes were not required to have "the ability to reflect" (ibid.). Secret counselors could read the documents only because "the secretaries were no longer responsible for keeping things locked and secret; they were themselves locked away" (109). A fantasy of secret reading depends on a bureaucratic fantasy of a division between scribes, who cannot read what they transcribe, and ministers, who can.

Con-Spirit-cies of the Law

> How can another see into me, into my most secret self, without my being able to see in there myself and without my being able to see him in me? And if my secret self, that which can be revealed only to the other, to the wholly other, to God if you wish, is a secret that I will never reflect on, that I will never know or experience or possess as my own, then what sense is there in saying that it is "my" secret, or in saying more generally that a secret *belongs*, that it is proper to or belongs to some "one," or to some *other* who remains some*one*? It is perhaps there that we find the secret of secrecy, namely, that it is not a matter of knowing and that it is there for no-one. A secret doesn't belong, it can never be said to be at home or in its place [*chez lui*]. Such is the *Unheimlichkeit* [uncanniness] of the *Geheminis* [secret].
>
> —Jacques Derrida, *The Politics of Friendship*[38]

To understand better how the secrecy of the law bears the divisibility of sovereignty, we need first to revise Jameson's mimetic account of allegory. As we have already seen in *All the President's Men*, allegory is not entirely mimetic;

rather, it endlessly redivides whatever opposed categories it makes similar and parallel, creating through the wasting of notes, as it were, an irreducible semantic indeterminacy that allows for TOTALLY paranoid/historicist readings of the history represented by the conspiratorial film.[39] Following Theodor Adorno's (1984) and Tom Cohen's (1994) more recent critiques of mimesis, we may observe that allegorical narratives depend for their presumed completeness on missing evidence that takes the form of documents that are, like notes, always divisible. To make these points concretely, let me turn briefly to Oliver Stone's conspiratorial film *JFK* (1991), perhaps the most postmodern conspiratorial film Jameson could hope for, in which a single note figures in a single but central pretrial scene. Jameson comments that Kennedy was the first media event.[40] Allegorizing history by allegorizing the divisibility of media, *JFK* tells the story of the failed prosecution of a Louisiana attorney named Jim Garrison (Kevin Costner) that used the Abraham Zapruder film of Kennedy's assassination as evidence in court. Even at the trial, the Zapruder film is not shown to the jury continuously from start to finish. Instead Stone cuts away from the courtroom screening to people in it and then back to the film, which re-edits to include footage, shot by Stone himself in different film stocks (8mm, 16 mm, 35mm)—just as the "Zapruder film" we see parts of at the beginning of the film is cut up, consisting partly of footage shot by different people the day of the assassination and partly footage shot by Stone, again all in different film stocks, spliced or "bled" together in one sequence.

JFK would seem to be a very postmodern film. It purports to tell the true story of the assassination, yet it undermines the notion of a single truth, distinct from fiction, by constantly alternating between color and black-and-white footage, often mixing them up in the same sequence. Consequently, one can't always tell whether the black-and-white footage is speculative or authentic. Stone's use of voice-over narration in court and in Garrison's office when preparing for court puts even greater pressure on the truth-value of black-and-white footage. At one point, Garrison talks in voice-over as we see black-and-white footage of Oswald being caught in a movie theater. Here we get a truly self-reflexive moment in which a film appears projected in Stone's film that might validate the power of film to provide evidence. Yet Stone shoots the sequence in such a harried way that the titles of the films are difficult to read on the marquee. This script says: "A double feature is playing—*Cry of Battle* with

Van Heflin and *War Is Hell*. He goes in. . . . Inside the theater, *Cry of Battle* is on the screen." But because the marquee puts the name of the star Van Heflin below *Cry of Battle* and above *War is Hell*, we cannot be sure unless we have seen the films if Van Heflin acts in both films or only one of them.

Instead of providing clear evidence of the authenticating and evidential power of film, Stone leaves his audience wondering if this part of the film is fiction or if Oswald really was caught at a movie theater showing this exact double bill.[41] The uncertainty Stone creates doesn't really matter, however. The genius of his film lies in the way it shows how any attempt to arrive at the truth through legal means will take the form of conspiracy theory. The law depends on mediatized evidence that is always haunted by a "spirit" of speculative reasoning, a spirit that is infinitely divisible and infinitely divides the referent effect it produces (spectrally).

Nowhere is the total deconstruction and divisibility of media more evident in the film than when it takes up a note. Garrison makes his first conclusion on the basis of a story about a note left by Lee Harvey Oswald (Gary Oldman) that was later destroyed. The story of the note is told as if in flashback (except that it is not subjective) in black and white. Stone then cuts to the pretrial scene, in color, with Garrison speculating on the note's content, his proof that it described the assassination being its destruction: what's not there produces what is there. Totally. Yet what is missing, the note, has to be singular, indivisible for Stone to be able to cinematically make the audience wonder what is authentic history in *JFK* and what is unproven speculation. The singularity of the note makes it possible to insert it in a single scene as well. Moreover, the note has to have been destroyed, its "existence" relayed orally through rumor, for the film's narrative of a conspiracy to become narratable. Because it is permanently indivisible, the (fantasy of a destroyed) note grounds an otherwise irreducible divisibility in legal reasoning that makes speculative reasoning impossible to tell apart from psychotic "un-reasoning."

Strangely enough, *JFK*'s formal inconsistencies—cutting between color and black-and-white film, different film stocks, and so on—undercut the mimetic allegory Stone wants to narrate. With the exception of the note, the divisibility of media is the condition of Stone's allegorical myth-making. The restoration of the referent through its destruction or recutting enables Stone to allegorize and mythologize Kennedy as the Oedipal father whose murder enabled the bad "son" President Lyndon B. Johnson to escalate the Vietnam War just as Kennedy was supposedly going to withdraw troops. Similarly, Jameson can restore the "social totality" as a postmodern, structural problem of representation: the increasing invisibility of new media makes them increasingly powerful. Oliver Stone's antimimetic allegory of total conspiracy theorizing remains as strong and as weak as Jameson's mimetic allegorical theory of totality as conspiracy. In *J.F.K*, Stone cuts up filmed history in order to recut extracinematic history: the allegorical economy of his film lies in making the notion of one authentic, original film invalid in order to validate a mythologized referent, the legend of *J.F.K* as it were: the film's narrative stands in for the fragments of film shown in it. *All the President's Men* reaches a similar end (the myth of journalism as the Fourth Estate preserving the Republic) through different cinematic means.

Sovereign Suspensions and Other Suspended (Death) Sentences

Unlike the postmodern conspiratorial films Jameson analyses, Fritz Lang's *Fury* (1936) and *The Testament of Dr. Mabuse* do not stop short of deconstructing the indivisibility of media, the law, and sovereignty.[42] Lang's cinematic default is already allegory: his film narratives operate in a Kafka-esque, if also realistic world. According to Tom Gunning, the overt allegory of Lang's early silent films, such as *Destiny*, continues to shape his later more realistic, sound films as early as *M* (1931). Resonant objects disclose character traits in *Fury* and Mabuse addresses the camera directly in one scene, talking and gesturing in ways that resemble Hitler in *The Testament of Dr. Mabuse*.[43] The common criticism of Lang's films, as Gunning points, is that their allegory is too obvious. But even cursory attention to the initial reception of both films suggests that Lang's conception of cinematic allegory is far more complicated: what seems obvious may not be and the seemingly obvious may also conceal something that is far from obvious. By Lang's own account, he fled Germany not because Hitler disliked *The Testament of Dr. Mabuse* but because Hitler liked it. Joseph Goebbels told him so (we have only Lang's word for it) and wanted him to make films for the Nazis.[44] If *The Testament of Dr. Mabuse* implies allegorically that Hitler is a master criminal who is also a madman, Hitler apparently either didn't see the parallel criticism or regarded it as a compliment. Once in Hollywood, Lang met with studio resistance to his proposed scripts serious enough to create a three-year-long hiatus between films, rejecting a script entitled *The Man from Behind You* "centered around a theme of . . . anonymous threatening letters. . . . Indeed, the signature scene of Lang's master criminal films occurs here, as [the protagonist, an attorney] Moran wonders aloud who can be responsible for the strange and obscene notes he finds in his office and Lang directly cuts to the [criminal] Professor testifying at the police office."[45] After Lang made *Fury*, MGM did not renew his contract.

Working from "internal un/readings" of the films alone, I will show that Lang's cinematic allegory is not dialectical, that it turns away from validating the capacity of film to reflect other media either by framing them within it or by framing itself as film-within-film. The self-reflexive moments in Lang's films turn away and tune out a dialectics of allegory. Insisting on the in/divisibility of media and the law, Lang profoundly unsettles character and object centered film criticism of Lang. Lang's allegorical cinema makes film itself divisible. No transcribed evidence—whether notes, photography, newspapers, or film itself—remains undivided, hence totally evident in his films. And Lang's allegorical deconstruction of supposed moral and political opposites such as the police and criminal organizations makes the law totally in/divisible, in/capable only of rendering verdicts that always arrive as suspended sentences. The legality of the sovereign's capacity to suspend the law from within the law is framed allegorically by Lang as a question of the law's suspension of its own sovereignty.

Although *The Testament of Dr. Mabuse* deals directly with the divisibility of notes, I want to turn first to *Fury* because it has a more expansive account of media as legal evidence. Moving backward chronologically, then, I will consider Lang's critique of the law's sovereignty in relation to his critique of media as sources of legal validation and authentification in *Fury* first. Critics have tended to divide the film in two narrative parts. Although *Fury* seems to begin as an antilynching social message film, the second half of the film seems to subvert this reading. As Tom Gunning puts it, the film's protagonist "Joe Wilson [Spencer Tracey] initially represented the typical citizen of a democracy, unexceptional and harmless, [who] later becomes a fascist character manipulating other people for his own ends."[46]

Yet the film does not turn on character so much as it does on the validity of film as legal evidence. The apex of this film concerns a courtroom scene in which the prosecutor introduces "mysterious evidence" after getting a series of witnesses to perjure themselves. The evidence is a film taken by a newsreel man during the attempted lynching. Garrett Stewart regards this scene as a vindication of the power of cinema, the stop action shots of three people involved in the "lynching" metaphorically putting a stop to lynching.[47] According to Stewart, "Lang's film may have cleared the way for a wider use of film in court, or 'movies' as Lang's headline calls them, a procedure that was subject until the 1930s. . . . Appellate judges repeatedly ruled against filmic evidence in the twenties because, unlike photographs, film could not be studied all at once as a portable document—only viewed and reviewed. Pictures on the strip were too small to see or at least for the jury to examine comfortably, and projected on-screen they were too swift to fix upon."[48]

This account of film as "Witness for the Prosecution" just won't do, however.[49] *Fury* puts into question the very clarity Gunning assumes cinema provides. Lang films the cameraman taking the film on a hotel room balcony during the attempted lynching. He says, "What a great shot," indicating that his film consists only of one long take. However, the film shown at the trial includes a great number of takes, many of them at ground level and in close-up. The mounted camera could not possibly have been moved. Even if one wants to argue that Lang is merely overriding realism for the sake of narrative economy to avoid having to repeat footage already shown earlier, one would have to account for other problems Lang goes out of his way to make evident. During the courtroom scene, for example, the projector keeps whirring even though the prosecutor refers to the freeze frame shots as "stop action." The shots of the defendants engaged in criminal acts are also shown on the screen in the courtroom from oblique, low, even German Expressionistic angles (the only such shots used in the entire film). When filming the attempted lynching, the newsreel cameraman says he had run out of film the one time we see him filming, and he tells the cameraman to reload the camera this time with the "new, hypersensitive film," and to attach a special lens. The long shot of the town's jail that follows immediately looks noticeably different from a similar shot of the jail that precedes the cameraman scene and that returns again shortly thereafter. Lang pointedly calls attention to the technical divisibility of his own film and of the film used as evidence in it. In addition, he invites us to notice crucial yet missing parts of the film, no doubt for reasons of narrative economy, when it is shown in court: the two men who light and throw the dynamite that blows up the jail and makes Wilson's escape impossible—"He'll never get out of there"—are not shown.

"Where Is the Corpse?"/"The Law Doesn't Know"

In any case, the cameraman's film is not decisive evidence in the trial. As in *The Picture Snapper*, the death of the condemned person is not shown in the film. Nevertheless, he is presumed dead, and newspaper banner headlines shown in the film indicate that he was burned alive. The defense points out that there is evidence establishing that Wilson did burn to death, asking, "[W]here is the corpse?" even though he also admits that objects known to have belonged to the dead person also count as evidence in place of the corpse. Even the corpse is not an absolute referent. A later shot shows a newspaper with a photograph of Wilson seen early on in the film now with the question "Is this man alive?" next to it. The question is meant, of course, as an empirical, legal one: Wilson is either alive or dead, the defendants are either guilty or innocent. Yet Wilson does not simply survive his fake death. When he escapes and returns to his brothers, he says, "I'm dead. I'm really dead. I'm legally dead." Yet if he isn't really alive the same way he was before he was almost lynched, he isn't legally dead either. Wilson says the mob watched him "burn alive." But they only thought they did. The coroner does not issue a death certificate for Joe.

To get a conviction for his "lynching," Wilson has to send an anonymously written letter and his partially melted engagement ring to the judge, and the judge himself has to be sworn in to be able to introduce it as evidence. Katherine, the single eye-witness who testifies that there was in fact a lynching, begins to recognize that the letter, even though made up of letters cut from newspapers, has been composed and sent by Joe. When going up the elevator to the courtroom earlier, she had recognized a tear in Joe's coat she had sewed up, and noticed that one of his brothers was now wearing it; she is further startled when he takes peanuts, Joe's favorite food, out of the pocket. Katherine also notices that the letter misspells "memento" as "momentum," exactly the way Joe did. Nevertheless, she sticks to her testimony when she is recalled to the witness stand and is asked to examine the somewhat melted ring; she confirms that it is the ring she gave Joe when she last saw him. Much of her testimony is not given in the film, however. After Katherine is sworn in, the film cuts to Wilson listening to it on the radio, but then turning the radio off. After she testifies, Katherine confronts Joe's brothers, saying, "He's alive, isn't he?" But she ends up concluding "He's dead" after they refuse to tell her the truth. But Lang's film is even more bizarre because the film shows the jury foreman reading out acquittals of two defendants and three convictions out of the twenty defendants on trial because Wilson appears in court to show that he is alive before all of the verdicts are read. Wilson says he will pay for what he did when addressing the judge; Wilson's presence in the courtroom neither convicts him nor exonerates him; nor does it even establish his guilt. How will Wilson pay for what he did? What exactly did he do? Send the letter and ring to the judge? Yet he didn't sign the letter, and Wilson's "evidence" may have been rejected by the jury during deliberations. Similar questions about Katherine remain unanswered. She notices the slip of the prosecutor and misspelling of "memento." But she is not asked about the spelling by the defense attorney, who of course can't know that there's a question to ask. And she apparently can't just say what she knows even in the form of a confession, as does the woman defendant who says, "We're all guilty," before fainting in court, because Katherine is not on trial, not accused of anything. All she does and all she can legally do is correctly to authenticate the ring.

Law on the Fritz

Fury ends with a speech by Wilson about what the "law doesn't know," a phrase that he puts at the beginning of his last two sentences. In the final shot of the film, Joe and Katherine embrace and kiss. Lingering questions about the innocence or guilt of the "good" and "bad" characters are not merely side effects of the necessity to close the film with a happy ending but arise from the film's interrogation of what the law does and doesn't know. Almost as if it had been written by Kafka on a good day, the ending of *Fury* suspends the law by intensifying a recurrent uncertainty about evidence of guilt and innocence, of life and death, haunting the film and leaving us uncertain about who is alive and who is dead, about who is guilty and of what. A subplot remains equally divided and unresolved: the governor calls up the National Guard after the sheriff notifies him that a mob is gathering, but his order is overturned by one of his officials for the sake of re-election. The governor goes along with his subordinate, but later a member of the mob yells, "The soldiers are here," without our ever being told who sent them. In any case, they arrive too late, and the governor gives his official a newspaper showing him that the lynching was a fiasco. We never learn the fate of these elected officials, but it hardly matters given that Lang's purpose is to show the strange ways they operate—the governor's order suspended by a nonsovereign for extrajudicial reasons.

Even the sheriff will not testify to what he saw for fear, he implies, of being lynched himself (the reason the writer of the anonymous letter gives for not signing his name or writing the letter by hand). Lang frequently repeats moments that need to occur only once for the narrative to advance. For example, two shots show superimpositions of the defendants to indicate Joe's guilty conscience, one when Wilson turns off the radio during Katherine's testimony, and the other after the cop walks by and momentarily looks back at him. The inscription on the ring—"from Henry to Katherine to Joe"—makes Katherine's name into a double referent: "Henry" and "to Joe" are engraved in different fonts, but "Katherine," engraved in the same style as "Henry," refers both to Katherine and her mother, also named Katherine. Joe first says "momentum" for "memento" when Katherine departs on a train, and she corrects him (a mistake she has corrected "many times"). Before the letter with "momentum" misspelled appears in court, the same mistake occurs in a handwritten letter we see in close-up with the something close to "memento" crossed out and the same mistake, "momentum," written above it. In Joe's next, now typewritten, letter, many apparently misspelled words have been corrected by XXXXs typed over them. Wilson does not bother to make a clean copy of his letter before mailing it. Similarly, the reward poster the sheriff shows Joe after arresting him lists the suspects as three men and a woman in a car with an Illinois license plate, an exact parallel to Joe's car, his two brothers, and Katherine. Lang's plot reversals do not divide *Fury* into two parts then, but keep redividing it, driving the plot by oscillating between fits and mis-fits.

Lang's antimimetic allegorical rendering not merely of objects and characters but of the law and media suspends the sovereignty of the law in order for the law to continue to be (legally?) practiced. As we have already seen, the sheriff and the judge both declare states of exception of different sorts. The judge acts out this suspension in an extremely odd performance: after making the extralegal decision to admit the letter into evidence, he momentarily and legally leaves the court without a judge so that he can take the witness stand and allow the prosecutor to introduce the letter and ring into evidence. The judge remains seated in the witness box during the prosecution's entire discussion of the letter and its contents until recalling Katherine to the stand. Moreover, the judge never replies to Wilson at the end of the film. He remains off-screen and on mute. What kind of justice can be delivered when the law has to suspend its capacity to decide in order to operate?

Notes on Lang's Allegory of Death

> Perhaps it is the encounter of death, which is only ever an imminence, only ever a suspension, an anticipation, the encounter of death as anticipation with death itself, with a death that has already arrived according to the inescapable: an encounter between what is going to arrive and what has already arrived. Between what is going to come (*va venir*) and what just finished coming [*vient de venir*], been what goes and comes. But as the same. Both virtual and real, real as virtual. . . . Death has just come from the instant it is going to come.
>
> —Jacques Derrida, *Demeures*[50]

> Everything that was recorded in files could therefore become *lex*. . . . [N]otes were a further preventive measure against falsification, since they attest to the orderly procedure of the *senatus consulat.*
>
> —Vismann, *Files*[51]

In dividing *Fury* into two parts, Gunning proceeds, like Jameson, to link the "dead" Joe Wilson mimetically to the criminal masterminds of Lang's earlier films such as *Dr. Mabuse: The Gambler*, and *The Testament of Dr. Mabuse*; Gunning similarly links the trial scenes in *Fury* to the "trial" held by the criminals at the end of *M* (1931). All of these masterminds are also masters of media, Gunning says, the difference in Joe's case being that he can only receive radio broadcasts, not make them as both Mabuses do in Lang's earlier films.[52] A character-centered analysis of Lang's films may usefully call attention to Lang's recycling of certain themes, but to understand how deeply his German and Hollywood films pose challenges to European liberal democracy as much as they do to Hitler, we must first grasp how allegory is not mimetic but a mediatized process of transcription and transference in which apparent opposites such as life and death, the police and criminal organizations, not only become parallel but are rendered divisible. *The Testament of Dr. Mabuse* explores varied ways in which the law's procedures for catching, convicting, and confining criminals by exposing one kind of guilt while concealing others derail justice as opposite terms innocence and guilt become inseparably crisscrossed by media, even if they remain distinguishable. As in the case of *Fury*, Lang is not interested in using the cinema to reform the law so that it functions better.

To be sure, Lang never simply collapses the police into criminals, as if the two were identical. Dr. Mabuse (Rudolf Klein-Rogge) plans and directs a series of crimes telepathically and through writing and radio dictations from his cell in an insane asylum until he eventually takes over the asylum's director, Dr. Baum (Oscar Beregi, Sr.). When one of Mabuse's henchmen, Thomas Kent (Gustav Diessi), turns against him with the support of his girlfriend Lili (Wera Liessem), Mabuse tries and fails to kill them. With Kent's help, police inspector Lohmann (Otto Wernecke) gradually discovers that Baum is Mabuse and ends up putting Baum back into Mabuse's cell in the insane asylum. Yet even the seemingly most allegorical scene in *The Testament of Dr. Mabuse* where Mabuse resembles Hitler is complicated by the way Mabuse has taken over Dr. Baum's personality. The topical allegorical parallel between Mabuse and Hitler folds into a parallel between Baum and Hitler, Baum being a puppet being mastered by Mabuse, who is nevertheless inside his puppet. These kinds of multiple analogies without a clear referent structure Lang's films as well as accounts of Lang as a film director. For example, David Kalat regards Lang and Mabuse as doubles: "Dr. Mabuse had not abandoned Fritz Lang, and in many ways it is as if the mad conspirator had traded identities with the film director" (92).[53] Yet to read the "Mabuse as Hitler" scene in Lang's film allegorically in these one-to-one ways is to ignore the way Lang allegorizes the secrecy of the law as the unreadability of Mabuse's notes. Mabuse writes all the time, but much of what he writes is gibberish; Lohmann retraces the writings of Mabuse and others, and he also recalls police files from the archive to his office. *Testament* oscillates between kinds of secret writing, only some of which the law has some power over: criminal writing (secret, psychotic, opaque, or illegible marks on pages of paper immediately discarded) and crime scene writing (disclosed, neurotic, transparent writing assembled into police reports that are bound—literally tied up in knots) and that are housed in a police archive. Witnesses who might testify, including an undercover cop who has gone so deep under cover that Lohmann thinks he has gone rogue, are killed or helpless.

Allegory in Lang's film is not mimetic, equating one term with another, but full of doubles and analogies that are not mirror images, or, we may say always funhouse mirrors the reflections of which are misrecognized by characters as accurate: an insane asylum and an academic lecture hall, hypnosis and transference, pages of writing and their projections on slide, a lecture hall and a movie theater, and so on. Lang's *M* famously draws parallels between the police and organized crime, the latter doing the work of the law up to the point at which the law intervenes to stop a crime in progress or about to be committed. Even in *M*, however, no verdict is rendered after the police stop the murder "trial" held by the criminal kangaroo court and take the suspect (whom we know to be guilty) off to jail. *Testament* intensifies a Langian logic of the law going into effect only when the law's capacity to suspend the law is itself suspended—and suspended by the law, too. Rather than draw parallels between completely discrete and indivisible sides, Lang allegorizes the secrecy of the law as the antimimetic folding, unfolding, and refolding of distinctions between seemingly opposed terms.

Lang's manner of allegorical un/folding may be glimpsed best at a number of points in the film that have to do with notes. *The Testament of Dr. Mabuse* gradually brings into relief links between Professor Baum's lecture notes and the notes of his criminal double, Dr. Mabuse, notes that are an assemblage/compilation of his automatic writing/dictations/audio transmissions (heard only by characters in the film). Mabuse produces his notes outside the law (he writes them in a insane asylum) and they are shown through a slide projector to medical, not law students. Yet Mabuse is reducible to the criminal in the insane asylum who bears his name. Mabuse has no single location. Lang departs from his earlier 1923 silent version *Dr. Mabuse, the Gambler* by not immediately revealing the criminal mastermind behind all the crime.[54] Instead, Mabuse and Baum are doubled up, made into a relay of recordings, note taking, note assemblage, and so on. Since we see Baum in the lecture hall and Mabuse in the cell (they are spatially located in these ways), we cannot determine who is sending the commands, Mabuse or Baum, and at what point Baum is taken over by Mabuse or takes over Mabuse. In other words, the film creates a series of narrative folds that make it impossible for us to locate an origin, a cause of crime, in a single person.

Whereas notes are always legible and written on bound notebooks in *All the President's Men*, they are initially illegible and scattered in *Testament*, picked up from the floor of Mabuse's cell. Dr. Mabuse's "testament" turns out to be a collection of his "Aufzeichnungen," or "notes."[55] The cover page has been typed, given a title, and dates assigned, but one cannot determine who typed the notes or bound them. When Baum's colleague Dr. Kramm (Theodor Loos) accidentally stumbles across them while looking for a book to read while waiting in Dr. Baum's office, Mabuse's writings are shown in close-up with a typed cover page entitled "notes." Dr. Kramm also refers to them as "Mabuse's notes" when asking Baum "who else knows about" them. More pointedly, Dr. Baum, possessed by Mabuse, explicitly renames the "testament" as "notes" when speaking about the genius of Mabuse to Inspector Lohmann (Otto Wernicke) in the morgue over Mabuse's corpse: "Of course, not testament in the ordinary sense of the word," Baum says to Lohmann, "just some of his notes." At all points, then, the notes are divided: we have only some of Mabuse's notes, not all of them, not one of them.

As *Testament* proceeds, Mabuse's notes not only become more and more legible as such but also explicitly cinematic. Baum's lecture on Mabuse is accompanied by slides of Mabuse's writings, and is preceded by a shot with Baum shuffling two lecture notes on the desk in front of him. As Baum tells the students Mabuse's case history and the lights darken, we see them all in unison sit up straight in their seats, stop writing, and start listening. The camera then cuts from them to what they have been looking at, namely, a slide of Mabuse. The darkened lecture hall is like a cinema, as some critics have noted, but for Lang cinema crucially comes into being through writing and then projects images—of writing.[56] The greater cinematic import attached to the writings is established in the very next scene when we see Mabuse in the act of writing and numerous pages of his writings for the first time followed by the film's first use of trick photography (a ghost or hallucination produced by superimposed footage). Baum's assistant's collection of Mabuse's writings from the floor calls up a phantom double of Mabuse, preceded by the phantom's shadow, an extra-cinematic double of a cinematic double, as it were.

Once the assistant gathers the pages of writing and they are named as "notes" in a later scene, Mabuse's power becomes dialectically more detectable as it becomes stronger and runs ahead of any attempt to put a stop to the crimes his notes transmit. Dr. Kramm literally stumbles across the notes in Baum's office and proceeds to pick them up on the floor after accidentally knocking them off of the desk. In this scene, we see them still unbound but with a cover page entitled "notes" for the first time. Since the scattered pages are unnumbered, Kramm has to work as an editor to reassemble them in the correct order. As Kramm begins to make sense of what he initially regarded as "junk," he recalls a newspaper story about a jewelry robbery he has apparently read earlier that day and matches the notes to the newspaper, realizing that the notes appear to be the robbery plans, which Kramm compares to a blueprint. As Kramm reads the notes after he reassembles them by hand, the cause and effect links between the notes and crimes committed in the film become clearer. Although Kramm detects Mabuse's hand, Mabuse detects his detection, so to speak, and this scene is immediately followed by audio orders to have Kramm killed and then, in the following scene, his murder.

Mabuse's notes next appear in what I call the film's transference scene, where Mabuse, his powers at their height, appears as his phantom double and takes possession of Baum. I call this a transference rather than a possession or haunting because it strikes me as a deeply psychoanalytic moment in the film. Even more than the scene in Lang's *Spies* (1928), where a letter is copied at a post office from the imprint the writer made in the support he wrote it on, Lang's attention to the transcription of notes as transference and telepathy recalls Freud's oft-cited "Note upon the Mystic Writing Pad" (1961).[57] Lang seizes on the two meanings Freud assigned the transference. Initially, transference meant the displacement of unconscious materials and affect to representation; subsequently, transference meant the therapeutic process in which a patient identifies with the analyst or someone else and recollects and reen/acts out the patient's traumas in therapy.[58] Lang puts both meanings into play into this scene but shows how they cannot be harmonized. In Lang's (anti-)therapeutic *Testament of Dr. Mabuse*, the medium of (anti-)transference and (non)transportation (one goes forward only to go nowhere) is enabled by misdirection and mismatches between various media, and more or less explicitly thematized as a (going off) track or trajectory (destiny or coincidence), a flipping (out) of a liberal character into a fascist or the reverse, through different analogues to recoding media, whether electronic or print, in each of his films. Lang thereby replays and plays out a tension in Freud's theoretical metapsychological theory that led him to view his own work as paradoxically seeing the "clearly unclear".[59]

In this scene, Lang renders cinematically what I earlier called the production of secrecy and referent effects in my discussion of Vismann's account of files. As a superimposed phantom, Mabuse is both transparent and opaque. Whereas in *All the President's Men*, we saw Bernstein move from giving his notes to Woodward, then summarizing and dictating them from memory, the lack of any clear causal logic in Lang's almost totally silent scene of telepathic transference, makes it extremely difficult to assign dictation and writing to a single person. Merely by reading the notes, Baum, almost as if he were already unconsciously Mabuse, seems to call up Mabuse's phantom and activate the transference of (un)consciousness. During the transfer, Mabuse pauses behind Baum and moves a set of pages from the top of one stack of notes over to the one in front of Baum.[60]

But just what is Baum reading? The notes in this transference sequence differ from their appearance in earlier sequences in more explicitly connecting their potency to their assemblage and integration, on the one hand, while making their potency lie in their hieroglyphic in the form of handwritten, historiated letters. The typed title page of the notes is now seen first, looking like the page Kramm saw but with new dates, establishing the notes Baum is now reading as the most recent installment and perhaps a development of Mabuse's earlier notes that Kramm had read in Baum's office. The first close-up shot of the notes shows a word and image and partially links them together so that the letters become something like hieroglyphs. Above the word "gas" is a gas mask, and the eyes in the gas mask, two "O"s, do double duty as zeros that appear to be part of a number, 1,000,000. Similarly, something like the word "Mord" is part of a drawing of a gas mask, with the "O" serving as the mouth. But the letter serving as the nose appears not as an "m" but as either a "u" or "w." One has to read the nonsense word "U/Word" as the word "Mord" by projecting "U/Word" forward, so to speak, and taking the U/W as a literal double U-turn (from U or W back to M) as the consequence of people breathing poison gas. After turning several pages, the introduction of sound marks a new stage in the notes' integration as Baum pauses at what is effectively the title page of the notes, "Herrschaft des Verbrechens," or "Empire of Crime," and reads the words aloud for the first and only time. Furthermore, the title page is illustrated, much like the first page of the notes we saw moments earlier on Baum's desk.

This time, however, the notes make more sense. Now the word "Mord" (murder) appears spelled correctly in the lower left. At the center of the page is a drawing of a large hand with a stop watch on it, and a time bomb in the upper right seems to double as a radio transmitter repeatedly sending out the word "crime." After the transference of Mabuse into Baum is complete, we see that another significant development has occurred: the notes that Mabuse's phantom has placed in front of Baum are bound. Marking yet a further stage in the assemblage of Mabuse's writings, the bound notes show the letters of four nouns doubling as drawings of what the words mean. Some of the letters become historiated: the "t"s, looking like capital letters, in "attentate" ("assault," in English) are also crosses; the words "railroad train" are part of a drawing of a railroad train; a gas tank is drawn in the large "O" of "Gasometer"; and several letters in "chemical factory" double as the smokestacks of a drawing of a chemical plant.[61]

When viewed near the end of the film for the final time, Mabuse's notes become fully cinematic. As Lohmann finds the notes on the desk and reads them aloud, the shot dissolves into an image of flames. The film then cuts to a close-up of the notes with Lohmann reading them aloud; the shot dissolves into a shot of the chemical plant now on fire, the attack having succeeded. Whether the notes are read aloud, as Kramm and Lohmann do, or are read silently, as Baum mostly does, does not matter. Even when the notes are deciphered and decoded, they may be sequenced only putting them just before the law, inaccessible to the law itself. Reading about crime becomes almost criminal.

Like the transference scene when Baum reads the notes aloud and calls up the phantom of Mabuse, so Lohmann's reading of the notes calls up the chemical plant explosion. The film footage of the chemical plant ablaze refers both inwardly to Lohmann's subjective visualization of what he is reading and outwardly to what is happening at the very moment he is reading. In catching up to Mabuse by "seeing" his notes, Lohmann also puts himself before Mabuse, as if responding unconsciously, as Baum may have been, to Mabuse's orders.

The film's nonmimetic allegory destabilizes its narrative structure: on the one hand, the film moves in linear, accelerated fashion from the opacity of Mabuse's written notes to their cinematic transparency and immediacy when Lohmann examines Baum's notes in his office and takes far less time Lohmann takes to make sense the notes than Kramm did Mabuse's; on the other hand, that same cut through a superimposition of a shot of the notes and a shot of the chemical plant burning involves a recursive movement back toward opacity. Even when Lohmann finds the notes while searching Baum's office, he twice refers to them as "something else," a supplement not visible at first. This recursion and opacity appears at all stages in which we see the notes being assembled, ordered, and bound as they become increasingly more cinematic. Baum's assistant picks up the notes from the cell floor in which Mabuse is imprisoned and Dr. Kramm knocks them on the floor and then picks them up again. Baum's lecture on Mabuse more explicitly narrates a progression in the clarity and readability of Mabuse's writing: the writing begins as apparently meaningless gestures that are then interpreted as pantomime writing that is then recorded on paper as automatic writing that is first regarded as nonsensical and then gradually made meaningful.

However, Baum's lecture has a recursiveness at odds with the way Mabuse's writings become progressively more legible and readable each time they appear on screen. Looking over his notes, Baum says he will recount a "Vorgeschichte" of Mabuse. The Criterion DVD translates "Vorgeschichte" as "history" in the subtitles, but the film makes a pun on the German word. Most obviously, Baum means "case history." Yet "Vorgeschichte" also means "prehistory." In addition to Mabuse's case history, Baum is telling the backstory, summarizing, in effect, the plot of *Dr. Mabuse, the Gambler* for viewers who haven't seen it or refreshing the plot for those who did see the film but who don't remember it well. By "recount," Baum means not merely tell, then, but retell. This is a story he has told before: "Look, here he goes again," a male student says to a woman student, just after Baum begins to lecture. Baum's two notes are doubled in Baum's slides of Mabuse's writing, shown either in two pages or in one page with two columns.

Baum's lecture also performs a passage from opacity and empty gesture to transparency. Before Baum begins to lecture, he looks over two pages of his lecture notes, neither of which we see in close-up. Upon review, the scene looks less proto-cinematic than precinematic: we don't see close-ups of Baum's lecture notes, and we see in the slides Baum projects not a film made from a script but of the "script" (text and handwriting) that precedes film—namely, script that is readable and unreadable, that combines letters of words with lines of a drawing. As we saw earlier, Kramm's decoding of the notes in Baum's office is similarly recursive.

Lang makes this recursive movement in the film both more and less legible as the film proceeds. A movement away from legibility back toward illegibility in the process of reading Mabuse's unbound and bound notes occurs as Baum turns the pages of Mabuse's notes during the transference scene. The camera cuts away twice from the notes just before Baum finishes turning a page. These encrypted pages, if seen while the film is put on pause, reveal what paranoiacs would call the film's "subliminal" messages, the kind of thing encrypted in David Fincher's *Fight Club* (1999) in the form of footage inserted so briefly that it is visible only when the film is viewed in slow motion. On the first, partially visible, encrypted page, "Tot," or dead," appears on the side of a drawing of a coffin with a cross on top of it. On the second encrypted page, a skull (echoing those seen in Baum's office during this sequence) with lightning flashes coming out of its mouth stands at the top center of the page flanked by the words "suggestion" and "hypnosis." The German word "Tot" and the skull name and personify death, linking allegorically the notes to the extracinematic; the turning of the pages marks the threshold between the cinematic and extracinematic. Lang also links the notes both to cinema and the extracinematic in the shot of this second page of encrypted notes by showing the new set of bound pages on top of the unbound notes, part of which are seen in the right part of the screen image. The contiguity of the encrypted bound notes and partly visible unbound notes constitutes yet another example, then, of the way the film loops back and forth between Mabuse's unbound, illegible notes and bound legible notes.

In addition to being performed in ways that are both clear yet encrypted to the point of being almost totally invisible as projected film, this double movement is literalized in a close-up of a page of the bound notes in the transference scene. The notes on this page are a palimpsest of two different texts, the first apparently written either with a lighter pencil or with a dark pencil that has been partially erased, the second written with a darker pencil over the first. The page as palimpsest qua overwriting is also visually registered by the way the underlining of some of the words written more darkly double as lines through some of the fainter words earlier.[62] Though the notes written in dark pencil are fully legible, they are at the same time haunted by the partly visible, partly crossed out notes written in lighter pencil or partially erased. In yet another recursive moment, the dissolve from Lohmann reading the notes to the factory on fire repeats these overwritten notes: the dissolve "crosses out" one image by superimposing another on it.

After having drawn numerous parallels between Lohmann's retracings of writings and Mabuse's "writings" such that the law reaches its limits, *Testament* ends by suspending the law when Lohmann stands outside of Baum/Mabuse's cell, repeatedly saying, "[T]here's nothing left here for a police inspector to do, nothing more to do." When carried out, the law's mission is in effect a transmission in remission, a truce but not an autoimmunization against further outbreaks, or breakouts, of crime. Pointedly, Mabuse rips up his writings; they are redivided, even torn up, but they are never destroyed. Thus, Mabuse's notes may potentially be reassembled and reactivated in the future. (Lang made a third version of the film in Germany in 1960, *The Thousand Eyes of Dr. Mabuse.*) And as the film ends with a fade to black, we hear the sound of paper still being torn by Mabuse as the door shuts, leaving us virtually inside in the fully darkened dark room with the insane criminal Baum/Mabuse. After the film ends, Mabuse reappears through the sound of a ticking time bomb, recalling the ticking bomb that almost killed the reformed criminal Thomas Kent and his girlfriend Lili. Again, a differentiation within Lang's film—sound without image—marks its enigmatic and antimimetic allegory of secrecy of the law, an allegory achieved through the most ordinary of cinematic special effects such as superimposition. Like *Fury*, *The Testament of Dr. Mabuse* offers us only a judgment that does not judge, a law without force, and a force without law, a boxed-in, unreadable fragments of Mabuse's torn-up notes.

LangesTod, or Notes from Beyond an Unreasonable Doubt

> But what are we saying when we say that a character in fiction forever takes a secret with him? And that the possibility of this secret is readable without the secret ever being accessible? That the readability of the text is structured by the unreadability of the secret, that is, by the inaccessibility of a certain intentional meaning or a wanting-to-say in the conscious of the characters and *a fortiori* in that of the author who remains, *in this regard*, analogous to that of the reader? . . . The interest of "Counterfeit Money," like any analogous text in general, comes form the enigma constructed out of this crypt which gives to read that which will remain eternally unreadable, absolutely indecipherable, even refusing itself to any promise of deciphering or hermeneutic.
>
> —Jacques Derrida, *Given Time: I. Counterfeit Money*[63]

> Technology and death itself are inscribed in *Condor*'s opening sequence.
>
> —Jameson, *The Geopolitical Aesthetic*[64]

Much more powerfully than the postmodern conspiratorial films Jameson discusses, Lang's allegorical films call into question the indivisibility of life, death, testimony, reason, justice, the archive, the sovereign, media, and testimony. By turning briefly to Lang's productions notes on his last American film, *Beyond a Reasonable Doubt*, we may understand how the history of Lang's films cannot be contained by biography and linear chronology, but further divide life and death. Gunning relates a fascinating anecdote about an intensely uncanny encounter he had with Lang "years after his death with words in [Lang's] handwriting" when Gunning was teaching a class on Lang. Gunning had prepared a slide of Lang's "notes" for *Beyond a Reasonable Doubt*, which Lang divided into two columns, one for what the film showed the audience, and one for what the film did not.[65] Gunning writes:

> My attention was drawn to an obscure line at the bottom of the right column, enlarged as I projected it on the screen for my class. The line is in Lang's handwriting, but seems to have been partially erased, or whited out. Closer examination showed it read: "[T]he dead never leave you."[66]

As Gunning points out, the line does not fall into either column of notes and does not seem to refer to anything specific in the film. Is it possible, Gunning asks, that "this note is a personal note of Lang's? And why . . . was it erased, particularly in the manner it was—obscured, but still readable?"

Gunning is no doubt right to refuse answers to these questions and to insist that the meaning of the note will always be a matter of speculation. I would suggest, however, that there is a recursive structure in Lang's films from the notes in the film back to the notes for the film. The issue is not a single referent, a match between one film and another or others, but a pattern. This encryption/inscription of Lang's note, "[T]he dead never leave you," does not lead us back to an original secret, which may be disclosed and decoded, but instead puts us in a loop from meaning to the catastrophic, explosive destruction of meaning to its uncannily doubled reconstitution as another meaning. The looped note is therefore not fully narratable: though it can be momentarily paused, its disclosure can never arrive at closure, since the notes are always only partly legible. Lang's encrypted, handwritten note has to be enlarged, blown up, if you will, and "projected" by another medium, like a slide, in order to be made (il)legible. In Gunning's account, we move from Lang's own notes, to their reproduction as a photograph in a reproduction in a book where they become only partly legible, to a slide of the photograph, projected on a screen in an academic lecture hall, then recognized as a note, decoded, retranscribed again into writing, that Gunning "anecdotalized" in print in his own book, missing the anec-note, become a "post-it-note," in the anecdote.[67] "LangesTod" encrypts and performs the way handwritten notes and cinematic inscription and projection live and die in the recursive delays and relays of the note as it is posted from one medium to another and—if I may be permitted a neologism with a triple pun—destin(t)erred.[68] Lang's encrypted note (to himself?) loses its indexicality through its reanimation or re-sui-citation in other media: it gets detached from the notes to *Beyond a Reasonable Doubt*, from other films by Lang, and even from Lang himself, as the note's possible referents, even if they are the usual suspects, proliferate.[69] The hand and hand writer are divided and doubled up, or, perhaps, doubled down. Putting a Langian perspective on the shared practices of note taking in legal trials, scientific research, and film production and narrative cinema, we might say that the criminal justice system, like science and film, always works in terms of a double-columned (in)visibility, inscribing a haunting kind of deathlike absence or loss, in its workings that decides what may be noted (down) by the jury and the public and what may not.

"That's What They All Say": The Force of Law after the Law

> First Citizen: The first thing he did was phone Chicago for his lawyer.
> Second Citizen: That's the first thing a guy like that will do.
>
> —Two men at a bar who become members of the lynch mob in Fritz Lang's *Fury*.

> At Prague again, just a few months ago, just before an arrest and an investigation without trial during which the representatives of the law asked me, among other things, whether the philosopher whom I was going to visit was a "Kafkalogue" (I had said I had come to Prague to follow the tracks of Kafka); my officially appointed lawyer had told me: "You must feel that you are living a story by Kafka"; and upon leaving me: "Don't take it too tragically, live it as a literary experience." And when I said that I had never seen the drugs that were supposed to have been discovered in my suitcase before the customs officer themselves saw them, the prosecutor replied: "That's what all drug traffickers say."
>
> —Jacques Derrida, "Before the Law"[70]

Lang's *Fury* and *Testament of Mabuse* and his note on *Beyond a Reasonable Doubt* are as funny as they are unsettling about legal and political sovereignty, whether democratic or authoritarian. Any authoritarian regime to come and any democracy to come are equally troubled by Lang's suspension of the law's capacity to suspend itself: precisely because the law has no force, Lang's films deliver neither justice nor injustice. The only justice we get is what just is. Lang's films offer a way into understanding the secrecy of the law not only through notes and other media but because his dis/closure of the law's unreadability, its narrative recursions returning to a referent that is not there—in the form of a corpse or the form of an imprisoned madman—brings the questions of being before the laws and the force of law together as a question of the law's aftermath. The secrecy of the law is reducible neither to indivisible media that are more or less obsolete nor to an instrumental understanding of media technologies.

Attention to many of Lang's other films and the more recent examples of the conspiratorial films that Jameson examines may further our understanding of the secrecy of the law by developing its implications for sovereignty and bio-thanato-politics.[71] If the distinction between life and death, fiction and testimony, the rule and the exception, are unsettled by the law's inaccessibility and unreadability, then the archive and the paperwork and divisibility of what Giorgio Agamben calls "bare life" (1995) become that much more important to examine—as notes, passports, and even death certificates retroactively secure the geopolitical borders they allow their bearers to cross.[72] Even dead bodies may decompose so that they are no longer a locatable referent but a left-over. Costa Gavras ends his film *Missing* (1982), about an American student murdered during the CIA-engineered coup d'etat in Chile, with a rather long take of a coffin with his name on it that stopped just after it has begun to be unloaded from a jet airliner that has landed in the United States. An autopsy, Jack Lemmon says in voice-over, was made impossible by the seven-month-long delay in shipping it home. Like the coffin that encloses and stores the "unreadable" corpse, the "evidence necessary to provide proof remains classified secrets of state." That's what they always say. Attention to the law's paperwork as "posthumographic" writing, of archiving organic "human" life before and after inorganic death, would allow the problems of sovereignty and biopolitics to be read allegorically and more widely in relation to the unreadability of law in literature, film, and media theory, and philosophy as well as in political theory.[73] What does the law know? What doesn't it know?

Notes

1. Jacques Derrida, "Before the Law," in *Acts of Literature*. Ed. Derek Attridge (New York and London: Routledge, 1992), 181–220; at 205.

2. Frederic Jameson, "Totality as Conspiracy," in *The Geopolitical Aesthetic: Cinema and Space in the World System* (Bloomington, IN: Indiana University Press, 1992), 49.

3. Cornelia Vismann, *Files: Law and Media Technology*. Trans. Geoffrey Winthrop-Young (Stanford: Stanford University Press, 2008), 56–57.

4. Derrida notes that Jean Bodin, Thomas Hobbes, and Jean-Jacques Rousseau all "used the very word *indivisible* to qualify the essence of sovereignty or sovereign government" (Jacques Derrida, *Rogues: Two Essays on Reason*. Trans. Anne Brault and Michael Nass (Stanford: Stanford University Press, 2005), 75, emphasis in original). Similarly, the "pledge of allegiance to the United States" ends with "one nation indivisible with liberty and justice for all."

5. See Jameson, *Geopolitical Aesthetic*, for the genre label "conspiratorial films."

6. See Vismann, *Files*, 102, on "the sovereignty of words" and the word as sovereign. On biopower and biopolitics, see Michel Foucault, *History of Sexuality, Volume 1: An Introduction*. Trans. Robert Hurley (New York: Vintage, 1980); Foucault, *The Birth of Biopolitics: Lectures at the College de France, 1978–1979*. Ed. Michel Senellart, Arnold I. Davidson, and Alessandro Fontana (New York: Picador, 2008); Giorgio Agamben, *Homo Sacer: Sovereign Power and Bare Life*. Trans. Daniel Heller-Roazen (Stanford: Stanford University Press, 1995); Jacques Derrida, *The Animal That Therefore I Am*. Trans. Marie-Louis Mallet and David Wills (New York: Fordham University Press, 2008); Derrida, *The Beast and the Sovereign, Volume I (The Seminars of Jacques Derrida)*. Trans. Geoffrey Bennington (Chicago: University of Chicago Press, 2009), esp. 413–43.

7. Jürgen Habermas, "Reconstructing Terrorism," in *Philosophy in a Time of Terror*. Ed. Giovanna Borradori (Chicago: University of Chicago Press, 2003), 46–81.

8. George W. Bush, cited in "Woodward Shares War Secrets," CBS News, *60 Minutes*. "Woodward Shares War Secrets," April 18, 2004.

9. Andrew McNamara and Peter Krapp, "Introduction," *South Atlantic Quarterly* 101, no. 3 (summer 2002): 441–48; at 442.

10. Jacques Derrida, *Archive Fever: A Freudian Impression*. Trans. Eric Prenowitz (Stanford: Stanford University Press, 1995).

11. Peter Krapp, "Screening the Secret," *Religion: Derrida / Vattimo*, ed. Ludwig Nagl (New York: P. Lang), 43–68.

12. Maurice Blanchot and Jacques Derrida, *The Instant of My Death/Demeure: Fiction and Testimony*. Trans. Elizabeth Rottenberg (Stanford: Stanford University Press, 2000).

13. Michel Foucault, "The Life of Infamous Men," in *Michel Foucault: Power, Truth,*

Strategy. Ed. M. Morris and P. Patton; tr. Paul Foss and Meaghan Morris (Sydney: Feral Publications, 1979), 76.

14. Franz Kafka, "Before the Law," in *Metamorphosis and Other Stories.* Trans. Michael Hofmann (London: Penguin, 2008). For Derrida's introduction of the phrase "democracy to come," I direct the reader to Jacques Derrida's *Specters of Marx: The State of the Debt, the Work of Mourning and the New International.* Trans. Peggy Kamuf (New York and London: Routledge, 1994); and Derrida, *Rogues*, esp. 86–87 and 165n. 26 for his elaborations of it. On Agamben, Carl Schmitt, and the secret, see Derrida, *The Politics of Friendship*. Trans. George Collins (London: Verso, 2006).

15. Derrida prefers to ask about waiting in a register that sounds very similar to Kafka: "While waiting—and we will have been talking about here is precisely what *waiting* means—can one speak democratically of democracy in this chateau?" (*Rogues*, 77).

16. Carl Schmitt, *Political Theology: Four Chapters on the Concept of Sovereign.* Trans. George Schwab and Tracy B. Strong (Chicago: University of Chicago Press, 2006).

17. Vismann writes of "the last secretary of the chancery to peruse records. He stood at the threshold of the decoupling of archiving and administering. For archival purposes, he was the very last to read the files that the registered, so that no one else had to read them after him" (*Files*, 99).

18. Walter Benjamin devoted separate essays to Kafka and violence. See Benjamin, "Franz Kafka," in *Walter Benjamin: Selected Writings, Volume 2, 1931–34.* Ed. Howard W. Eiland and Michael W. Jennings (Cambridge, MA: Harvard University Press, 1999), 794–820; and Benjamin, "Critique of Violence," in *Walter Benjamin: Selected Writings, Volume 1, 1913–26.* Ed. Marcus Bullock and Michael W. Jennings (Cambridge, MA: Harvard University Press, 1996), 236–52. Derrida followed suit, devoting separate essays to Kafka's "Before the Law" in Derrida, "Before the Law," 181–220, and Benjamin's "Critique of Violence" in Derrida, "Force of Law: The 'Mystical Foundation of Authority,'" in *Acts of Religion.* Ed. Gil Anidjar (New York and London: Routledge, 2002), 228–98.

19. See Vismann, *Files*, 12–29, 158, for a discussion the law's unreadability in Kafka's "Before the Law" and *The Trial.*

20. Jacques Derrida, "Nietzsche and the Machine," in *Negotiations: Interventions and Interviews 1971–2001.* Trans. Elizabeth Rottenberg (Stanford: Stanford University Press, 2002), 215–57.

21. Hans-Jörg Rheinberger, "Scrips and Scribbles," *MLN* 118, no. 3 (April 2003): 622–36. See also Rheinberger, *An Epistemology of the Concrete: Twentieth-Century Histories of Life.* Trans. Timothy Lenoir (Durham, NC: Duke University Press, 2010); and Rheinberger, *On Historicizing Epistemology: An Essay.* Trans. David Fernbach (Stanford: Stanford University Press, 2010).

22. Ibid., 628.

23. Ibid., 631. One could productively pursue the relation between notes, the secrecy of the law, biopolitics, and sovereignty in a science-fiction disaster film such as *The*

Andromeda Strain (dir. Robert Wise, 1971), *Outbreak* (dir. Wolfgang Petersen, 1995), and *Splice* (dir. Vincenzo Natali, 2009), among others.

24. National Center for State Courts' Report, "*State-of-the-States Survey of Jury Improvement Efforts*" (May 2007), 33–34. The report is online in pdf form at http://www.ncsconline.org/D_Research/cjs/state-survey.html.

25. Bernhard Stiegler, *Technics and Time 3: Cinematic Time and the Question of Malaise*. Trans. Stephen Barker (Stanford: Stanford University Press, 2011), 170.

26. For a positivist account of the hard drive and "inscription" that overtly ignores Paul de Man's work, see Matthew G. Kirschenbaum, *Mechanisms: New Media and the Forensic Imagination* (Cambridge, MA: MIT Press, 2008).

27. See Avital Ronell, *The Telephone Book: Technology, Schizophrenia, Electric Speech* (Lincoln: University of Nebraska Press, 1989). See also Laurence Rickels, *The Case of California* (Baltimore, MD: Johns Hopkins University Press, 1991).

28. Jameson, *The Geopolitical Aesthetic*, 68. Jameson discusses "conspiratorial films" of the 1960s, 70s, and 80s such as *Blow Up* (dir. Michelangelo Antonioni, 1966), *The Conversation* (dir. Francis Ford Coppola, 1974), *Three Days of the Condor* (dir. Sydney Pollack, 1975), *The Parallax View* (dir. Alan Pakula, 1974), *All the President's Men* (dir. Alan Pakula, 1976), *Blow Out* (dir. Brian De Palma, 1981), *The Dead Zone* (dir. David Cronenberg, 1983), and *Videodrome* (dir. David Cronenberg, 1983).

29. Jameson, *The Geopolitical Aesthetic*, 14–15.

30. Ibid., 76–77, my emphasis.

31. Jacques Derrida and Maurizio Ferraris, *A Taste for the Secret* (Cambridge: Polity, 2001), 51–52.

32. Vismann, *Files*, 64.

33. Jameson, *The Geopolitical Aesthetic*, 79. In *Billion Dollar Brain* (dir. Ken Russell, 1968), a traitor is seen through a video monitor putting index cards into a supercomputer to falsify the record.

34. Jameson, *The Geopolitical Aesthetic*, 78.

35. Ibid., 79.

36. For an update of this scene, see *National Treasure* (dir. Jon Turtletaub, 2004).

37. Similar kinds of recursive narrative looping can be seen in *Blow Up* and *Blow Out*.

38. Derrida, *The Politics of Friendship*, 92.

39. See Theodor W. Adorno, *Aesthetic Theory*. Trans. C. Lenhardt (London: Routledge and Kegan Paul, 1984); and Tom Cohen, *Anti-Mimesis: From Plato to Hitchcock* (Cambridge and London: Cambridge University Press, 1994).

40. Jameson, *The Geopolitical Aesthetic*, 47.

41. For the screenplay, see "Arrest at the Texas Theatre: Oliver Stone's JFK: The JFK 100: JFK assassination investigation: Jim Gwww.jfk-online.com."

42. Recent conspiratorial films include, among others, *Se7en* (dir. David Fincher,

1995), *The Game* (dir. David Fincher, 1997), *Conspiracy Theory* (dir. Richard Donner, 1997), *Dark City* (dir. Alex Proyas, 1998), *The Thirteenth Floor* (dir. Josef Rusnak, 1999), *Anti-Trust* (dir. Peter Howiit, 2001), *The Manchurian Candidate* (dir. Jonathan Demme, 2004), *National Treasure* (dir. Jon Turtletaub, 2004), *The Stepford Wives* (dir. Frank Oz, 2004), *The Forgotten* (dir. Joseph Ruben, 2004), *Flightplan* (dir. Robert Schwentke, 2005), *Zodiac* (dir. David Fincher, 2007), *Shooter* (dir. Antoine Fuqua, 2007), *National Treasure: Book of Secrets* (dir. Jon Turtletaub, 2007), *Max Payne* (dir. John Moore, 2008), *Beyond a Reasonable Doubt* (dir. Peter Hyams, 2009), *The Conspirator* (dir. Robert Redford, 2010), *The Girl with the Dragon Tattoo* (dir. David Fincher, 211); and *Source Code* (dir. Duncan Jones, 2011). A Desert Storm veteran's notebook appears forty minutes into *The Manchurian Candidate* (dir. Jonathan Demme, 2004) along with drawings and incomprehensible writings on a wall of his apartment. Both notebooks and wall scribblings are staples of the genre; films in this genre unconsciously and persistently recycle Lang's Testament of Dr. Mabuse films. For a discussion of some of the films mentioned above and others, see Richard Burt, "Stupid Shit: (In)security in the Age of Twilightenment," *ArtUS*, no. 11 (February 2006): 29–37. Library and archive scenes in disaster films such as Roland Emmerich's *The Day After Tomorrow* (1999) and *2012* (2010) and procedurals are also worth examining in relation to the conspiratorial film genre.

43. On the oft-perceived parallel between Hitler and Mabuse (possessing Dr. Baum), see Tom Gunning, *The Films of Fritz Lang: Allegories of Vision* (London: BFI, 2000); and David Kalat's audiocommentary on the Eureka: Masters of Cinema and Criterion DVD editions of *The Testament of Dr. Mabuse.*

44. See Gunning, *Films of Fritz Lang*, 471–72.

45. Ibid., 212–13.

46. Ibid., 219.

47. Garrett Stewart, *Between Film and Screen: Modernism's Photo Synthesis* (Chicago: University of Chicago Press, 1999), 62–63.

48. Ibid.

49. Ibid., 56–62.

50. Blanchot and Derrida, *The Instant of My Death/Demeure*, 64, 65.

51. Vismann, *Files*, 50, 52.

52. See Gunning, *Films of Fritz Lang*; and David Kalat, *The Strange Case of Dr. Mabuse: A Study of the Twelve Films and Five Novels* (New York: McFarland, 2001), 68–91.

53. Kalat, *Strange Case of Dr. Mabuse*, 92.

54. In *Dr. Mabuse, the Gambler*, Lang makes counterfeit banknotes the centerpiece of Mabuse's criminal operations.

55. Translated into English, the German word "Aufzeichnungen" means both "notes" and "notations."

56. On the lecture hall and cinema analogy, see Gunning, *Films of Fritz Lang*; and Kalat, *Strange Case of Dr. Mabuse.*

57. On Lang's silent film *Spies* (1928) and Freud's essay on the mystic writing pad, see Gunning, *Films of Fritz Lang*, 140; and Sigmund Freud, "A Note upon the Mystic Writing Pad," in *The Standard Edition of the Complete Psychological Works of Sigmund Freud, Volume XIX*. Ed. James Strachey (London: Hogarth Press, 1961), 227–34.

58. For the former meaning, see Sigmund Freud, *The Interpretation of Dreams*, in *The Standard Edition of the Complete Psychological Works, Volumes IV–V*. Ed. James Strachey (London: Hogarth Press, 1953). And for the latter meaning, see Freud, "Further Recommendations in the Technique of Psychoanalysis: Recollection, Repetition and Working Through," in *The Standard Edition of the Complete Psychological Works, Volume X*. Ed. James Strachey (London: Hogarth Press, 1958),145–56.

59. As Samuel Weber writes: "[T]he 'observation' that Freud opposes to rationalistic speculation emerges as being of a most peculiar kind. For its medium is not clarity but obscurity, not light so much as shadow." Weber, "The Divaricator: Remarks on Freud's Witz," *Glyph* 1, no. 5 (1997): 5.

60. Making Baum's writing desk be the site of the double and of a double reading (matching news clipping to the reassembled notes) is perhaps predictable. See Friedrich Kittler, "Romanticism—Psychoanalysis—the Double," in *Literature, Media, Information Systems*. Trans. John Johnston (Amsterdam: G + B Arts, 1997), 50–84.

61. The shots of the bound sections of the notes, with no sound, are intercut with shots of the criminals listening to a radio voice (Mabuse/Baum) directing each section to do the attack outlined in a given section of the notes. So the link between notes and cinema is made clearer, as we move from silent notes to cinematic voice-over.

62. The text is read aloud in voice-over by Baum, like a film script, and then continued by the phantom Mabuse sitting across the desk from Baum.

63. Jacques Derrida, *Given Time: I. Counterfeit Money*. Trans. Peggy Kamuf (Chicago: University of Chicago Press, 1992), 152.

64. Jameson, *The Geopolitical Aesthetic*, 13.

65. Gunning, *Films of Fritz Lang*, 479.

66. Ibid.

67. On the "anec-note," see Richard Burt, *Medieval and Early Modern Film and Media* (New York and London: Palgrave Macmillan, 2010), 6–7; 121–83; 240n17.

68. See ibid., 130–36.

69. These kinds of multiple analogies without a clear referent structure Lang's films as well as accounts of Lang as a film director.

70. Derrida, "Before the Law," 218.

71. On biopolitics, see Foucault, *History of Sexuality*; Foucault, *Birth of Biopolitics*; Agamben, *Homo Sacer*; Agamben, *The Open: Man and Animal*. Trans. Kevin Attell (Stanford: Stanford University Press, 2004); Agamben, *State of Exception*. Trans. Kevin Attell (Stanford: Stanford University Press, 2005); Derrida, *Beast and the Sovereign*.

72. On the death certificate, see Derrida, *Specters of Marx*, 48. See also "This is your

death certificate," *After.Life* (dir. Agnieszka Wojtowicz-Vosloo, 2009); and the death certificate with "cause of death: fright" in *The Tingler* (dir. William Castle, 1959).

73. On posthumography, see Richard Burt, "Putting Your Papers in Order: The Matter of Kierkegaard's Writing Desk, Goethe's Files, and Derrida's Paper Machine, or the Philology and Philosophy of Publishing after Death," *Rhizomes* 20 (Summer 2010).

Index

Index

The Amherst Series in Law, Jurisprudence, and Social Thought

EDITED BY

Austin Sarat, Lawrence Douglas, and Martha Merrill Umphrey

Imagining New Legalities: Privacy and Its Possibilities in the 21st Century (2012)
Law as Punishment/Law as Regulation (2011)
Law without Nations (2011)
Law and the Stranger (2010)
Law and Catastrophe (2007)
Law and the Sacred (2007)
How Law Knows (2007)
The Limits of Law (2005)
Law on the Screen (2005)

The authorized representative in the EU for product safety and compliance is:
Mare Nostrum Group
B.V Doelen 72
4831 GR Breda
The Netherlands

www.ingramcontent.com/pod-product-compliance
Lightning Source LLC
Chambersburg PA
CBHW051256200926
51612CB00002B/61
9780804782593